The HEN HARRIER

The HEN HARRIER
– In the Shadow of Slemish

Don Scott

Whittles Publishing

Published by
Whittles Publishing Ltd.,
Dunbeath,
Caithness, KW6 6EG,
Scotland, UK

www.whittlespublishing.com

ISBN 978-1904445-93-7

Printed by
Bell & Bain Ltd., Glasgow

For Linda and Douglas

And also for my harrier colleague of 21 years, Philip McHaffie

G.D'arcy 08

Gordon D'arcy

A mating pair of hen harriers courtesy of the artist

Contents

Acknowledgements

Without the support and understanding of my long-suffering wife Linda and son Douglas, my studies of hen harriers in Northern Ireland would never have come to fruition. Many days and long weekends were given up to fieldwork and I will always appreciate the sacrifices they have made for me over the past 24 years. The writing of this book gives me the opportunity to thank them both sincerely for their wholehearted support. My late mum and dad, Margaret and William, were also great supporters and financial backers of my harrier work and they are both greatly missed by all the family.

When I first met Philip McHaffie in March 1989, I little suspected that we would still be great friends and harrier colleagues 21 years later. This quietly spoken, even-tempered and modest man has been my constant companion through good times and bad, during our forays into the Antrim Plateau and the Sperrins to study the sometimes elusive, yet always captivating hen harrier. He has been a true friend in every sense whose company, friendship and advice I value greatly.

I also owe thanks to another long-time friend and fellow birder Gary Wilkinson, who introduced me to hen harriers in April 1986 at Slieveanorra in the Antrim Plateau. The same habitat is frequented by another good friend and merlin aficionado Larry Toal and so our paths cross each season to exchange vital raptor information. Michael Devlin has also been a great help to me in recent years, as has Cliff Dawson, who kindly provided me with important information about a depredated male hen harrier in the Sperrins in County Tyrone.

I sincerely thank Jim Wells MLA for taking the time from his busy work schedule to write a foreword for this book; it is greatly appreciated. As the highly respected chairman of the Northern Ireland Raptor Study Group since its inception in 1992, there is probably nobody in Northern Ireland better qualified for the task. Jim's 30 year study of the peregrine falcon in Northern Ireland is legendary.

I am extremely grateful to my raptor colleague Keith Glasgow for kindly agreeing to provide the superb paintings and drawings for this book. Keith has a unique ability to portray birds of prey in their natural habitat and the picturesque scenery of the Antrim plateau. I am absolutely delighted that his stunning artwork graces the pages of this book.

My sincere thanks go also to George Gordon, the Records Secretary for the Northern Ireland Birdwatchers Association, for providing me with numerous records of hen harriers, and to Stanley Black, the estate manager at Cleggan Lodge, for generously granting me access to the estate during my ongoing studies. The late John McGhie (formerly of the Forest Service) and the late Dr. William McDowell were also a great help to me over many years, as was the late C. D. (Jimmy) Deane OBE.

Dr. Tim Hipkiss, assigned to Quercus at Queen's University Belfast, studied hen harriers with me in the Antrim Plateau in 2006 and 2007. Although his real passion was probably owls, he took readily to studying hen harriers under my guidance and his part in this story deserves recognition. From across the border in the Republic of Ireland, I thank Dr. Stephen Newton, from BirdWatch Ireland, Jimmy Walsh from Dublin, Frank King and Barry O'Donoghue from Kerry. I could not leave out David Scott from Dalkey who studied hen harriers in Wicklow in the 1960s and 1970s. David sadly died in 1998 but he had a major influence on me and his enthusiasm for harriers in Ireland was infectious.

I am proud to have known Donald Watson who died in 2005 aged 87. It was a privilege for me to visit the great man at his home in Scotland. I would like to thank two more people working with harriers there: Brian Etheridge (RSPB Highland) for his positive advice and help, and Harry Bell from the Tay Raptor Study Group who provided me with daily advice and information about a pair of nesting marsh harriers in County Down in 2009.

In the early 1980s I had the pleasure of meeting Colin Shawyer, then Director of the Hawk and Owl Trust. Colin has always been a great supporter of my harrier work in Northern Ireland and both he and his wife Val have remained firm family friends and raptor colleagues for well over 25 years. It was Colin who introduced me in 1991 to the late Dr. Roger Clarke. Our mutual interest in harriers led not only to a friendship but to a seventeen year joint study of tree nesting hen harriers in Northern Ireland.

Had it not been for the timely intervention of Colin Shawyer, Roger Clarke and Donald Watson, along with further support from Bill Bourne from Aberdeen, my unique discovery of tree nesting hen harriers in County Antrim would probably have gone unnoticed and unrecorded.

I would also like to thank Stephen Murphy from Natural England and Gary Jenkins, who both study breeding hen harriers in the Forest of Bowland in Lancashire. Both have provided me with important data, not only about the ups and downs of harriers in that area, but also about their depredation by the resident pair of European eagle owls. Fellow author John Miles from Cumbria has provided me with important harrier data from his local patch.

My long-time friend and harrier colleague from Wales, Iolo Williams, kindly agreed to write a foreword for this book. Iolo and I have corresponded and liaised about hen harriers since the early 1990s.

A big thank you goes also to harrier colleagues Henk Castelijns in Holland, Igor Fefelov in Russia and David Baker-Gabb and Wally Klau in Australia for kindly sharing data on their local hen and spotted harrier populations.

I also sincerely thank the Hawk and Owl Trust (HOT) which for many years financially supported my harrier work here in Northern Ireland and also in India. Were it not for its generous funding, my annual studies would probably not have been completed. Thanks are also due to the Northern Ireland Environment Agency (NIEA), formerly the DOENI, which granted me a licence to study these wonderful birds of prey.

Finally, I am indebted to Keith Whittles from Whittles Publishing in Caithness for taking on the onerous task of editing and publishing this book. His help in many ways is greatly appreciated.

If I have failed to mention anyone who may have helped me with my hen harrier studies in County Antrim and elsewhere over the past 24 years, I sincerely apologise. Their absence from the acknowledgements section of this book is not intentional.

Foreword by Iolo Williams

Hen harriers have been in my blood since I was a very young boy. I remember skipping off the Berwyn moors as an 11 year old having found my first hen harrier nest, tucked amongst the tall heather in a small isolated upland valley. Later in life, I was lucky enough to be able to pursue my interest in these magnificent birds whilst working as Species Officer for the Royal Society for the Protection of Birds in Wales and as the hen harrier co-ordinator for the Wales Raptor Study Group.

It was whilst working for the RSPB that I first came to hear about a remarkable chap called Don Scott who was studying hen harriers in Northern Ireland. Incredibly, news soon filtered through that Don had found tree nesting harriers within his study area. In Wales, we had recorded hen harriers nesting in bracken and moor grass, as well as on the forest floor amongst some very tall Sitka spruce, but never a tree nesting pair. I had to speak to Don!

Thus began a correspondence that led to a friendship that has lasted almost 20 years. This book is the result of a lifetime's work and is the Irish hen harrier bible. From these pages, you will learn not only a great deal about hen harriers but also about the trials and tribulations of monitoring birds of prey. Anyone willing to sit on his backside on wet ground for weeks on end through rain, hail and snow before walking through acres of thick Sitka spruce, then returning to watch once more, deserves a medal. To do this every spring and summer for 24 years deserves a knighthood.

Although the book concentrates on breeding hen harriers, Don has also monitored nesting goshawks, short-eared owls, red kites and marsh harriers, the last returning in 2009 to nest in Northern Ireland for the first time in over 150 years.

It would be a fitting tribute to his work if the book were to end on a successful note. The truth, however, is that hen harriers are struggling in Northern Ireland, as they are throughout much of the United Kingdom. Human persecution is rife in many areas and takes its annual toll, as do habitat degradation and neglect, but this incredible bird of prey continues to struggle on against all the odds.

Don Scott has brought the plight of the hen harrier and birds of prey in general in Northern Ireland to the public eye. It is now up to the decision makers and landowners to ensure that these magnificent birds are here for future generations to admire.

Iolo Williams
Naturalist and broadcaster
Montgomery, mid Wales

Foreword by Jim Wells

As a result of centuries of habitat destruction and persecution, Northern Ireland has lost many of the raptor species which once graced its uplands, woods and coastline.

Nine raptor species, including owls, now maintain a foothold in Northern Ireland and several, such as peregrine falcon, sparrowhawk and buzzard, not only survived the pesticide era but saw their populations increase to record levels. Unfortunately, kestrel numbers have declined sharply in recent decades and there is a growing concern that land-use changes are having a profound impact on the population of this attractive raptor.

Golden eagle, osprey, marsh harrier and red kite no longer nest in the province but hopefully, as a result of population increases elsewhere in the British Isles and reintroduction schemes, we will once again see these magnificent raptors soaring in our skies.

Whilst all birds of prey enthusiasts have their favourite species, there are few who would deny that the sight of the ghostly grey silhouette of a male hen harrier quartering moorland is one of the most thrilling wildlife experiences to be witnessed in Northern Ireland, or indeed anywhere.

I have vivid memories of my first encounter with a hen harrier. As a young student I searched Ballypatrick Forest, an area well known to the author of this book, for several days looking for a species that had eluded me for years. I was just about to give up when I walked round the corner of a Sitka plantation to find myself staring at a stunning male perched on a post within feet of me. I froze and for several minutes marvelled at his perfect plumage and steely gaze. I suspect that what eventually prompted the harrier to fly off was the sound of my heart pounding. That was 32 years ago but every subsequent encounter with the hen harrier has provoked a similar reaction. I can fully understand why Don has devoted so much of his life to the study of this magnificent bird.

It is not often that research carried out in Northern Ireland leads to a world first in the field of ornithology, but Don's discovery that hen harriers in County Antrim were nesting in trees completely changed our understanding of the breeding ecology of this species. Whilst this remarkable find eventually prompted widespread interest well beyond these shores, it also provided further evidence of the pressures that are so evident in our upland areas. It is almost certain that tree nesting was a response to the totally unsustainable levels of grazing and burning which afflict heather moorland in Northern Ireland. This is a recurring theme in this book and it is imperative that the relevant authorities study Don's findings carefully and implement policies which will restore our uplands to their former glory.

I commend this book to anyone with an interest in birds of prey, moorland ecology or forestry and I hope that it will encourage many more people to support the conservation of this wonderful bird.

Jim Wells MLA
Chairman, Northern Ireland Raptor Study Group

Preface

During my formative years my interests lay mainly in sporting activities but I always maintained a fond and respectful appreciation of wildlife. Birds of prey in particular have captivated me since I was a small boy. It was not until 1969, though, when a career move forced me to leave my native Bessbrook in County Armagh for Holywood, County Down, that I became involved in the fascinating world of ornithology.

Birds of prey instantly stamp a powerful and lasting impression on anyone observing them for the first time: the strong hooked bill, the powerful gripping feet and talons, the keen vision and great command of flight. No wonder, then, that I was permanently hooked on harriers of all species all those years ago but I freely admit that none of them has had a bigger impact on me than the hen harrier.

Donald Watson's classic monograph on the hen harrier, published in 1977, the only book to date solely dedicated to this beautiful raptor, was based on 17 years of study in Galloway, south west Scotland. My study, carried out mainly in County Antrim, began a decade later in 1986 and spans an unbroken 24 year period to 2009: hence the need for another book, particularly one that exclusively covers the life and untold story of this species in Northern Ireland.

At the start of my harrier studies, the late David Scott from Dublin advised me to keep detailed notes of my harrier activities. 'Young man' – and I can still hear those words ringing in my ears – 'you will be glad of it if ever you decide to write a book'. How perceptive he was for when I started writing this, my second book on harriers, I had already recorded nine-tenths of the text to be included.

The title came about as a result of a conversation I had with Roger Clarke during the summer of 1995, when we were both observing a hen harrier tree nest from a prominent moorland vantage point in south Antrim. Basking in the warm sunshine, totally enthralled by the comings and goings at the nearby nest site, I revealed to Roger that my long-term ambition was to write a book about the local hen harrier population.

'And what title would you give the book?' he asked quietly. 'Just look behind you', I replied. Our idyllic backdrop was the Slemish Mountain, one of the most famous and historic landmarks in the county. Slemish, at 450 m, can be seen almost everywhere you go in Antrim and as hen harriers regularly pass over its daunting slopes, I have named my book in its honour.

Until recently, only three of our ten species (including the sporadic short-eared owl) of breeding raptors and owls in Northern Ireland were monitored on an annual basis, the monitoring of barn owls by the Ulster Wildlife Trust having started in 2008. I have monitored the hen harrier population since 1986 and make annual counts of goshawk and short-eared owl, but it is vital that the other six species be studied, as virtually nothing is known about their present ecology.

This book is based on my experiences and life with the hen harrier in the Antrim Plateau over the past 24 years but also includes encounters I have had with several other raptor species along the way, three of which – goshawk, short-eared owl and marsh harrier – I have shown to have successfully bred here. Another, the red kite, attempted to breed for the first time in any part of Ireland for over 200 years. I have included many other relevant observations of other birds of prey, even if their visits to our shores were only fleeting.

I have lived through exciting times with hen harriers over the years and some sad and disappointing moments too. All are included, to be lived again by, I hope, both the raptor enthusiast and the casual birder. My passion for harriers will be obvious. The maltreatment and mismanagement of this elegant raptor over the years have led me to speak frankly but any criticisms expressed are meant constructively.

As a result of my long-term and original studies of the hen harrier in Northern Ireland, I was extremely proud to be awarded a degree in biology in September 2001 by the Institute of Biology in London. In January 2008, I was duly elected as a serving committee member of the Northern Ireland branch of the Institute of Biology.

I am also a founder member (1992) of the Northern Ireland Raptor Study Group and presently serve on the committee. For over fifteen years I was the Hawk and Owl Trust's representative for Northern Ireland. I also served a five year term as Honorary Treasurer of the Northern Ireland Birdwatchers Association where I was also the co-compiler of the Northern Ireland Bird Report. Over the years, I have also been asked to peer review the occasional book and scientific paper on raptors for several highly respected ornithological journals.

I end this introduction with a sobering thought from my first book on harriers by my good friend David Hollands:

'They have never enjoyed the celebrity status of eagles or falcons and apart from a few species, remain very little known … Many harrier species need marshes and heathlands, both habitats which are increasingly threatened all over the world, but harriers seem unlikely to be considered in any development plans for such places.'

Nothing since has changed in Northern Ireland nor in many other parts of the UK. I hope this latest version of the hen harrier story sheds further light on the lifestyle of this enigmatic species in the degraded uplands and alien forests of County Antrim.

Don Scott CBiol MIBiol
Dundonald, Northern Ireland

The harrier's range

Sixteen species of harrier are recognised worldwide, ranging across every continent except the Arctic and Antarctic. That figure has grown from the ten species proposed in 1973 by Dutch taxonomist Ebel Nieboer and the thirteen proposed ten years later by the American researchers Dean Amadon and John Bull. Advances in DNA testing and the work of Professor Michael Wink of Heidelberg University and Dr. Robert Simmons of the University of Cape Town brought the figure to sixteen in 2000. There is also one recognised subspecies, *Circus aeruginosus harterti,* the North African race of the Western or European marsh harrier. It is sparsely found in Algeria, Morocco and Tunisia with individuals occasionally occurring at locations in southern Europe.

Of the sixteen species, a quarter occur in the UK and Europe: hen harrier, Western marsh harrier, Montagu's harrier and pallid harrier. Of these, only the first three breed in the UK, with the pallid harrier breeding mainly in eastern and central Europe. Until recently, only the hen harrier bred in Ireland but the Western marsh harrier made a very welcome return to Northern Ireland in 2009.

The northern harrier is the only species to occur in North America, while the cinereous and long-winged harrier are resident in South America. In southern Africa we find the African marsh harrier and the endemic black harrier and, on Madagascar, the Madagascar marsh harrier.

On the much smaller island of Réunion, in the western Indian Ocean, there is the aptly named Reunion harrier, while Asia hosts two species in the form of the pied and Eastern marsh harrier. Australia is home to the spotted and swamp harriers with the Papuan harrier found in Papua New Guinea.

Most of these 16 species and the one subspecies of harrier are usually feathered in black, white, grey and various shades of brown plumage. The most colourful, unsurprisingly, tend to be the adult males but three of the 17 – the black harrier, African marsh harrier and spotted harrier – show both sexes sporting similar plumage details. Plumage patterns and colours are probably significant for species recognition and camouflage and possibly for choice of mate, but also signal sex, age, status and individual identity in all harrier species.

Hen harrier ecology

The hen harrier is a handsome and elegant bird of prey, a highly skilled acrobat and a formidable hunter. Its prowess as a predator was probably best described by Watters in 1853: 'Searching for food at a later hour than any of the hawks, the Hen Harrier is repeatedly observed at twilight circling and searching over the fallows as minutely as the Owl; hunting in pairs, each bird selects a separate beat, traversed so correctly that, observing the birds passing a particular place, by returning at the same time on the succeeding evening, the bird is certain to occur to our observation'.

Hen harriers belong to the largest raptor family, Accipter, one of 16 worldwide members of the genus *Circus*. It is a medium sized hawk of slim build, with a longish tail and very long wings relative to body weight which assist its buoyancy when in flight, allowing it to forage for long periods. It is a diurnal raptor that mainly frequents open country, alternately flapping and gliding on wings held up in a shallow dihedral or V shape.

The hen harrier has the most northerly breeding range of Europe's four species of harrier and the widest distribution, stretching west to Ireland and east to Asia. It is also the least migratory of the three British species of harrier, in contrast with the Western marsh, Montagu's and pallid harriers of Europe, which migrate south to Africa and Asia shortly after the end of the breeding season. Of all 16 species and one subspecies of harrier worldwide, the hen harrier is the most studied, documented and, sadly, the most persecuted, particularly on the UK's uplands and grouse moors, where it is now considered a rarity.

The average weight of hen harriers, quoted by Brown and Amadon (1968) is 357 g for males and 483 g for females. To survive they require an average daily intake of food equal to 12.5% of their bodyweight in spring and summer and 15.8% in autumn and winter. The hen harrier, like all harrier species, shows reversed size dimorphism (RSD), the females being larger than the males. The degree of RSD varies from species to species of harrier, with hen and pallid harriers exhibiting a high degree of RSD mainly because of a diet rich in birds, while Montagu's harriers, which feed on more lowly prey such as lizards and locusts, show a lower degree. This supports the theory that bird-eating raptors are more highly size-dimorphic. The greatest RSD shown by any harrier species is in the long-winged harrier of South America, with females around 42% heavier and 1.5 times larger than the male. The average weight of females from the remaining 15 species, including the hen harrier, is around 34% greater than males.

The first real description of the hen harrier in the UK was written by Dr. William Turner in his *Avium Praecipuarum* of 1544, the first printed bird book. Turner gives the name as Hen Harroer and leaves no doubt about the reason: it 'gets its name among our countrymen from butchering their fowls' (hens). At that time he was referring to the grey adult males and considered the brown female, or ringtail, as a different species, due to their contrasting plumage differences, though he that does correctly note that the two caught their prey in the same manner.

Hen harriers fly as low to the ground as necessary to maximise their chances of surprising and capturing prey, using vegetation and the lie of the land to mask their approach. Hen harriers both look and listen for prey, their pronounced facial discs concealing large ears which are probably used in a similar manner to those of the unrelated owl. Several biologists, though, have questioned the role of the facial disc, or ruff, on harriers and believe its use may be purely social rather than functional.

When a hen harrier detects a sound, it is able to position its head to point directly towards it. Prey is then swiftly seized, pinned to the ground and held firmly in the talons, helped by the harrier's specially evolved long legs. As in all raptors, the sharply taloned toes extend automatically when the leg is outstretched towards prey and contract as the harrier's weight bears down and pulls on tendons in the legs. Foot and claw size are probably the best indicators of predation potential.

The hen harrier usually nests on the ground, mainly on heather moorland at altitudes of 200–250 m (650–820 ft) above sea level. In Northern Ireland, however, some hen harriers habitually nest in trees, one of only two species to do so, the other being the exquisite spotted harrier from Australia. Outside the breeding season, the hen harrier can be seen over lake margins, reed beds, salt marshes, farmland stubble, marginal farmland, cutaway bog and even close to the coast.

Most raptor species are monogamous but harriers are an exception. Hen harriers are known to be more polygynous than any other species of raptor, the male mating with more than one female during a breeding season, and are occasionally polyandrous, the female mating with more than one male. These behaviours on the breeding grounds are only occasionally successful.

The silvery blue-grey plumage of the male hen harrier has attracted local names like white kite, white hawk, seagull hawk and, most appropriately, moor hawk. These names probably derived from the sight of the male bird quartering low against the dark backdrop of a hillside or heather moorland. Hill farmers in north Antrim refer to the male as a blue hawk while in many parts of Ireland the hen harrier, like the buzzard, is known locally as a kite. The name undoubtedly derives from the harrier's long wings which carry it floating and flapping lazily overhead, like a kite on string.

The Irish Gaelic name, *Clamhan Luch*, means mouse hawk and the female and brown-plumaged young of the year were always referred to as ringtails. Various Old English spellings of the word ringtail include *ringteal*, *ringteale* and *ringtayle*. In Holland the hen harrier is known as the *blauwe Kiekendief*, in Spain as a*guilucho pálido* and in France as *le busard Saint-Martin*, due to its arrival on or around 11 November, St Martin's Day, every year.

The Old English name for the hen harrier dates back to at least the 16th century, derived, as in Watters' account above, from its liking for domestic chickens. The word harrier is rooted in the Old English *herigan,* meaning 'to harass by hostile attacks'. The Latin name for the hen harrier is *Circus cyaneus, Circus* from the Greek *kirkos,* implying a bird of prey that flies in circles, *cyaneus* also derived from the Greek, *kuaneos* meaning dark blue, the colour of the male's back and upper wings. The collective noun for a large gathering of birds such as harriers is a swarm.

The hen harrier must be the UK's most controversial bird of prey and is heavily persecuted, particularly on upland moors where it comes into conflict with the interests of gamekeepers and red grouse chicks during the breeding season. On my home patch in Northern Ireland, with the red fox its only natural threat, the hen harrier is not thriving as it should. Man is its greatest enemy, considering it more often an inconvenience than a wonder of the natural world.

The history of the hen harrier in Ireland

Hen harriers were once thought to be a widespread breeding species throughout the island of Ireland wherever suitable upland habitat existed In the course of the 19th and 20th centuries, however, they declined drastically in both range and population due to a combination of habitat loss and persecution. According to William Thompson, writing in 1849, the 19th century breeding strongholds were in Counties Wicklow, Kerry, Waterford and Tipperary, and in Antrim and Londonderry in what is now Northern Ireland.

Alluding to Antrim and Londonderry, Thompson stated that 'in suitable localities, such as prevail throughout the greater part of the county of Antrim, the adult birds remain during the year and the male is always conspicuous from his light coloured plumage – appearing at first sight like a sea-gull'. With regard to County Londonderry, Thompson wrote: 'A sporting friend informs me, that there are many 'white hawks' (hen harriers) on his mountains at Ballynascreen (near Drapertown), whose nests he has met with in the heath'.

Ussher and Warren (1900) specifically mention that the hen harrier also bred in three other counties in Northern Ireland: on the Mourne Mountains near Rostrevor (Down), near Lack (Fermanagh) and also in the Sperrins (Tyrone) but apparently not in County Armagh.

By 1954, the hen harrier was uncommon enough to be described as 'a rare vagrant' in C. D. Deane's *Birds of Northern Ireland*. It had been recorded only four times in Northern Ireland since 1900. One of these four records involved a male and female seen on 7 September 1952 in the Mourne Mountains (Down) well after the breeding season had ended. It seems reasonable to suggest that these birds may have bred there during the summer months but had gone unnoticed due to the lack of birders in that area.

The first mention of a noticeable decline in breeding numbers appears in the mid 19th century in what is now the Republic of Ireland. Thompson states 'that near Clonmel (Waterford), it was now very scarce, in 1849, whereas 11 years earlier, in 1838, he had been told that eggs and young were easily obtained there'.

In present-day Northern Ireland, the decline may have started as early as 1845 as Thompson mentions that 'the species must be rare in that district (referring specifically to County Down), as the first adult male which came under the notice of the gamekeeper at Tollymore Park (near Newcastle), in the Mourne Mountains, was not seen until early February of that year'.

Further evidence of the continuing decline throughout Ireland comes from John Watters (1853) as he categorically states: 'This species appears to be of considerable rarity upon the eastern portion of the island, although for the present it still occurs in considerable numbers, both north and south'.

Persecution by so-called sportsmen and collectors, who regarded most birds of prey as vermin, was probably causing a more general decrease than was realised in Ireland at that time but, at least for the moment, a good number of hen harriers survived in the more remote breeding haunts. During what were turbulent years for our resident raptors, golden and white-tailed eagles also disappeared from their mountain and coastal haunts as did the marsh harrier from our inland marshes and heaths. When William Thompson described the status of the hen harrier in Volume 1 of his *Natural History of Ireland* (1849–1856) he opened with the callous treatment meted out to our resident birds of prey during the 19th and early years of the 20th century: 'The first Hen Harrier that came under my own notice appeared when a friend and I were in search of snipe, in a boggy spot among the Belfast Mountains (Antrim), when a female bird hovered above us in the manner of a Kestrel, and was not alarmed by our presence, nor by that of our dogs engaged in beating the ground immediately beneath – her life fell a sacrifice to my gun'. To this day, the hen harrier is scarce in that area.

By the end of the 19th century, there was no longer any doubt that the population had been greatly reduced wherever it bred and by the start of the 20th century the hen harrier was considered extinct as a breeding species in what is now the Republic of Ireland. It probably died out as a breeding species at around the same time in the north but a lack of proven records and the scarcity of ornithologists during the first half of the 20th century mean that we can only speculate.

The hen harrier was suffering elsewhere too. In the UK, and Scotland in particular, the 19th century saw its indiscriminate slaughter, along with other raptor species, mainly on private estates. The Glengarry estate in Inverness-shire was particularly brutal (Ritchie *et al.* 1920). Between 1837 and 1840, more than 75 harriers died at the hands of ruthless gamekeepers.

An unnamed writer in the Quarterly Review, December 1845 (mentioned in Thompson, 1849), dwelling on 'Highland Sport' and the so-called enemies of red grouse, states: 'Hawks of all sorts, from the eaglet to the merlin, destroy vast numbers. But, the worst of the family, and the most difficult to be destroyed, is the Hen Harrier! …Living wholly on birds of his own killing, he will come to no laid bait and hunting in an open country he is rarely approached near enough to be shot!' The horrific fate that awaited these birds appears to have changed little in more than 160 years.

One of the best known instances of mass killing by gamekeepers occurred between 25 June 1850 and 25 November 1854, when 351 hen harriers were said to have been killed on two south Ayrshire estates (Watson, 1977). Within a few years hen harriers were, not surprisingly, regarded as virtually extinct in Ayrshire and neighbouring Wigtownshire as well as in the border counties of England (Gray and Anderson 1869).

According to the late David Scott, the hen harrier suffered many lean years in southern Ireland but never died out as a breeding bird, as was once supposed. The odd pair apparently still bred on the Tipperary-Waterford border and it may well have survived in the Slieve Bloom Mountains on the Laois-Offaly border as well. Indeed, according to Scott, the hen harrier continued to breed in a few parts of the southern counties in the first half of the 20th century and bred sporadically in others.

The words of Kennedy, Ruttledge and Scroope (1954) sum up the ill-fated history of the hen harrier in Ireland: 'It is regrettable to have to record that ruthless extermination is the fate awaiting individuals of this species, which is not, except rarely, detrimental to game preservation and poultry-rearing. Few sportsmen seem capable of sparing these large, slow-flying birds of prey which are so confiding. I could probably include the Hen Harrier's much larger cousin, the Marsh Harrier, in these sentiments as well, as the same fate also awaited them in Ireland'.

And yet the recovery of the species and its eventual recolonisation of southern Ireland seem to have begun in about 1950 and is best described by the late Father P. G. Kennedy SJ in his *Birds of Ireland* (1961). 'Since 1940 it has occurred more frequently and has been an annual visitor to Counties Kerry, Wexford and Wicklow. It bred in Kerry, formerly one of its strongholds, in 1908 and probably in some subsequent years, and on the Knockmealdown Mountains (which separate Counties Tipperary and Waterford) up to 1913'.

In 1954, after a lapse of 41 years, there was satisfactory proof that the hen harrier had once again bred in Ireland. A year later it bred successfully in at least two counties and in autumn and winter was recorded in all four provinces. In 1956, at least 11 pairs bred successfully in three counties and in winter the hen harrier was regarded as widespread. Successful breeding then occurred in four counties in 1957 and then in five counties by 1958. Their range extended gradually as the years went by, with birds breeding in at least seven counties by 1967.

By 1971, there had been a sudden spread of nesting into 13 counties throughout the whole island and, probably for the first time in the 20th century, two pairs successfully nested and fledged young in the north Antrim area. It is possible that these birds may have come from the Mull of Kintyre in Scotland, only 11 miles (7 km) from the coast of Northern Ireland, but they may also have spread northward from a nucleus in the Irish Republic.

The recovery in Northern Ireland's uplands continued, due mainly to the extensive planting of young conifers, especially in County Antrim, during the 1960s. At the end of the Second World War, many upland areas of the UK and Ireland had been covered by blanket forestry, with harriers remaining to breed in the resulting young conifer plantations until the trees grew too tall and before the eventual closure of the canopy. These man-made forests, both young and mature, provided vital sanctuary for this species in the absence of deep tracts of heather moorland. The hen harrier would place its nest at the base of the conifers, still only one metre high, with the site wide open on all four sides. By the mid to late 1970s, some 20 pairs were breeding in the Antrim Plateau but once the trees grew taller and the canopy began to close, the harriers deserted the spruce plantations and returned to open moorland, which by now was showing the first signs of overgrazing by sheep. Furthermore, very few nests, if any, have been found in Antrim in areas felled and replanted, which does not bode well for the long term future of the species in conifer forests and sadly, since the early 1980s, hen harrier numbers have been in decline. Continued overgrazing resulting in poor ground cover, widespread depredation by the large fox population and the neglect and mismanagement of our uplands are all taking their toll.

Breeding biology: from courtship to fledging

In early spring, the pale grey, ghost-like male can often be seen 'sky dancing'. The term was coined by the great Frances Hamerstrom as she carried out a 27 year study (1957–1983) of the marsh hawk on the prairies of Wisconsin, and describes the breathtaking aerial display performed as the male starts to establish his breeding territory. Again and again he climbs to more than 100 m above the ground before spiralling downwards, spinning and tumbling, seemingly out of control, calling excitedly throughout his death-defying performance. Just when it seems impossible for him to avoid crashing to the ground, he suddenly regains control and sweeps upwards again to the same height, immediately resuming his impressive sequence of undulations.

Newly arrived females watch intently from prominent perches on a nearby mound, a fencepost or halfway up tall Sitka spruce trees, as the male attempts to attract one or all of them to join him in his aerial display. Occasionally, a female will instantly follow suit but her display is never as vigorous nor as prolonged as his.

During his bouts of sky dancing, it is not uncommon for the male to complete over 100 undulations each time he displays and, if unsuccessful, the whole process is repeated many times, after several well-earned breaks. Generally, though, his initial efforts tend to be successful and it is not long before he and at least one of the females can be observed circling and diving in unison over the moorland, their conspicuous white rump patches, or uppertail coverts, clearly visible to the naked eye.

Once a breeding pair has been formed, repeated sequences of copulation take place, usually on the ground, with the female obligingly crouching down while the male precariously stands on her lower back for several seconds, his wings fully outstretched and slowly beating the ground to maintain his delicate balance.

Although the male will initially select a potential nest site, the female has the final say when deciding its exact location. The nest is built by the female, with the male collecting his fair share of nesting material, carried by both sexes in either their feet or bills.

Male hen harriers occasionally build what is known as a cock nest which they do not appear to line with nesting material. Donald Watson suggests that they are built when males outnumber hens or when a male has lost his mate. This behaviour may also be triggered by excessive human disturbance at the nest site or when a male's original nest has been lost to a passing predator very early in the breeding season. Whatever its function, I have never observed cock nest building in the Antrim Plateau but have seen it on at least two occasions in southern Scotland during 2007 and 2008.

In Antrim, most of my ground nesting records have occurred during the first two weeks of May and none in April but dates can vary and egg laying can be delayed if the weather conditions are unfavourable. Clutches laid in Antrim range between three and six eggs, the commonest clutch being five eggs. Incubation is said to start when the second egg has been laid, but it does occasionally start with the first and may even be delayed until the clutch is complete.

In plantations where tree nesting is prevalent, nesting does not usually take place until two or sometimes three weeks after that of harriers which preferred to ground nest. This may be due to the time it takes for a pair to choose and then construct an intricate tree nest, compared with a generally straightforward ground nest. Clutch sizes range from two to four eggs, very rarely five, with the start of incubation following the same pattern as for ground nesting harriers.

Freshly laid hen harrier eggs generally have a pale bluish-green tint which fades to off-white within a week of being incubated. They vary in shape from rounded to somewhat elongated. Freshly hatched or broken hen harrier eggs can be recognised immediately by their attractive ice-green inner shell. The eggs are relatively small for the size of the bird, with the mean dimensions of 901 hen harrier eggs, measured by Eddie Balfour on Orkney, being 46.3 × 35.6 mm. In comparison, the average for 100 Montagu's harrier eggs, given by the *Handbook of British Birds,* was 41.5 × 32.7 mm. A newly hatched hen harrier chick weighs on average 19.8 g.

If the original clutch is lost, the female may well lay a replacement, provided the season is not too far advanced, which then results in the abandonment of nesting for that year. During the crucial incubation period, which lasts around 30 to 32 days, and for two weeks after hatching is completed, the female is totally dependent on the male for food. By the time the brood is a few weeks old, a distinct range in sizes is clearly noticeable due to asynchronous hatching. The smallest chick is least likely to survive as its larger siblings claim the majority of the spoils.

It is during the incubation period that females begin to moult and this continues until after the young have fledged. Grey males, however, do not usually begin to show signs of wing and tail moult until the chicks are a few weeks old. The complete moult for both sexes may therefore extend over several months.

In years when the food supply is poor or when inclement weather prevents regular hunting forays, the weakest chick will die and will be diligently fed by the female to the eldest chicks. The female will occasionally remove decaying or half-eaten prey items and hatched eggshells to keep the nest clean and free of predators, occasionally eating the shells as an extra source of calcium after the long incubation period.

Prey deliveries by the male during incubation and the early stages of brooding tend in Northern Ireland to consist of small birds like meadow pipit, skylark and starling but in other parts of the UK, hen harriers frequently rely on small mammals like rabbits, short-tailed voles and red grouse and their chicks.

Most prey items are delivered to the female by means of the aerial food pass, a not-to-be-missed moment when the male briefly stalls in mid-air to drop the prey, his mate turning on her back to receive it in her sharp talons. During poor weather the female rarely leaves the nest so the prey items are delivered to her or dropped into the nest by the industrious male. Once the brooding stage has ended, the female immediately resumes her hunting duties, with both adults playing an equal part in the rearing of their offspring.

All species of harrier have the same basic mode of hunting: flying rather slowly, usually low over the ground; they flap for a few metres and then gracefully glide on for a similar distance. They meticulously work every inch of the ground on their flight path like a well-trained pointer or spaniel. They quite often fly into the wind to slow down their ground speed, which is particularly useful when looking down into dense vegetation for prey. Once prey has been located, a hen harrier can strike with amazing speed and agility, even within a small gap in the heather or other rank vegetation.

Wilhelmus (Wim) Schipper from the Netherlands carried out extensive studies of hunting behaviour and a comparison of prey brought to the nests of Western marsh harriers, Montagu's harriers and hen harriers, concluding that the last were the most agile and prolific hunters of passerine birds in flight. These findings undoubtedly refer to males, which are generally more agile and lighter and are known to capture more small birds than do the much heavier females. His findings also showed that males of all three species hunted over larger distances to obtain prey items than did females.

When the harrier cannot strike immediately, it will hesitate over its quarry until it finds the right moment or reluctantly fly on empty handed. During an attack, it dives straight down onto its intended prey, feet first, wings upraised, or stalls by spreading its tail before dropping through the air in a characteristic sideways movement. If the prey is not seen until the bird passes by, the harrier can double back with amazing speed, assisted by the wind into which it has been flying. Despite these skills, it is reckoned that only a low percentage rate of all strikes, maybe no more than 10–15%, is successful.

In defence of her nest and chicks, a female hen harrier can be particularly aggressive towards humans. It's a rare but hair-raising experience. Donald Watson found that hen harriers which showed most aggression towards human intrusion at nest sites were the most successful at rearing young to the flying stage but did go on to say that even the mildest of females can have successful nests as well.

Prior to fledging, young harriers are extremely active on the ground, rushing off into heather to hide from predators, hastily returning to the centre of the nest when either adult arrives with food. Similar activity has been observed and recorded at hen harrier tree nest sites in Northern Ireland.

The sexing of young in a ground nest is best done when the chicks are two to three weeks old and can be based on three important criteria: body weight, leg thickness and the colour of the irides which are cloudy grey in males and chocolate brown in females.

Fledging occurs at around 30–35 days for the much lighter males and approximately three to four days later for the noticeably heavier female chicks with both sexes fully dependent upon both adults for at least two or three weeks before their dispersal from their breeding grounds. The average weight of chicks at fledging is given by Scharf and Balfour (1971) as 472 g, but female chicks may be as much as 100 g heavier than males.

Mortality rates are highest amongst harriers in their first year of life with more than 60% and even 70% failing to survive to twelve months. Despite these high mortality rates amongst young fledglings, hen harriers, in the absence of persecution, are fairly long-lived with males known to survive to ten years old and females to twelve.

Those that do survive the rigours of their first winter will probably return to their natal area the following spring but are unlikely to breed. Breeding generally occurs when hen harriers are two or three years old but individuals have been known to breed in their second calendar year. This is most noticeable in males which are still in partially brown (ringtail) plumage but which quite often breed successfully despite their immaturity.

Throughout most of their first year of life, young male hen harriers remain in brown (ringtail) plumage similar to that of adult females. The moult into grey plumage occasionally begins as early as the March of their first calendar year, but the first grey feathers on the head, breast and greater wing coverts do not generally appear until July or August of that year. What happens to the young males in eclipse plumage before they attain the plumage of a full adult male is a continuing puzzle to me. They are a very rare sight even at winter roost sites and are only occasionally seen attempting to breed. Where do they go? Do they migrate and find territories elsewhere or do most of them fail to reach adulthood? Is their scarcity in Antrim due simply to the low fledging rates that have continually dogged this species in recent years? In 24 years of studying hen harriers I have failed to find the answer.

Nesting European Eagle Owls, now pose a big threat to breeding Hen Harriers, in the UK. (Courtesy of Gary Jenkins)

Above: A superb brood of five young Hen Harrier chicks. (Courtesy of Stephen Murphy)

Left: The author in action. (Courtesy of Keith Glasgow)

Below: A male Hen Harrier in characteristic hunting mode. (Courtesy of Bob McMillan, Skye-Birds.com)

Right: An adult male Hen Harrier. (Courtesy of Bob McMillan, Skye-Birds.com)

A Common Snipe

Two week old harrier chick

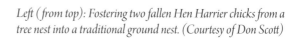

The formidable Goshawk

Hen Harrier chicks sheltering under their mum from the heavy rain. (Courtesy of Fred Quinn)

A close-up of a female Hen Harrier at her nest. (Courtesy of Don Scott)

Study of nestling Hen Harrier

Below right: The author with a young Black Harrier in South Africa. (Courtesy of Don Scott)

Male & Female, near Slemish

Slemish Mountain in County Antrim - right in the heart of Hen Harrier territory. (Courtesy ofDon Scott)

Right: Learning to dissect harrier pellets, with the late Roger Clarke. (Courtesy of Don Scott)

Female near Byvore Bridge, Slieveanorra

The author and his captive bred Great Grey Owls. (Courtesy of Don Scott)

Male over peat stack, Capanagh Forest

Young Curlew chick

Close-up study of young harrier brood

Left: Slieveanorra - former tree nesting and tree roosting habitat for Hen Harriers. (Courtesy of Don Scott)
Right: A 'sky-dancing' male Hen Harrier. (Courtesy of Bob McMillan, Skye-Birds.com)

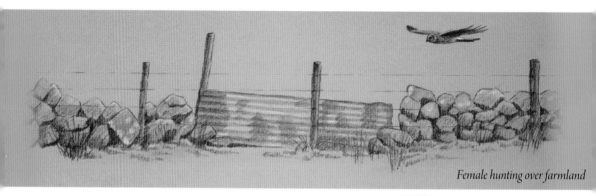

Female hunting over farmland

Male circling at, Slieveanorra

Female returning to Slieveanorra Forest

Right: Female Marsh Harrier landing at her nest. (Courtesy of Bob McMillan, Skye-Birds. com)

Below: A hunting female Marsh Harrier. (Courtesy of Bob McMillan, Skye-Birds. com)

Meadow Pipit in typical pose

Study of a young rabbit

A soaring female Hen Harrier. (Courtesy of Bob McMillan, Skye-Birds.com)

Close-up of a female harrier chick

Above: Bowland in Lancashire - A rare roadside sign promoting their Hen Harriers. (Courtesy of Gary Jenkins)

Male crossing the Glendun River, Slieveanorra

The 'Kiekentellers' (harrier observers), monitoring winter roosting Hen and Marsh Harriers, in Holland. Left to Right: Don Scott (N.Ireland), Andre Bourgonje (Holland), the late Roger Clarke (England), and Heinrich Belting (Germany). (Courtesy of Henk Castelijns, Holland)

A female Hen Harrier guarding her tree nest. (Courtesy of Bob McMillan, Skye-Birds. com)

Female in typical hunting pose

Hen harrier diet in Antrim

Food studies are central to our understanding of raptor behaviour and ecology. Not only are the form and structure of a particular species closely related to its prey and hunting technique, but so too are various aspects of that species' ecology, including population density, distribution, breeding performance and mortality. Furthermore, raptors may be unwittingly exposed via their prey to harmful pollutants so a thorough knowledge of their diet is important for the conservation and management of both hunter and prey.

Most detailed studies of diet, including that of the hen harrier, have been made during the breeding season as prey is generally brought to the nest, making it easy to collect large numbers of pellets and discarded remains. Pellets and prey remains can also be collected at ground roosts and below tree roosts and, less often, at favoured plucking posts.

Until 1991, there had been no comprehensive study of the diet of breeding hen harriers in Northern Ireland. As a result, virtually nothing was known about the feeding ecology of this scarce Red Listed raptor. And, despite detailed studies of breeding hen harriers in the neighbouring Republic of Ireland carried out from the early 1960s to the 1980s by accomplished ornithologists such as Doran, Jones, O'Flynn and Scott, their diet remained virtually unknown there as well.

With the guidance of Roger Clarke, I mastered the skills of pellet dissection and the identification of prey remains and in 1991 we began methodical studies of hen harrier diet. Pellets, prey remains and moulted feathers were collected annually from ground and tree nest sites. Over a five year period, 160 hen harrier pellets were collected from all the known nest sites in County Antrim. They were dried and analysed and found to contain 260 prey items.

The results showed that only three species of small birds – meadow pipit, skylark and starling – dominated 74% of the harrier's food intake. The high dependence on small birds was unsurprising given the absence of voles in Northern Ireland. In total, avian prey made up 78.5% of the diet with red grouse, snipe and several unidentified passerines also recorded. Mammals such as rabbit and hare also featured at 13% with smaller species like pygmy shrew and wood mouse at 4% and unidentified beetle remains making up the remaining 4.5% of the diet.

The low importance of red grouse (0.8%), in the harrier's diet was not a surprise as there are only small pockets of this rare game bird in the Antrim Plateau and elsewhere in Northern Ireland. David Scott told me that his own studies of hen harriers in the Wicklow Hills in the neighbouring Republic of Ireland during the 1960s and 1970s had also shown the red grouse to be a 'rare bird'. The statistics show that Antrim is not like Scotland, where hen harriers rely heavily on red grouse during the breeding season, yet they are still wrongly blamed by the shooting fraternity for preying on grouse.

This criticism has in recent years undoubtedly seen rogue elements taking the law into their own hands to unlawfully kill adults and chicks in north Antrim and elsewhere in Northern Ireland. The sneaky removal of the female's eggs late in the incubation period or the sudden disappearance of downy chicks are part of a strategy to severely disrupt the harrier's breeding cycle. Yet if Antrim's hen harriers depended on red grouse as their main source of food they would have died out long ago. More importantly, my study of their diet clearly shows that hen harrier numbers are more likely to be influenced by the numbers of small passerines than by the numbers of red grouse.

Lagomorphs (rabbit and hare) were found to be the most popular mammal (13%) and were probably taken by females, which are on average 40% heavier than males. Males, with their smaller size and greater agility, are widely thought to hunt more passerine prey. Also of note over the five year study period was an overall decrease in skylark remains which diminished in line with a decline recorded throughout the UK. Conversely, there was a rich supply of juvenile and adult starlings in the Antrim Plateau just as the harriers had hatched their eggs and they soon became their second most important prey species.

A second batch of 310 hen harrier pellets was collected from nest sites in the same area over a 10 year period between 1996 and 2005. This was my first real test. I had built up an extensive reference collection of feathers, skeletal remains and hair and fur samples from small and medium-sized mammals but until now had analysed only a few hen harrier pellets found at winter roosts in Counties Antrim and Tyrone and on my travels in India and the Gambia.

This large sample quickly demonstrated that Antrim's hen harriers had a more diverse diet than we had thought. 193 more prey items were identified comprising eight different species of bird. Again meadow pipit, skylark and starling dominated, making up 75% of the harrier's total diet. More significantly, skylark numbers had decreased by 2.2% with meadow pipit and starling increasing by 0.5% and 2.9% respectively. Red grouse showed at only 1.1%, with snipe 2.6%, curlew 1.8%, chaffinch 0.9% and finally house sparrow at 0.7%. Several curlew chicks and snipe were also found on the forest floor and clinging to the upper branches of four tree nests.

Lagomorphs (rabbit and hare) were again the dominant medium-sized mammals at 9.5% but had decreased by 3.2% from the previous study, with small mammal numbers – pygmy shrew (2.2%) and wood mouse – remaining stable. One pellet found below a tree nest contained just a large ball of hair and specific analysis showed that it belonged, oddly enough, to a badger (0.2%). A foraging hen harrier, probably a female, had obviously found a badger carcass but had been unable to feed on it due to its thick coat and skin.

Unidentified black beetle casings were again recorded at 3.1% with scales from viviparous lizard (0.9%) appearing in pellets for the first time. Mammals and other non-avian species accounted for only 18% of the hen harrier's total diet in Antrim.

A third batch of 130 pellets was collected from ground and tree nest sites in County Antrim over the four year period from 2006 to 2009. These contained a total of 240 prey items similar to those found in the 470 pellets collected since 1991. Meadow pipit, starling and skylark again dominated, making up 73% of the hen harrier's total diet, with male blackbird and male stonechat appearing for the first time as did brown rat. The complete make-up of the diet over this period can be found in the Tables section at the end of this book.

The analysis of 600 pellets over a 19 year period from 1991 to 2009 would make it seem reasonable to suggest that Northern Ireland, and Ireland as a whole, have never supported a large hen harrier population because of an absence of short-tailed voles. In the UK, voles are an essential part of the hen harrier's diet during the breeding season, probably governing the harrier's numbers during poor vole seasons, which on average occur every three to four years. Yet there are no voles on the nearby Isle of Man and the island supports a substantial and productive hen harrier population with around 30–40 breeding pairs annually and record numbers of wintering birds, with past counts exceeding 100 and reaching 50 on average.

Having observed the breeding habitat for hen harriers on the Isle of Man and compared it with that found in Antrim, I have concluded that harriers on the Isle of Man suffer little disturbance, no persecution and minimal predation. Antrim does not provide these basic requirements and so fails to support a successful and productive hen harrier population.

Do hen harriers hunt at night?

Recent observations by Bill Hesketh and Bill Murphy, who study breeding and winter roosting hen harriers in the Forest of Bowland in Lancashire, provide growing evidence of nocturnal hunting by diurnal raptors such as hen harriers. They, like me, have always assumed that hen harriers hunt by day and communally roost at night but their recent and potentially groundbreaking findings call this into question.

Remote locations and fading light make winter roosts extremely difficult to monitor precisely but these two competent observers have, on several occasions, while crossing moorland by torchlight at the end of their evening watches, seen ringtail hen harriers pursuing fieldfares. They have also glimpsed, as late as 10 p.m., the occasional ringtail in the headlights of their car. This behaviour has never before, as far as I am aware, been recorded or documented.

Hesketh and Murphy have also, at morning watches, observed harriers rising with full crops, indicating that they had fed prior to leaving the confines of the roost site. These particular individuals would land nearby, staying on the ground for a considerable time while others with empty crops flew off hastily, presumably to hunt. Were the birds with full crops hunting during the night or was a larder, as the two observers have suggested, situated within the roost itself? At evening watches in Northern Ireland, I have observed harriers arriving with full crops but never departing with a full crop the following morning.

Hesketh and Murphy have also witnessed three females and two male harriers settling at an evening roost, with none emerging the following morning. This suggests either that they had been disturbed by a predator or that they had taken flight during the night for other reasons. Disturbance by a predator is probably the more likely explanation for their early departure.

While watching evening roosts in Northern Ireland and on the Isle of Man, I have counted birds in at night and out again next morning and ended up with two completely different figures. Could these different totals be explained simply by disturbance from a predator or had the birds left to hunt prior to sunrise? If a minority had left due to a marauding predator, then why had they not all left, as usually happens when roosting harriers and other avian species are disturbed?

At one site I have watched for the past 18 years, the harriers tend to remain high up in the surrounding conifers when a red fox enters the birds' roosting quarters. When I leave, well after sunset, they are still perched in the tree-tops where they probably remain overnight. Hen harriers are known to have an alternative roost site, which is occasionally nearby, so it is possible that the missing birds had used it at some stage during the night. Perhaps, though, the missing harriers, as the two Bills have suggested, were away hunting during the hours of darkness.

It would be interesting to pursue the theory of night hunting and feeding but obtaining definitive proof would be extremely difficult. I have never seen hen harriers hunting at night but I have observed them hunting at dusk, which Donald Watson also mentions in his famous 1977 Poyser monograph. I have also observed hen harriers arriving well after sunset at my local roost and at a mixed harrier species roost in India so it is possible that we have underestimated these birds' flight capabilities. Hen harriers' ear apertures are extremely large and comparable with those of owls rather than other diurnal raptors so this could be a nocturnal adaptation. Nocturnal hunting and feeding by diurnal raptors may not be that unusual, as recent studies of goshawk (2003) in Hamburg and peregrine falcon (2006) in New York have shown, while a 1991 publication records the North American Northern harrier flying and presumably migrating at night.

I do know that I will now be watching harriers more closely at winter roosts and during late evening forays during the breeding season as this fascinating behaviour, like tree nesting, may have gone unnoticed for many years.

Communal roosting

A melee of hen harriers over their communal winter roost is an awe-inspiring sight, one not to be missed under any circumstances either by the serious harrier student or the casual birder.

The earliest reference to communal roosting by hen harriers appears to come from Selby (1831): 'It roosts upon the ground in very long heath or ling and generally in companies of five or six together, males and females indiscriminately.' However, it is not certain whether Selby's observations preceded those of his friend Sir William Jardine or, indeed that he discovered the behaviour independently, as the two gentlemen regularly corresponded and made field trips together with Jardine giving a more comprehensive account a few years later.

Communal roosting outside the breeding season is known to occur in most species of harrier apart from the Australian spotted harrier, about whose winter behaviour little is known. Roosts can range in altitude from 15 m (50 ft) to 427 m (1400 ft) above sea level. In winter, birds approach the roost site from about 30 minutes to one hour before sunset and first form pre-roost gatherings, usually near or on the edge of the roost itself, on mainly bare ground, short grass and the tops of low bushes. They then stand facing into the wind, doing nothing more than preening and observing their surroundings.

Shortly before sunset they will begin to leave these pre-roost areas and on arrival at the roost itself will often fly about, criss-crossing each other's flight paths or gently soaring if a fresh wind is blowing. Chattering calls are sometimes heard during these final flights but the spectacle of harriers roosting is otherwise a strangely silent affair.

Before they begin roosting there may be an instant or two when all or most of the birds are in the air together above the site. This is known as milling, the birds generally circling low and then high in a clockwise and then suddenly anti-clockwise direction before dropping into the surrounding vegetation.

At other times, especially during heavy rain or when there is little wind to assist their flight, birds may arrive and roost immediately with no more than one or two in sight at any given time. Occasionally, the larger females oust the males from where they were roosting, sending them flying to and fro, hesitating over other possible places to roost and perhaps landing a few times before finally settling for the night.

Hen harriers roost individually in gaps in vegetation and on flattened patches or tussocks known as forms, often within a few metres of each other but sometimes much further apart. In the UK a variety of open habitats are used, with about half of the sites discovered so far on fresh or salt marsh, in reeds, sedges, rushes and long grass. Other sites are on dry rough grassland, in heather on lowland heaths or higher up on heather moorland, in young conifer plantations, amongst crops and occasionally in dunes near the coast.

In Northern Ireland, harriers have been recorded roosting on heather moorland, in a mixture of rushes and grass, in vacated tree nests and near the tops of tall conifers when the site was deemed unsafe due to the presence of a fox. Numbers at individual roost sites throughout the UK can vary from just a few birds to, exceptionally, over 100 and even single birds can persist in using the same site on a regular basis. At two known sites in Northern Ireland, the maximum number recorded has been eight and six birds respectively.

The departure next morning is usually swift and less spectacular. The harriers start to leave their roosting quarters about half an hour before sunrise, occasionally settling to preen before dispersing from the area. They may leave singly in all directions, or in twos and threes in a favoured direction, but all will have left the area by about 15 minutes after sunrise. Hen harriers are known to travel quite a distance from their roost sites in a day, the maximum distance recorded being 16 km (10 miles).

Towards sunset, hen harriers, possibly the same ones, can be seen returning to the communal roost, which will be used for an unpredictable number of days, weeks and months each winter. These winter roost sites can act as useful indicators of the success of a breeding season, with the young of the year tending to arrive with the adult birds. A small local roost may also reveal the exact breeding population in that particular area, as many of these roosts tend to be adjacent to the birds' breeding grounds. The small and scattered breeding population in Northern Ireland, however, makes the roosts particularly difficult to find, let alone to monitor each winter, and roosts are not always used every year.

A history of communal hen harrier roosts in Northern Ireland

A hen harrier winter roost site in Northern Ireland is of great ornithological importance, as a lack of regular observers in the uplands during the harshest months of the year mean that very few have been recorded. Alternative sites are sometimes used but harriers tend to be faithful to their roosts. Many of the instances described below indicate that the same birds returned nightly, indeed year after year, to the same site.

Early historical records

Before 1992, the only winter roost known to me in Northern Ireland was at Reedy Flat, on the southern shore of Lough Neagh in County Armagh. During the winter months of 1990–1991 and 1991–1992, I had regularly seen up to three ringtails (adult females or young of the year) roosting there. In the winter of 1992–1993 an adult male and female were regularly present, followed in 1993–1994 by a single male, his dingy plumaged upperparts signifying that he was a very young individual.

I made four visits to the area during the course of the 1994–1995 winter, recording during two of those visits only an occasional passing male or female, apparently roosting elsewhere. Only the occasional harrier was recorded after that, but not apparently roosting at Reedy Flat. The site, based on grass and rushes (juncus), has hardly been used in recent years, thanks mainly to disturbance by wildfowlers and the intrusion of a large herd of grazing cattle which flattened the rushes.

In the late 1970s, a small roost was known of in a forest to the north of Ballycastle in County Antrim. Up to four hen harriers were seen by Fred Quinn, a member of the Forest Service, on most evenings during the autumn and winter months but after the introduction of clay pigeon shooting to the area, the site was vacated and apparently never used again.

For at least two winters a male roosted amongst dead bracken at Murlough Nature Reserve (County Down). It was first seen by National Trust warden Richard Ellis on 17 January 1984 and again from 5–8 February of that year. During the 1984–1985 winter, a single adult male again roosted within the reserve and was taken to be the same bird because of distinctive plumage markings.

During the mid 1980s there were apparently two well-known hen harrier winter roosts in the Sperrins, one close to Slieve Gallion (Londonderry) and the other further to the south west near Fivemiletown in County Tyrone. To my disgust, harriers arriving to roost at both these sites were ruthlessly shot. They were presumably ambushed on arrival as they milled over the sites before going to ground. They were soon driven from these areas, never to return.

In 1987 and for a few years thereafter an adult female regularly roosted on a small man-made island at Lough Na Cranagh which lies directly behind the famous basalt promontory of Fair Head in County Antrim. This lone female was observed roosting on several occasions by Clive Mellon while he worked in the area as a National Trust warden. There were also unconfirmed reports of individual birds roosting on at least two occasions on the adjacent moorland.

In November 1993, several wildfowlers reported a grey male going to ground close to a small coniferous wood to the east of Ballymoney (County Antrim) although on subsequent visits I was able to record only sparrowhawk and merlin. During the winter months of 1997–1998 an adult grey male roosted on several occasions amongst the tall reeds and sedges at the outer edges of Lough Money (County Down). The bird roosted close to the home of the warden Sean D'Arcy-Burt from the nearby Quoile Pondage NNR, an area also favoured by hunting harriers during the winter months.

Overwintering harriers have in recent years also been observed at other locations in County Down: the Quoile Pondage mentioned above, the remnants of the Downpatrick Marshes, Strand Lough and around the St. John's Point area. The harriers at this last location may have been moving to and from the nearby Isle of Man.

The Copeland (Islands) Bird Observatory also receives a thin but regular autumn passage and records show that the month of October is the best time to see migrating hen harriers. Rathlin Island, off the north east coast of County Antrim, also hosts the occasional migrating hen harrier, probably from the nearby Mull of Kintyre in Scotland.

Roost monitoring

On 20 September 1992, I began a comprehensive and long term survey (17 years and 240 watches to date) of a hen harrier roost site 1.3 miles into a mature conifer plantation in the Sperrins, County Tyrone and about 250 m above sea level. The site is in a now unused turbary, an area of land used by peat cutters over several generations. Only two other roost sites in the UK have a higher elevation: one on Dartmoor (England) at 300 m, the other in Ayrshire (Scotland) at 450 m above sea level. The main roost, which lies less than 100 m from a narrow forest track, has a long history of roosting hen harriers with one relevant record dating back to a wet and cold February afternoon in 1981, when at least six adult males were seen circling above the site by a Forest Service employee, Albert Crooks, just as he finished work for the day. Three harriers were noted on at least three further occasions in subsequent years and there were even earlier, if imprecise recollections of roosting dating back to 1978.

The site was rediscovered by luck in mid August 1992 by my raptor colleague Larry Toal after a chance meeting with Albert during Larry's end of season merlin studies. I made two initial visits to the site on 12 and 16 September with Albert, Philip McHaffie and Roger Clarke, where we found several fresh pellets, excreta and moulted feathers amongst the deep heather to the rear of the site, directly behind a cluster of four large willow bushes, proving that harriers were still visiting the area.

Exhileratingly, on the first evening of my survey a few days later, two pale plumaged grey males roosted in the long heather. This certainly exceeded my expectations, considering an overall success rate of 75% and the site's high elevation which made it more susceptible than lower roosts to harsh weather.

The two most successful months for observing roosting hen harriers were October and February, with the two least successful months being December and March. The vast majority of harriers observed at the roost were grey males (85%) with females and ringtails (first year birds) rarely recorded (15%). In the UK, grey males tend to be more numerous at roosts in western areas like Northern Ireland while at eastern roosts, the larger females and brown plumaged ringtails predominate.

The largest number of harriers recorded at this site was eight, a Northern Ireland record, but this has unfortunately occurred only once, on 28 September 1997. Five have been recorded on a handful of occasions and four recorded 12 times, with three 25 times, two on 55 occasions and a single bird recorded more than 60 times.

Over the winters of 2005–2008, only single birds were recorded and quite often none at all, with several others apparently avoiding the site to roost elsewhere. This was almost certainly due to the regular intrusion of red foxes, which in later years forced the harriers to roost in the tops of the surrounding conifers. One such intrusion, witnessed by Michael Devlin on 10 October 2001, saw a fox bobbing through the deep heather carrying a male hen harrier in its jaws, so the birds would have moved to a much safer roost elsewhere.

This is an important area and habitat for our raptor species. Hen harriers once bred at this traditional roost site, it was visited by a red kite on 22 September 1997 and goshawk and buzzard are both now resident. Further monitoring will, I hope, reveal the reason for the premature abandonment of this site and allow for its reversal. The red fox intrusions, the arrival of the goshawk and buzzard and the recent harvesting of half of the surrounding conifers, which sheltered the site from the harsh elements, may all be playing their part.

Another hen harrier winter roost was discovered by sheer good luck on 13 November 1994. Philip McHaffie and I were having a welcome cup of hot coffee at a popular raptor watchers lay-by on the Altnahinch Road, which conveniently overlooks a vast expanse of Slieveanorra Forest in north Antrim, when, at about 2.40 p.m., we had a chance sighting of a single adult male roosting, unbelievably, near the top of a block of tall conifers about 100 m from our vantage point.

The following week, on 20 November, I visited the area again with my wife, more in curiosity than any real hope of seeing another harrier unconventionally roosting in the tree tops. Then, at 3.45 p.m., we saw what was almost certainly the same pale plumaged male from the previous week, circling above the tall conifers and landing suddenly in one, about 2 m from the top, in what I reckoned was the same part of the forest. This very pale male, almost white when seen against the dark green of the forest canopy, had been observed breeding in this area for the past four years. How good it was to see him again.

It now became quite obvious why this bird was tree roosting. The heather moorland was useless for such a purpose and a high density of foxes made it much safer for this wise and seemingly adaptable old harrier to be up a tree rather than on the ground. Although no more harriers were recorded that evening, I hoped that others would follow suit over the coming weeks and months. I was not to be disappointed.

On 27 November, all roads thankfully led to Slieveanorra again (where else would I have gone?) but on this memorable occasion I was regrettably on my own. Over a three hour period, from 12.50 p.m. until 3.50 p.m., a total of six hen harriers – four adult males, a female and a young ringtail – roosted high in the tops of the tall conifers in the same general area as the previous two weeks, This was considered a record attendance for a hen harrier winter roost site in Northern Ireland, only eventually surpassed at the Sperrins site in September 1997.

Also present that evening were a male and female sparrowhawk and a male peregrine falcon, none of which had been present on our two previous visits. The reason for their arrival in the area became clear at around 4.15 p.m. when approximately 1500 starlings and a flock of 200 fieldfares suddenly appeared above the forest canopy before they too roosted in the tall conifers. In fading light, I watched the peregrine snatch one of the starlings from the mass, with both sparrowhawks also awaiting their chance of a late afternoon meal.

On 4 and 11 December, Philip and I again watched the site. On the first occasion, two males and an adult female were present. Our watch the following week was eventually abandoned due to hill fog, but not before we observed our old friend, the pale plumaged and ghost-like adult male, tree roosting once again. Five further watches from 17 December to 14 January 1995 drew complete blanks, with one again prematurely abandoned due to dense hill fog.

On 18 February, the same male roosted again. 'What a beautiful bird this is,' I murmured to myself, seeing his silvery-white upperwings and body as he came to rest on a 20 m high Sitka at 2.50 p.m. Two further watches before the start of the 1995 breeding season saw three harriers (two males and one female) going to roost on 11 March, with the same two males present, identified by their distinctive plumage markings, on 18 March. This was a remarkable first winter at Slieveanorra and I was hopeful that the trend would continue during the 1995–1996 series of roost watches.

The first watch of the 1995–1996 winter took place on 8 October 1995 with five harriers – three males and two females – roosting in the tall conifers, with singles of both sexes recorded on the 15th and none on the 21st, although small parties of several hundred starlings were seen congregating for the first time. Not surprisingly, a female peregrine, two kestrels and a male merlin were observed hunting the arriving starlings, which simply scattered in all directions to escape their sharp and deadly talons.

On 28 October, two males and two females roosted, with one male seen pre-roosting for the first time on the adjacent moorland. Six further watches from 18 November to 3 February 1996 had a 50% success rate culminating with the return of the pale- plumaged male on the last day. Starling numbers had peaked by 25 November with over 3000 roosting in the same area along with a mixed flock of several hundred fieldfare and mistle thrushes.

Two final watches on 3 March and 17 March produced two grey males and a surprise visit on the 3rd from a sub-adult golden eagle, with a male and a female seen half-heartedly displaying on the 17th prior to roosting. We were full of anticipation about what the following winter would bring at this superb roost site.

To our dismay neither tree roosting harriers nor any other raptor species materialised at Slieveanorra during the 1996–1997 winter. Gone too were the thousands of starlings and thrush species which had also roosted in the same area. This unique hen harrier roost, which had also attracted four other raptor species, was undoubtedly linked to the large number of roosting starlings and thrushes so when they suddenly moved away, so did all the harriers. Thankfully, the odd roosting harrier is still to be seen at Slieveanorra today but sadly not, as far as I am aware, tree roosting.

Other hen harrier tree roosts

Until the tree roost at Slieveanorra was discovered back in 1994, I knew of only one other exceptional site where harriers were not roosting directly on the ground. This male- dominated winter roost site was discovered in 1962 by my harrier colleague Frank King from County Kerry. Here, up to 10 adult males, with no females or ringtails, spent the night completely off the ground, roosting in a low ragged hawthorn hedge.

The hedge was on neglected farmland and many of Frank's observations were made only in October, over a two year period, when the hedge was still leafy. He doubted that it would provide sufficient cover later in the winter. It is interesting that the information gleaned from both the Slieveanorra and, to a lesser extent, the Sperrins roost sites appears to tie in with similar observations made in Kerry by Frank King, providing evidence of a phenomenon quite rare in the context of the species ecology and overall European range.

Since then, and after an extensive search of the harrier literature, I have managed to find a further three instances of hen harriers roosting in trees. The first of these was recorded during the winter of 1968–1969 in southern Germany at a semi-mature spruce plantation surrounded by young pine trees between 3 and 3.5 high. (Andris, Saumer and Trillmich, 1970).

Surprisingly, this rarely recorded behaviour occurred only once, with the harriers soon reverting to roosting exclusively on the ground during the remainder of that winter and in subsequent years. Andris surmises that the gradual growth of the spruce and pine trees and the resulting disappearance of a sufficiently large open grassy area nearby, once favourable for roosting, could have been the cause of this behaviour, previously unobserved in Germany.

The same three observers then recorded hen harriers tree roosting for a second time, on this occasion in a pine forest in the southern Upper Rhine plain during the winter of 1977–1978. The birds sought out an 11–14 year old plantation and roosted in the upper fifth of the 7–12 metre trees. The observers specifically mention that the roost site was never along the forest edge but always in the middle of the plantation (as at Slieveanorra Forest in Northern Ireland) in an area covering several hectares and in trees of approximately the same age. In both these instances the number of roosting harriers was not mentioned by the observers.

During the winter of 1976–1977 a third hen harrier tree roost was discovered in the Rench plain (central Baden) in south Germany. On this occasion, a pine wood provided the actual roost site in an area of about three hectares situated on the fringes of a large and mixed deciduous wood of around 400 hectares (Kropp and Munch, 1979).

Discreet observations were made during February, March and April 1977 from a camouflaged hide within the pine wood, This showed that at least five or six harriers settled in trees around 20 metres high, mostly on dead branches about three or four metres below the tree tops. Over 300 pellets were found under at least 30 different trees during several collections, showing that the roosting sites must have changed several times over what had to have been a considerable period of time. Interestingly, all the known roosting sites were situated within an area of one hectare.

Other records now show that tree roosting by hen harriers during the winter months is not exclusive to Northern Ireland nor to the neighbouring Republic but that this unconventional form of roosting is still rarely recorded in any part of the world where harriers freely congregate after their breeding season has ended. More importantly, they also show that the hen harrier in particular has great survival skills and, in difficult conditions, is apparently able to adapt immediately to its surroundings, no matter how alien they may at first appear.

Tree roosting in vacated tree nests

Before the discovery of the tree roosts at Slieveanorra Forest and in the Sperrins, hen harriers in Northern Ireland had been observed roosting during the winter months in vacated tree nests.

The first definite signs of tree roosting by a hen harrier were discovered on 6 February 1993 when I was inspecting the old 1992 tree nest in south Antrim with Philip McHaffie and George McGrand, formerly of the Forest Service. The ground below the 2 m high nest was heavily soiled with freshly deposited excreta and a secondary feather from an adult male was also found on the forest floor.

A second early-morning visit was paid to the site on the 13th and as I approached the nest, I inadvertently flushed an adult male, proving that tree roosting was already occurring. During visits in January and February 1992 to the long vacated 1991 tree nest, small amounts of fresh excreta had been noticed on the ground, but tree roosting by hen harriers was not then considered a possibility.

Similarly, on 26 March 1994, a visit was paid to the vacated 1993 tree nest and on arrival I found the forest floor soiled black, a sign of old excreta, but also heavily splattered with much recent crystallised white excreta, with several pellets and a large primary from a female also present. A second and much later inspection of the 1993 tree nest on 25 March 1995 again revealed the presence of fresh excreta, which indicated further use of the nest for roosting purposes in consecutive years.

When a tree nest was subsequently discovered in Antrim, we took care to visit it during the winter months, as long as it remained intact, to see if tree roosting was still taking place. The answer we got was an emphatic 'yes'. The majority of my tree roosting records are of adult males, given that, as I have already emphasised, the majority of harriers attending roosts in Antrim and the Sperrins are grey males.

Provided that enough suitable trees are available in plantations, it's likely that tree roosting and roosting in vacated tree nests during the winter months will persist in the Antrim hen harrier population, just as tree nesting has persisted since at least 1990, given the unsuitability of the moorland for roosting and nesting.

It is highly unlikely that another large ground or tree roost will be discovered in Antrim or the Sperrins in the near future, due to the fragmentation and overall decrease of the hen harrier population in these areas. One can therefore expect more single birds roosting in future years, probably in similar circumstances to those described above, which does not bode well for the future of this species over the next decade.

---

1   On Sunday, 23 November 2008 at around 3.30 p.m. and similarly on Saturday, 6 December, Philip McHaffie and I observed two grey males going to roost in either the trees or in a long-vacated tree nest in the original tree nesting forest in south Antrim. For the first time in 20 years, no tree nests had been found in the plantation in 2008 or 2009, so were these birds using a previously used arboreal nest or were they simply tree roosting? Information from the Forest Service in July 2009 suggests that a small ground roost is in operation about 200 m to the south west of the plantation. This will, I hope, be observed during the winter of 2009–2010.

Why harriers tree nest

Several species of harrier can nest in trees just like any other arboreal bird. The majority of records are from Europe but other instances have occurred in North America, Australia and New Zealand, with only one in the UK (Northern Ireland). This strange behaviour has mystified even those of us who have studied them closely but there are complex and varied reasons why it happens.

Instances of tree nesting have been recorded in five (31%) of the world's 16 recognised species of harrier *Circus sp.* and I strongly suspect it in another. The definite records are for the spotted harrier from Australia and Western Indonesia, the swamp harrier from Australia and New Zealand, the hen harrier and the Western marsh harrier from Europe and the Northern harrier from North America and Canada. During personal observations in 2004 and from recent photographs, there is a distinct possibility that an isolated island species, the Reunion harrier, may also be tree nesting.

Spotted harrier

Until 1991, the spotted harrier from Australia was recognised as the only species of harrier habitually to nest in trees. Spotted harriers were probably once ground nesters like other harrier species and so have subsequently adapted and become arboreal probably for the same reasons as those quoted for the hen harrier in Northern Ireland. It is not generally recognised that they sometimes practise another habit unique among harriers: they have two breeding seasons per year, in autumn and spring, especially when prey is abundant.

The spotted harrier builds its own flimsy nest, which is unusually flat for a raptor, often positioned on the smaller outer branches of a tree rather than in a fork and on occasions quite low down. Due to their flimsy nature, the nests of this exquisite species are more commonly blown out of trees during bad weather than are those of other Australian raptors (D. Baker-Gabb). Several hen harrier tree nests, equally flimsily constructed, have also been blown out of trees during exceptionally wet and windy weather.

This suggests that the spotted harrier adopted arboreal nesting relatively recently in its evolution, perhaps in response to high predation pressure from numerous mammals and to poor ground cover in the arid and semi-arid areas where it breeds. Nests have been found in a variety of trees, including the many species of eucalypts and casuarinas, from as low as 2 m but more often between four and eight metres. The spotted harrier rarely nests higher than 12 m above the ground but at least two nests have been known to be above 14 m and 15 m respectively.

In treeless areas like the Nullarbor Plain in South Australia, spotted harriers have been known to build their nests on telegraph poles. One nest has even been found on the ground (W. Klau). The spotted harrier is regarded as a highly nomadic species, similar to the short-eared owl, and its movements, particularly during the breeding season, are often associated with the availability of food. This explains its sudden arrival in desolate and treeless areas.

Hen harrier

I have found only three instances of hen harriers using another bird's nest or nesting in a tree. These records pre-date the discovery of habitual tree nesting in Northern Ireland during the summer of 1991 and almost certainly in 1990. I must emphasise that none of the following three records involves hen harriers building their own tree nests.

Firstly, an extract by P. V. Plesskiy (1971) describes an interesting and abnormal find of a hen harrier tree nest in the Kirov-Chepskiy district of Russia in 1936. The nest was found on 19 July 1936 at a height of nine metres in a large pine wood where the trees were exceedingly tall. When examined, the nest was found to contain three fully feathered chicks. Near the nest the female was found shot and on 21 July, the male was found to have died in a similar fashion (I. Fefelov).

Confusion now surrounds what exactly happened to the three young. The original extract states that the chicks were taken into captivity and apparently then ended up in Plesskiy's own private collection. Another extract (a translation) by Professor Alexander Shepel states that all three chicks fledged from the nest at the end of July.

To complicate matters even further, the extract ends by saying that the fledglings from this nest were to be found at the local museum and were examined 60 years later (1996) by V. N. Sotnikov. However the story really ended, this is undoubtedly a historic and unique record for this species and shows that even 72 years ago, hen harriers were prepared to nest in trees if necessary.

Secondly, on 29 May 1978 in Bohemia, now the Czech Republic, a pair of hen harriers was found nesting on an old red squirrel drey 20 metres up a spruce. The base of the nest was, not surprisingly, very small, measuring only 20 cm × 30 cm, yet somehow contained four eggs when found. Sadly, the nest failed prior to hatching.

The third instance refers to a pair of hen harriers using a 1977 sparrowhawk nest in 1978, again in what is now the Czech Republic. The nest was five metres up a European larch in a young forest of mixed tree species. When the nest was discovered, it contained three nestlings of between three and five days old.

On 28 June, one chick was found dead directly below the nest and a few days later the remaining two chicks had also fallen to the ground. Both were retrieved by children who immediately took them to a falconry centre. One was found to be dead on arrival, the other, identified as a male, was in a poor state of health. Due to the falconer's dedicated care it survived and was later returned to the wild.

Persecution and human disturbance were undoubtedly responsible for the birds' deaths and the failure of these three nests.

Western marsh harrier

The Western or more familiarly the European marsh harrier has also occasionally been known to nest in trees. Two records come from the Czech Republic: the first dates from June 1989, 14.8 metres above the ground in the top of a pine tree, and the second from July 1989, a 3.5 metre high nest found in a willow shrub. Thirdly, in May 1982 in central Germany, a 13 metre high nest was found in a weak oak near Bernburg. In all three instances the marsh harriers had carefully constructed their own arboreal nests.

It is thought that in the last instance the marsh harriers may have been trying to nest as near as possible to a traditional nest site where the ground habitat had become unsuitable. This valid explanation for tree nesting was put forward by Gleichner and Naumann (1985) as damage from winter flooding and ice had totally destroyed a nearby reedbed, meaning that it offered no cover for nesting. Records also show that both the Western marsh harrier and the swamp harrier (see below) build larger and bulkier nests on the ground and in trees than does the hen harrier.

A further two records are worthy of inclusion. On 8 June 1986, approximately 60 km. east of Prague, a marsh harrier nest with three chicks was found 3.75 metres above ground on the top of a snowberry bush. Then, on 11 June 1991, a nest which also contained three small chicks and an unhatched egg was discovered on a common elder bush 90 cm above the water level in south Moravia, in the eastern part of the Czech Republic. Both nests had apparently been built by harrier pairs.

Swamp harrier

The swamp harrier has also been recorded nesting in trees, in New Zealand. In total, six instances have been documented at heights of 15m, 12m, on two occasions at 7m, 4.5m and at 2.5 metres. There is also a single record of a nest on the disused drey of a ring-tailed possum high in the top of a tea tree.

The nests at 15m and 12m are highly unusual, as they were built in consecutive years in a single tawa tree, probably by the same pair of swamp harriers. The two nests at 7m and the one at 4.5 m were found in native mahoe trees. In most of the cases mentioned, suitable ground nesting habitat seemed to be available nearby, yet these birds apparently preferred to tree nest. What's more, the harriers appeared to have built these bulky structures themselves.

Northern harrier

There is a single but vague reference to tree nesting in North America by the Northern harrier (formerly known as the marsh hawk). The famous American editor and ornithologist Ralph S. Palmer (1988) mentions a report from 1946 of the Northern harrier, at that time considered the North American race of the European hen harrier but now a separate species, nesting in an old Swainson's hawk nest. 6 metres up in a willow bush, Unfortunately no further details are given because the reference, probably a local journal, was given as 'missing'.

Reunion harrier

I can only speculate as to whether or not the Reunion harrier is tree nesting but if it is not, then it is surely likely to do so soon, given its extraordinary arboreal abilities and the unique circumstances in which it now finds itself.

I spent a week making comprehensive observations of this species on the island of Réunion in the western Indian Ocean during late October and early November 2004. The lower parts of this 50 km × 70 km island are now densely populated and highly dependent on agriculture, mainly sugar cane, and tourism. This rare and endemic species with the smallest range of all the world's harriers now therefore finds itself relegated to the surrounding hills which are densely covered in trees and rank vegetation.

This bird, which should be more at home over wet and open areas at ground level, has now adapted to living and foraging above and below the canopy of these trees. Its wings are much shorter and rounder than in a normal harrier species and its hunting technique and flight are more akin to those of a buzzard or goshawk. A recent photograph shows a pair of these amazing birds nesting not on the ground but several metres off it, on top of the sloping hillside vegetation.

Tree nesting

en harriers in Northern Ireland began tree nesting very recently in comparison with the Australasian spotted harrier. That bird has always been known to nest in trees while the arboreal history of the hen harrier can only be traced back with certainty to 1990. Although the first tree nest was not discovered until 14 July 1991 there were signs that the site had been occupied the year before: evidence found on the forest floor, the large size of the nest and two chicks seen nearby even though no ground nest was ever found.

The two species favour completely different breeding habitats and strongholds. The cosmopolitan hen harrier mainly inhabits upland areas which tend to be damp, covered with rank vegetation, mainly heather, and generally surrounded by dense conifer plantations which the birds also utilise. By contrast, the spotted harrier is found in more open and sparsely wooded country adjacent to huge wheat-growing paddocks (fields) in tropical and temperate areas and also in Australia's arid and semi-arid zones.

The spotted harrier uses a wide variety of tree species for nesting whereas the hen harrier has only been known to use Sitka spruce which have lost their tops, or more exactly their leading shoots, during the early stages of growth. Nest sites discovered over the past 19 years have ranged in height from 2 metres to 13 metres, with an average height of 9.83 metres, similar to those of other harrier species that have been known to tree nest.

During my many visits to tree nests in dense and claustrophobic Sitka plantations, I have always been particularly fascinated by the behaviour of other resident birds. Robins and wrens, both probable prey species, will forage and nest within feet of a harrier's nest and I have watched enthralled as cheeky chaffinches come and perch close by. When the young of these small birds have fledged, they can be seen scuttling about the outer branches of the nest and those of the neighbouring Sitkas, seemingly unconcerned by the harriers' presence. I have on several occasions observed a brooding female, and later her young chicks, totally entranced by their close attendance yet making no attempt to depredate them. On open moorland, all three species would probably have been preyed upon yet in their own environment they apparently feel safe with harriers as next door neighbours.

Interestingly, ground and tree nests can be found simultaneously in both relatively young and mature conifer plantations in – and only in – County Antrim. No records of habitual tree nesting have occurred elsewhere in Northern Ireland, the neighbouring Republic of Ireland, the UK nor throughout the species' vast European breeding range.

Thanks mainly to decades of overgrazing by sheep and to poor habitat management, Antrim's uplands do not have the deep and widespread tracts of heather moorland required by hen harriers for nesting and communal roosting. As a result, with the Antrim Plateau providing poor ground cover, the nests of hen harriers and other ground nesting species are highly exposed, rendering them vulnerable to predators such as the red fox.

In comparison, the more westerly and southerly counties of Tyrone and Fermanagh are blessed with favourable ground conditions and nesting harriers are rarely found in young or mature conifer forests, although the occasional ground nest has been discovered in recent restock areas. With no records of tree nesting in these counties and similarly no evidence that harriers in Antrim have ever nested in restock, Northern Ireland's hen harrier population can only be described as an enigma. It is as if there were two separate species of hen harrier in the Province, with harriers in Tyrone and Fermanagh appearing to have completely different nesting and ecological habits from those in Antrim, no more than seventy miles away. The reason, sadly, is that one population faces severe habitat problems while the other does not.

It is probably in light of these problems that habitual tree nesting evolved in County Antrim. It is also likely that arboreal nesting occurred simply as a reaction to the degeneration of moorland rather than as a straightforward evolutionary change. Both possibilities have been considered by harrier experts and, whatever the answer, some sort of a giant leap forward, evolutionary or otherwise, did take place in 1990. I for one am glad it did or the Antrim population might have decreased dramatically. Thankfully, both young and mature conifer plantations were conveniently adjacent to open moorland and provided, in the absence of deep heather, both vital protection and necessary ground cover. If these man-made forests had not existed there would probably have been a greater dearth of breeding hen harriers in Antrim's uplands.

Hypothetically, the basic instinct in those bird species, including harriers, which habitually ground nest is to revert to nesting in trees when their habitat is deemed unsuitable. This is true of the Northern Ireland merlin population which formerly nested on the ground but which for at least 30 years has exclusively nested in trees along the edges of mature conifer forests. In many cases, though, suitable ground habitat was available nearby, in the form either of long grass, heather moorland or marshes yet harriers appeared hellbent on arboreal nesting. It is interesting to speculate whether all harrier species have, at some point in their history, nested in trees.

The implications of tree nesting for future conservation

In England and Scotland, where the hen harrier is more heavily persecuted than in Northern Ireland, tree nesting in conifer plantations could be safer than ground nesting. Both hen harriers and red grouse live and nest on heather moorland, bringing the harrier into constant conflict with the shooting fraternity, so a mature conifer forest would make the harrier and its nest less conspicuous and less easy to find.

On the ground, harriers in the UK are also subject to extreme depredation pressures from a much wider variety of mammals than in Northern Ireland. Mortality rates of chicks in ground nests and of recently fledged birds can be as high as 60% or 70% so tree nests might appear to be the answer to all the hen harrier's problems.

Sadly, though, that has not been the case in Northern Ireland. Long-term studies (1990–2006) show that fledging rates of harrier chicks from tree nests in County Antrim are much lower than those from ground nests, despite depredation and persecution at the latter. Tree nests had a mean clutch size of 3.11 but the mean fledged brood size was only 1.51 chicks per nest. In contrast with ground nests, no incidents of persecution were detected at tree nest sites.

A study of a similar number of ground nests showed that they had a mean of 4.05 eggs per nest, with brood size at hatching averaging 3.00 nestlings and a much healthier 2.29 young fledged per nest. The true fledging figures would have been 2.6 young per fledged nest if there had of been no instances of actual or suspected human persecution to report.

It should be noted that during the tree nesting study, 20 young chicks were rescued from below the nests, successfully rehabilitated where necessary and released back into the wild. As these birds would have died without human intervention, they are excluded from the numbers of naturally fledged young used for comparison purposes.

This lengthy study (Scott and Clarke 1990–2006) resulted in three main findings. On clutch size, it found that there is no good reason to suggest that clutch size should be different in tree and ground nests. On hatching success, it found that losses during incubation at ground nests were more likely to be due to depredation, while nest instability during wet and windy weather was more likely to lead to losses at tree nests. On fledging success, it found that this was affected in tree nests by jostling but more by depredation at ground nests.

In the early stages of our study of tree nests, we speculated that although fledged brood size was reduced by the number of young falling from the nests, this may have been more than balanced out by the protection the tree nests offered from predators. The large gap between the mean fledging brood sizes of 2.6 young at ground nests and 1.5 young at tree nests now appears to render this hypothesis unlikely.

It is of course possible that a higher proportion of ground nests fail at an early stage due to depredation from terrestrial mammals to which tree nests are not exposed. This is, however, speculation and the persistence of the tree nesting habit is intriguing given its relatively poor success and its overall decrease in recent years.

Whether hen harriers born in and fledged from arboreal nests return as adults to nest in trees has been one of the most frequently asked questions since the inception of tree nesting, probably in 1990. After much discussion with the late Roger Clarke and my colleague Philip McHaffie, we came to the firm conclusion that this unusual form of nesting by hen harriers would become imprinted on chicks and that fledglings would eventually return to nest in trees, just as other arboreal species do. How otherwise would this trait have continued for so long in at least three County Antrim forests yet nowhere else in Northern Ireland? There is only a relatively small, unstable and unsuccessful breeding population in this area, thanks mainly to poor ground cover over the years. A percentage of the offspring hatched here, having been born and reared in an arboreal nest, have therefore been only too willing to attempt tree nesting in their turn.

There have been several instances over the past 20 years, including tree nesting immature females, but two cases in particular stand out in my mind. In 1995, a first year male still in brown ringtail plumage successfully bred with an adult female and fledged four chicks from a 10 metre high tree nest. The size difference in particular was unbelievable, the young male looking minute in comparison with his female partner. Then, in 1997, a sub-adult male also bred successfully with a mature female with their tree nest fledging three young.

I was hoping at one stage to have the chicks that had fallen from active tree nests wing-tagged, which would have proved conclusively that they do return to an arboreal nest to breed. My request was turned down by the DOENI (now NIEA) in light of the fact that many hen harrier chicks have been wing tagged in other parts of the UK and there are too many wing tags.

Although I am convinced that both male and female harriers reared in tree nests do return to tree nests to breed, there are probably still more questions than answers regarding tree nesting. Will there be any spread of this trait outside Northern Ireland? Are tree nests more successful than ground nests? Is tree nesting evolution in progress or do both strategies operate side by side, occurring simply in response to the available habitat? I would suggest the last, with a little bit of natural selection playing a part.

With regard to tree nesting evolution, this study has clearly shown that tree nesting by hen harriers in the Antrim Plateau is not advantageous to the long-term success and overall survival of this species. Only the return of vast tracts of deep heather moorland will allow this elegant raptor to thrive in our uplands once again. This will not happen in the short term, unfortunately, and probably never will, so hen harriers are likely to continue to tree nest in mature conifer forests provided that suitable trees are still available for this purpose. The fact that no tree nests were found during 2009 may appear to contradict this theory but that has more to do with decreasing numbers than with a lack of suitable conifers.

In February 1993, in time for that year's breeding season, we constructed three artificial platforms as an initial experiment to replicate tree nests, but they failed to attract hen harriers to occupy them. The platforms were carefully maintained for several years after they were built yet still did not provoke any interest from prospecting harriers, the birds simply finding their own nesting sites within the vast and dense conifer plantations. There are clearly local preferences in habitat and nest site selection, with the Northern Ireland hen harrier population apparently adapting to the environment immediately available to it.

As shown by the individual tree nesting records referred to in the previous chapter, almost all those harrier species which nest in trees seem to build flimsy nests, choosing materials similar to those used for ground nests. This probably makes them susceptible to collapse, particularly during wet and windy weather. Even the experienced spotted harrier is known to construct weak and vulnerable nests but several observed during my visit to Australia in 2006 were much more sturdily built than those of the Antrim tree nesters. Tree nesting may not seem to us the preferred option but these birds may have been faced with a dilemma: to tree nest, or not to nest at all? If I had been a hen or even a spotted harrier, I know what my answer would have been.

Threats to hen harriers

As the 2001 breeding season progressed, it became very clear that hen harrier numbers in the conifer forests of County Antrim had noticeably declined from 1999 and 2000. There had been a delayed start to the season due to foot and mouth disease restrictions which temporarily closed all the known forests in my study area for many weeks. At the time, Philip McHaffie and I had thought that a few pairs may have been overlooked prior to nesting, explaining the noticeable decline to only a dozen or so territorial pairs.

Sadly, by the end of the 2002 season we had confirmed beyond doubt that breeding hen harrier numbers in this unique population had declined to only 11–13 territorial pairs. We had no idea what could have caused this sudden drop in a normally stable population. For the past few years we had suspected that buzzard and goshawk were affecting numbers to a degree, but other factors were almost certainly to blame as well.

Then in 2003, County Antrim witnessed one of its worst ever years for breeding hen harriers since my studies began in 1986. Only 13 territorial pairs were located, with fewer than 10 pairs attempting to breed in the Antrim Plateau. As in 2002, only one pair was discovered nesting on open moorland and, for the first time since 1990, no productive tree nests were found. .

Comprehensive fieldwork, particularly over the four years from 2000–2003, had identified several major problems which were probably responsible for this alarming decline. We had to take into account the inclement weather, which badly affected the breeding success of hen harriers and other raptors in our uplands. The spring and summer of 2002 and 2003 were particularly bad, the former being the wettest on record. The effects of global warming were evident in the unfamiliar weather patterns we endured in Northern Ireland between 1999 and 2009, even if our some, like our former Environment Minister, Sammy Wilson MP MLA, chose to think otherwise.

The past 24 years have taught us that it takes only a couple of lean breeding seasons for hen harriers in particular to show a noticeable drop in numbers the following year. This time, though, the problem was more serious than that. There had been no reduction in foraging on adjacent moorland with prey still widely available and only a minimal decrease in suitably sized conifer habitat, so other factors were contributing to the decline. Disturbance caused by tree felling, the helicopter spraying of fertiliser on forests and car rallying almost definitely displaced several pairs of hen harriers and other protected species from at least five plantations between 2000 and 2003, especially when the work continued during the breeding season. Since then, there has been a more than substantial increase in common buzzard and goshawk, both of which are now highly visible in the majority of conifer forests, young and mature. The buzzard population has increased rapidly across the Province over the last decade, but particularly during the past five years (2004–2009). The goshawk is a very recent addition to our breeding list and is now apparently rapidly establishing itself in Antrim in particular. Its arrival, along with breeding short-eared owl and the attempted breeding of red kite in Antrim during 2002, appears to be putting our other resident birds of prey under immense pressure in these increasingly over-saturated conifer plantations.

Both buzzard and goshawk will harass and prey on smaller and more vulnerable raptor species like hen harrier, kestrel and merlin, occasionally to the point of local extinction. These two much larger and highly powerful raptors could potentially dominate our skies and most of the forests in Northern Ireland at the expense of other birds of prey and many vulnerable woodland bird species. In 1999, a pair of hen harriers was eventually forced to abandon its tree nest after harassment and depredation by buzzards resulted in the deaths of two fully feathered chicks. In 2002, another pair of hen harriers which had regularly ground nested within a mature conifer plantation in north Antrim failed to do so for the first time in six years. A pair of buzzards had hijacked a nest in a tall conifer, used in previous years by merlins and kestrels in turn. Both species were forced out of the immediate area and probably failed to nest in that plantation. More recently, in 2006, a rare hen harrier ground nest on an open hillside at least five km. from the nearest plantation was harassed on several occasions by a male goshawk. Thankfully that nest survived and fledged four young.

Harassment of both sexes of hen harrier has been clearly observed, mainly by male buzzards during their early season sky dancing displays and at the pre-egg laying stages. A lull was noticed during the incubation period but harassment resumed almost immediately after the young had hatched and prey deliveries to the nests had increased. It continued almost unabated until the sites were prematurely abandoned, resulting in the deaths of several chicks, subsequently depredated by the buzzards.

On 6 April 2008, Philip McHuffie and I watched a buzzard actually escort a male hen harrier out of a heather-covered turbary within the plantation where the harriers had previously bred, just to make sure that they would not return to breed there. Their greater size and dominance mean that buzzard and goshawk prevail in these coniferous forests.

In April 2003, in the same forest, four buzzards were observed displaying with a single goshawk in close attendance. Not surprisingly, hen harrier numbers in the area soon began to decrease with none recorded breeding there in 2007. A pair of hen harriers had regularly ground nested in another north Antrim forest until 1997 but, when a pair of goshawks moved into their territory and bred, the harriers disappeared and could well have been depredated. In 2001, the mature larch trees in this forest were felled, allowing the hen harriers to return, but for how long?

At Slieveanorra, the largest conifer plantation in County Antrim, Philip and I would regularly locate up to six or even seven pairs of breeding hen harriers a year. They either nested in trees or on the ground, with the area also famously hosting a winter roost for harriers during the mid 1990s. The arrival of several pairs of buzzard and, at one stage, two pairs of goshawk means that harrier numbers have dropped by half. In 2008, only two or possibly three pairs of hen harriers were present at Slieveanorra and, not surprisingly, none were in the vicinity when buzzards and goshawks were displaying

It is highly likely that the majority of these large forests hold more than one pair of goshawk but their secretive nature and unwillingness to provide raptor workers with regular sightings during the course of the breeding season mean that they are rarely observed.

At a relatively young plantation in south Antrim, where the conifers are around 6 or 7 metres tall, we were astonished to find another pair of goshawk displaying on the morning of 6 April 2003. Our records show that both hen harrier and short-eared owl have successfully bred there in the past and we wait to see what future years will bring, as the owl has not nested there since 1999. It is highly unlikely that goshawks will nest in this forest at present but there are two large copses of tall conifers nearby. Buzzards are also holding territory on the periphery of this young plantation, which does not bode well for the future of either the hen harrier or the short-eared owl.

Probably the most disturbing goshawk record so far was witnessed on 10 April 2008 in mid Antrim, at a relatively young conifer plantation where the trees were between 6 and 8 metres high. I had never until then observed a goshawk depredating or even harassing another raptor species in any of these forests, although I had always suspected that it was happening.

A week earlier, the forest had held two pairs of displaying hen harriers and I was unaware that goshawks were even present in the area. The only place they could have been living was in an adjacent plantation with tall deciduous and coniferous trees to the south east of this forest, where a pair of red kites tried unsuccessfully to breed in 2002.

At around 10.45 a.m., I noticed a large bird of prey flying towards me from a northerly direction and I at first took it to be one of the resident buzzards. As it approached, I noticed that it was a goshawk and that it was carrying a large prey item. As it passed directly over my head at a height of no more than 50 metres, I immediately identified the goshawk as a male, but was also able to identify the prey item – a male hen harrier.

The goshawk, as I expected, veered to the south east and seemed to dive down towards the plantation, but I lost sight of it and could not be sure where it landed. I returned to the area again on 13 April and as I walked along the forest path towards the south gate, I noticed a pile of feathers in front of me on the path. They were from the male hen harrier, left where the goshawk must have fed on it. The sheer force and destructive nature of these birds was there for all to see.

Only one pair of hen harriers remained to breed at the north end of this plantation: thankfully they were successful and apparently unhindered by these fearsome predatory birds.

A comparative three year study was carried out in two conifer plantations in south and mid Antrim, specifically during the winter months from October 2006 to February 2007, from October 2007 to February 2008 and from October 2008 to December 2008. It showed that buzzard and goshawk were surprisingly tolerant of hen harriers and other raptors in these forests.

Thirteen visits were made to each location during the study periods, making a total of 26 visits, each watch lasting six hours, meaning a total of 156 hours of observation with 78 hours spent in each forest. During this time, Philip McHaffie and I did not observe one single instance of harassment, depredation or displacement by either buzzard or goshawk. Harassment was in fact more likely to come from the resident sparrowhawk, kestrel and hooded crow populations. The study revealed a sharp contrast between breeding and wintering raptor populations in these forests, with buzzard and goshawk seemingly avoiding any interaction with hen harriers or other resident raptor species.

We therefore concluded that harassment, displacement and depredation were more likely to occur during the intensity of each species' individual breeding cycle. The saturation of both these forests, with up to eight species of breeding and competing raptors in any one season, has made territorial dominance a priority for both buzzard and goshawk so it was probably inevitable that the third largest raptor in these plantations – the out-of-place hen harrier – would be affected.

I find it both sad and shameful that eight of our ten breeding raptors and owls are highly dependent on young and mature conifer plantations for both nesting and roosting purposes. Fortunately, as far as we know, the peregrine falcon and barn owl do not live in dense conifer forests but they have their own problems, with the latter struggling to maintain a secure foothold in our lowlands. Unfortunately, little is known about the long-eared owl population, due to its nocturnal nature and its liking for coniferous forest, so it is possible that this rarely observed owl could also be affected by the dramatic increase in both buzzard and goshawk.

The hen harrier, merlin and short-eared owl now occupy the same nesting niche as five other birds of prey. Through no fault of their own, they have had no option but to nest in trees or on the ground in young and mature conifer forests, as their preferred nesting habitat in deep heather on open moorland hardly exists any more in Antrim. As a result, the majority of our forests are over-populated with diurnal raptors and owls and so interaction with other species is inevitable.

Unlikely though it is, the sooner the hen harrier, merlin and short-eared owl are returned to their traditional nesting and roosting grounds amongst prime tracts of deep heather moorland, the better their chances of avoiding harassment and depredation by true forest- dwelling raptors. The return of these three species to open moorland would immediately alleviate the overcrowding in the forests and should result in a better long-term future for all our raptors. We must continue to carry out annual surveys to ascertain the impact on all our birds of prey and owls of the various threats that face them: buzzard and goshawk, humans, our changing weather conditions, forestry operations and wind farms.

Thankfully we do not yet have breeding European eagle owls in Northern Ireland as they can also wreak havoc on breeding hen harriers. In the Forest of Bowland in Lancashire in 2007, evidence of the recent depredation by a pair of resident eagle owls of an adult female and a young hen harrier, its feathers still in pin, was found by Stephen Murphy at the owls' favourite plucking post. Stephen monitors hen harriers for Natural England at what he describes as the most successful breeding site for harriers in the country so losses which could have a detrimental effect on the population are a cause for immediate concern. Not surprisingly, both species are now being more closely monitored than ever.

These huge owls have no fear of humans nor of other large raptors like buzzard and goshawk so it's frightening to think what could happen if they were suddenly to arrive in Northern Ireland. For hen harriers and other vulnerable species, it could mean complete and violent destruction.

Problems in Antrim

After many years of detailed research in the Antrim Plateau, I identified a catalogue of problems which were obviously affecting the whole area, several of which dated back to long before my studies. The problems have almost certainly had an adverse effect on moorland dwelling species like hen harriers and probably explain why they have resorted to mature and young conifer plantations as possibly their last refuge.

The degradation of moorland by excessive peat-cutting, so-called agricultural improvement schemes, overgrazing by uncontrolled numbers of sheep and widespread depredation of ground nests by foxes was amongst the first of many problems I identified in this area. This was probably enough in itself to force hen harriers from the open moorland into the relative safety and seclusion of mature conifer plantations.

Red fox depredation alone can have a devastating effect on ground nesting hen harriers and I have found many ransacked nests in Antrim over the past two decades. Local farmers in this area cull large numbers of foxes before and during the lambing season but, despite their best efforts over many years, the fox has survived and even proliferated.

An interesting study of breeding hen harriers in Orkney from 1975 to 1981 by Nic Picozzi, showed that, in the absence of foxes, the main losses there were also due to depredation (31% of 281 nest failures). In total a massive 87 nests had been lost over a seven year period, which equates to 12.42 nests per annum. If those annual losses had occurred in the Antrim Plateau, there would have been no breeding harriers left in the area. The only ground predators in Orkney were a few feral cats and stray dogs but gulls *Laridae*, skuas *Stercorariidae* and crows *Corvidae* were plentiful, in particular the hooded crow, the main predator at harrier nest sites. Hooded crows are also numerous in the Antrim uplands and so are probably responsible for an unknown number of nest failures there as well.

Around 30 years ago, our now vulnerable merlin population made the same transition as have hen harriers and for probably the same reasons. They moved from being a ground nesting species to become an exclusive tree nester, using old crows' nests along the edges of conifer forests. I firmly believe, as does Larry Toal who studies merlins, that if these plantations had not been readily available to both these species then their numbers would probably have declined even further than they have.

During the course of my studies, now in their 24th season, I clearly identified many other serious problems and threats. Some date back decades, some are more recent, most are linked to man and all are affecting the ecology of the uplands in the Antrim Plateau with serious implications for the long-term future of our moorland species.

My research shows that up to ten species of birds are at risk of being permanently lost from this area, including meadow pipit, skylark, red grouse, hen harrier, merlin and short-eared owl. In recent years, I have also noticed a sharp decline in curlew and lapwing, with dunlin and golden plover probably now extinct as breeding species.

Also cause for concern are the illegal burning of moorland by farmers and vandals, the discharge of effluents on the moorland at Slieveanorra and elsewhere in Antrim and the training of gun dogs during the breeding season, illegally flushing incubating birds from their nests and causing desertion in most cases. Hill walkers, particularly teenagers on award schemes, can cause untold damage to the already degraded moorland by failing to use the designated paths.

Within conifer plantations, problems also arise from motorcycles, quad bikes, mountain bikes and even stolen cars, despite strenuous efforts by the Forest Service to prosecute those involved. Until recently, and unfortunately again in 2009, car rallies have taken place in Antrim's forests during the breeding season and disturbed breeding raptors, so these should in future be confined to the autumn and winter months.

The poisoning and shooting of raptors in our uplands and elsewhere have been on the increase in recent years. Particularly affected are common buzzards, peregrine falcons, almost certainly hen harriers and even visiting red kites. Peregrine falcons and hen harriers generally fall foul of disgruntled members of racing pigeon clubs and the shooting fraternity respectively.

In recent years that shooting fraternity has whipped up intense feeling over the relationship between raptors and red grouse. This has inevitably led to the persecution of hen harriers in County Antrim even though red grouse make up less than 1% of their diet in Northern Ireland. The persecution of birds of prey in remote areas is extremely difficult to monitor as it usually occurs secretly. Over the years, I have witnessed the illegal removal of several egg clutches from hen harrier ground nests and the disappearance of young chicks from other sites, all in suspicious circumstances. Most recently, several broods of hen harriers have been killed and birds have disappeared from their traditional breeding grounds in north Antrim. The slaughter of birds of prey and other wildlife may have been socially acceptable in the 18th and 19th centuries, but we are supposed to be living in the 21st.

One recent and well publicised instance of alleged hen harrier persecution occurred on 24 October 2007 on the Sandringham Estate in Norfolk, owned by Her Majesty The Queen. It apparently involved her grandson Prince Harry, third in line to the throne, a male family friend and the Estate gamekeeper. It appears that the reserve warden and two visitors were watching two hen harriers in flight over a protected conservation area, when they heard shots, before first one, then the second bird plummeted dead from the sky. It was alleged that the prince and his two companions were the only ones shooting in the area at the time and that they were illegally using lead shot. (Source: various UK newspapers, November 2007).

Regrettably, despite an intensive police inquiry, no charges could be brought as the bodies of the hen harriers were not found, meaning that there was no vital forensic or ballistic evidence to study. The case was closed but the Crown Prosecution Service commented that no one else was being sought for the crime.

In Northern Ireland during the 1990s there was evidence that the poisoned carcasses of rabbits and other animals were being distributed from a small plane onto the hills in north Antrim. This came to light only when the plane crashed, killing the pilot and badly injuring his passenger. More recently, dead lambs and woodpigeons have been laced with deadly poisons to lure young foxes and other species, including raptors, to their deaths. Hard-headed members of racing pigeon clubs are even said to have employed a 'hit man' to dispose of peregrine falcons at one well-known site in County Down.

Wind farms, which I regard as out-of-place monstrosities, can be found at two locations, in the Antrim Plateau and on nearby Rathlin Island. They do absolutely nothing to enhance these areas and, more importantly, vital moorland habitat has been lost during their construction. One site, on Slievenashanaghan Hill, is in prime hen harrier territory and on 13 January 2007 a male was found dead, its right wing completely sheared off, after a collision with one of the turbine rotors. During scheduled winter visits to the area between October 2005 and December 2007, Philip McHaffie and I also found the decimated remains of eight hooded crows, six ravens and a common buzzard, with a further two ravens found in February 2008. Crow species appear to be most vulnerable to collision. Observations over a number of years have shown that the area is prone to mist and hill fog even during the summer months so the granting of planning permission in early 2008 to extend the site was totally irresponsible.

With twenty turbines as of March 2009, the hillside is now uninhabitable for any species. These wind farms with their miniscule capacity to generate power seem to take precedence over important and vulnerable wildlife in this area. Too many people are, after all, making too much money from them.

In May 2008 a tidal turbine was installed for a trial period of five years in the fast-flowing narrows of Strangford Lough in County Down. Its two rotating blades, fully submerged, begin to generate power during the strong incoming tide and do so again as the tide starts to ebb. This revolutionary device is silent, and much smaller and less obtrusive than a wind farm yet has an output comparable to twenty turbines.

The long-term future of our wild places depends on managing the habitat to accommodate our rare breeding bird species and other wildlife. I firmly believe that if drastic measures are not taken soon to fully protect sensitive areas like the Antrim Plateau, then both our rare and our common birds will eventually cease to breed there. Regrettably, in the many years that I and others have studied raptors in this area, we have noticed very little action being taken by any of our local conservation bodies to fully protect this important and unique habitat. Neither have we seen firm action against those who wilfully and illegally cause disturbance and irreparable damage to the moorland. Sadly, a similar situation now exists in parts of the Sperrins, which border the westerly counties of Londonderry and Tyrone.

I have watched for well over two decades as the Antrim Plateau has been gradually eroded, and in many places completely destroyed, thanks to mismanagement and neglect. Humans can turn a unique habitat into a potential wasteland, an unattractive place for tourists and locals alike. The Antrim Plateau is an integral part of the world famous Glens of Antrim, quite rightly recognised as an Area of Outstanding Natural Beauty (AONB). I am appalled at how badly humans are allowed to treat this area without fear of prosecution.

Thankfully, 2007 brought some good news for hen harriers and merlins in Northern Ireland with the long-awaited designation of SPAs (Special Protection Areas) in the uplands of County Antrim and elsewhere in the Province. If they are not fully implemented, both EHS (the Environment and Heritage Service) and the Forest Service could incur huge fines from the European Union. I, though, am one of many who believe that it is probably too little too late for both hen harriers and merlin, as their numbers in the Antrim Plateau, particularly those of merlin, have not risen for many years.

It took thousands of years to create the vast expanses of moorland that formerly existed throughout the Antrim Plateau, yet it seems to have taken only a decade or so to destroy them completely. Protecting the environment and its wildlife is an obligation, not a choice, for our conservation organisations. We take for granted the fauna with which we have been blessed in Northern Ireland. We pay them attention only when they are in serious decline or vanish from an area which they have graced for centuries. Let's have some action now, before it is too late.

A chronological study of the hen harrier in County Antrim

1986–1989: the early years

The recent history of the hen harrier in the Antrim Plateau and in Northern Ireland in general is neither a very happy nor a very successful one, a series of peaks and troughs. For me, the early years of studying this most graceful of raptors in Antrim were the best.

I vividly remember the spring of 1986, when my long time friend and fellow birder Gary Wilkinson took me to see my first hen harriers at Slieveanorra Forest, a few miles north of the former Huguenot village of Newton Crommelin right in the heart of the Antrim Plateau. Slieveanorra, or 'Orra' as it is called by the local inhabitants, is a large area of mainly heather moorland surrounded by one of the largest conifer plantations in Northern Ireland around a 510 metre summit.

This is a desolate yet beautiful area of gently sloping hills, dotted with sheep grazing peacefully on the brown shoots of a carpet of seemingly degraded heather. One third of County Antrim is mountainous but this was my first visit to hill farming country. Although it was late April, it was easy to envisage how harsh the winter weather could be at this altitude. The sun shone in our favour throughout the day but a constant biting northeasterly wind reminded us that this was only just the start of spring.

The peace and solitude was occasionally interrupted by the welcome mewing of a buzzard or the croaking of ravens as they passed busily overhead. Although I was unaware of it on that particular April day, this was where I would eventually cut my teeth in my study of hen harriers. This picturesque place was the harrier's home and was to become my own second home for the next 24 years.

The rest of that first spring and summer were spent observing hen harriers and exploring the whole of the Antrim Plateau and its adjacent conifer plantations, from Ballyboley Forest near Larne in the south and northward through the historic and beautiful Nine Glens of Antrim to Ballypatrick Forest Park on the outskirts of Ballycastle. I was glad of Gary's company on the visits he made with me that summer but usually I travelled alone, finding my feet, observing and admiring these amazing birds. One year in their company and I was hooked.

Several things intrigued me about those birds that first summer. Firstly, the population for the whole of Northern Ireland at that time was estimated at between only five and ten pairs yet I had discovered at least eight, maybe ten pairs in Antrim alone. As I had very little experience either as an ornithologist or in the field of research, I didn't know whether I should chance telling anyone.

Fortunately, I knew the late C. D. (Jimmy) Deane, having joined him on field trips which he had organised around Northern Ireland. Jimmy was not only an experienced birder but a renowned journalist, author and photographer, who, in 1971, with Fred Quinn of the Forest Service, had photographed what were probably the first hen harriers to nest in Antrim in the 20th century. Thankfully, Jimmy believed me about the number of pairs I had found.

I was also anxious to find out why I had regularly observed hen harriers displaying and apparently preferring to nest in recently planted areas and in the more widely available mature conifer forests. Hen harriers are known to nest in young conifer forests and had done so in Antrim during the late 1960s and early 1970s, when the trees were only one metre high. The harriers had begun to thrive again in these nursery plantations but had declined suddenly by the end of the 1970s, once the trees had grown taller.

To try to find some answers, I bought a copy of Donald Watson's fine monograph of the species which stated that the hen harrier frequents and nests on open moorland and not in mature conifer plantations,. Why, then, had I found no evidence of this in 1986? This was the main question which I hoped to answer in 1987.

Why, too, had nobody in Northern Ireland studied hen harriers before? In other parts of the UK, they were classed as a problem species, particularly on grouse moors where they were repeatedly shot and disposed of by gamekeepers. Was their notoriety the reason why nobody bothered to study them?

I urgently needed a contact who studied hen harriers elsewhere in Ireland. Donald Watson put me in touch with David Scott, who had studied them during the 1960s and 1970s in the Wicklow Hills near his home south of Dublin. He had even observed breeding Montagu's harriers in Ireland.

From 1987 until his death in 1998 we regularly exchanged information. I still have all his letters, produced on his old but still effective typewriter. He always told me to 'Keep notes, young man, they will be valuable to you later!' and how right he was.

The next two years (1987 and 1988) were spent studying every aspect of the hen harrier's lifestyle and counting their numbers from a discreet distance. This was done mainly on my own but I did manage to coax my wife Linda to join me on my weekend forays into the scenic Glens of Antrim. I vividly remember her first sighting of a very pale-plumaged male hen harrier, which she took to be a herring gull.

But she was not the only one learning. I needed to gain vital field experience if I was to progress and gain the confidence to study these birds properly. During those two years I never did solve the problem of why hen harriers were associating and apparently nesting in mature conifer plantations when Donald Watson's book and my field guide said they should be nesting on open moorland. It only later dawned on me that birds do not read books.

The winter months of 1987 and 1988 were also spent in the Plateau, searching for a communal roost site, but sadly I failed to find one despite regularly encountering several males and an occasional female. On the afternoon of 12 December 1987 I found myself walking over moorland directly behind Fair Head, where our last golden eagles nested from 1953 to1961. I was heading for Lough Na Cranagh with its crannog (man-made island), now covered with long grass and a few windblown trees. It was there the previous week that Clive Mellon, who then worked for the National Trust, had observed a female hen harrier preparing to roost.

I had thought it a strange place for a roost site but concluded that it would protect the harrier from the many marauding foxes brought onto these hills by sheep farming. Sadly, there were no roosting harriers to be seen, but returning to my car, I could see and hear two common buzzards in the distance, circling and calling in a distressed and agitated manner.

Suddenly, as I got closer, an immature golden eagle rose from the heather carrying the fresh carcass of a partially eaten rabbit. It had probably pirated it from the buzzards, which looked tiny in comparison, but they were not to be deterred and obviously wanted it back. After several brief aerial skirmishes, all three birds flew towards the misty cliffs of nearby Murlough Bay. This was my first ever sighting of a golden eagle in Northern Ireland, a superb substitute for a roosting hen harrier.

In early March 1989 I received a very welcome letter from Colin Shawyer, then director of the Hawk and Owl Trust. A raptor enthusiast from north Belfast named Philip McHaffie wanted to get in touch with someone locally who studied hen harriers. We soon made contact and by April were making regular field trips into the Antrim Plateau. We had a terrific first year together and during one late April visit to the vast expanses of Slieveanorra encountered an amazing 13 hen harriers, both male and female, mainly displaying at several different locations. There were at least seven territorial pairs there in 1989, a stark contrast with around half that number twenty years later.

1990–1999: Antrim's heady harrier years

The 1990s were probably the most exciting time for hen harriers in Antrim since the return of the species in the early 1970s, when according to the late Jimmy Deane, some 20 pairs eventually nested. In 1990, a huge sweep of the area in spring showed that there were at least 14 or 15 territorial pairs in the Antrim Plateau, of which around ten probably attempted nesting. Of these, only two nests were discovered on open patches of degraded heather moorland, with the remainder seemingly within the confines of mature conifer plantations.

Both nests were discreetly observed from my car, one eventually fledging three young, the other four. While watching one particular forest where the trees were probably between ten and fifteen metres high, we got the impression that the birds were dropping down into open spaces between the uniform rows of Sitka spruce. Were there natural openings there or had several trees fallen and created good cover for a ground nest? The following year, this chance sighting would turn out to have historic implications for hen harriers in County Antrim, the UK and across Europe.

We did manage to solve one long-standing problem in 1990. We had wondered why the majority of hen harriers were frequenting forests containing mature conifers during the breeding season and not utilising the moorland to its full potential. Philip and I walked several transects in south, mid and north Antrim and found the ground cover abysmal in many places. We did not even manage to flush a single red grouse.

The heather was completely overgrazed and degraded by sheep. Instead of the thigh-high or even deeper tracts of heather that I've found in parts of Scotland, the cover was in many places no more than ankle-high and could easily be walked over in a pair of ordinary shoes. Almost any ground nest could easily be found and immediately depredated by foxes or destroyed by humans wishing to do the birds harm. We both predicted that very few ground nests would be found here in future unless overgrazing was limited or ended entirely, allowing the moorland time to recover. It turned out that we were right.

Once again no roost sites were located in the Antrim area despite regular sightings, mainly of males, during the winter months. Males seem to linger in their territory after the breeding season has ended, whereas most females and young of the year (ringtails) leave for much lower locations. Only when the weather is severe in the uplands and prey is scarce will they desert the area temporarily, returning within weeks or days once conditions have improved. With so many birds remaining, we felt they must surely have a communal roost site somewhere in Antrim or else be roosting individually in the areas they most favoured.

I had applied for a disturbance licence from the DOENI (now NIEA) but my application apparently arrived too late for the 1991 breeding season, which was very disappointing. I resolved to try again the following year.

The 1991 season started like any other, with our first visit to the breeding grounds during the last weekend of March. As usual there were several males idling about the forests awaiting the return of the females, which were in short supply at this time of the year. The weather was still bitterly cold and windy as we moved into the first fortnight of April with the majority of females still in no hurry to return to their preferred upland sites.

Those that had already returned appeared to take no notice of the few males that put in half-hearted bouts of sky dancing. At least two females at one location left the secluded confines of the forest to go hunting over adjacent rough pasture, one returning 15 minutes later, the other ten minutes after that. Both carried small avian prey items, probably meadow pipit or skylark.

By the middle of the month the weather had improved and it even felt reasonably warm in the spring sunshine. This was what the harriers had been waiting for, the chance to perform their acrobatic and sometimes frenzied displays. By the end of April most of the harriers we observed had paired off but those males that had not still displayed aimlessly in the hope of finding a partner.

It would not be long now before the birds would be breeding again, which in Northern Ireland is usually around the second week of May. The eggs are laid very quickly and it is crucial that the weather remains relatively stable during the incubation period with no prolonged downpours or dramatic drops in temperature which can chill the eggs, resulting either in small broods or, more likely, a failed nesting attempt.

On 9 June, Linda and I were walking along the forest track in a plantation when we inadvertently flushed a female from a ground nest containing five eggs. This was the first hen harrier ground nest I had seen in six years of studying the species. It was only two metres from the edge of the track and was very exposed in short grass amongst some old brash by a few dead young conifers which had been felled to widen the firebreak. It seemed inevitable that the incubating harrier would be disturbed by every passer-by and when Philip and I visited the area the following week to check on her progress, the eggs and the female had disappeared, although the nest remained completely intact. It appeared that someone had carefully stolen the eggs, for if a fox had got to them first the nest would have been completely ransacked, with telltale pieces of eggshell strewn around the nest site.

The weather surprisingly held up well that summer and by the end of June we were able, from our roadside vantage points, to observe males and females returning to the forests and to one open moorland site carrying numerous prey items to feed their broods. At another forest site the female must still have been brooding very small chicks as she returned rather swiftly to her nest after a traditional aerial food pass.

The non-stop flow of food continued into early July and was amazing to watch, showing us what prolific hunters these birds are when they need to be. One female was timed leaving the forest to hunt over an adjacent rushy sheep-walk: seven minutes later she was back at her nest with food. Fledging took place at most nest sites just before or just after mid July. This too was a sight worth seeing, the young fledglings precariously taking to the air for the first time, often simply to greet or beg from the adults who were usually carrying food just for them.

1991: an unexpected discovery

Sunday, 14 July 1991 was an exceptionally warm and sunny day and I had no intention of visiting Antrim to observe hen harriers. Philip was still on holiday until later that day and Linda was not free to join me in the field but she encouraged me to go out as it was too good a day for loafing about the house. After visiting one location, where a pair was still present, I moved on to check another forest made up solely of Sitka spruce. In the air were two adults and two recently fledged birds, probably from a ground nest at the south end of the plantation, and I almost certainly missed a double aerial food pass between them.

On my way north, a pair of merlin were screaming frantically over the main road, then suddenly disappeared into the forest. I stopped briefly to see what had caused the commotion and saw that it was down to their sudden arrival with food for at least two hungry chicks. The merlin is not only our rarest diurnal raptor but is also the smallest, so it was great to see them having some success. If the ecological balance is to be maintained, all birds of prey, not just hen harriers, need to do well.

I decided to go for a walk at the north end of the forest and after about three kilometres began to feel the effects of the searing heat and blazing sun. About halfway along the forest I headed down one of the main firebreaks which would eventually take me back to the main road.

When I got close to the end of the first large block of conifers a male harrier passed overhead followed by a recently fledged young harrier, with a female perched right on top of a tall Sitka spruce. The ground nearby was heavily soiled with fresh excreta, a moulted feather from the female and the discarded remains of several small birds. The most surprising thing, though, was that there was no ground nest nearby so where, I wondered, were these birds nesting? The female then took to the air and began circling low, repeatedly looking down into the trees only a couple of rows from the edge of the block.

Hesitantly and rather reluctantly I went to investigate and found on the forest floor another primary from the female, numerous pellets and lots of crystallized fresh excreta. Looking up, my attention was drawn to a nest in a Sitka spruce directly above my head. A young harrier was calling and wing-flapping on the nest so I immediately retreated from the area, reminding myself over and over again that harriers do not nest in trees.

When I got home I immediately told Linda about my unusual find and later that evening rang Philip to give him the details. While both were mystified, they did at least believe me, which is more than can be said for other people whom I contacted that week. The NIEA Wildlife Branch told me that I had probably seen kestrels and definitely not hen harriers nesting in trees. This was an insult to my intelligence but, even though I had studied hen harriers for six years, my confidence began to flag.

Over the next couple of days I referred again and again to Donald Watson's famous book and while the spotted harrier from Australia nests in trees, nowhere could I find any mention of hen harriers doing the same. I was now beginning to doubt both my sanity and what I had clearly observed on 14 July, but being *throng*, or adamant, and still believing that I was right, I refused to take no for an answer. As a last hope I rang my good friend Colin Shawyer, the former Director of the Hawk and Owl Trust, and carefully explained the situation to him.

To my amazement and delight he believed my story. Here was someone who knew me well enough to trust what I had just told them. Colin took my word completely and went to Roger Clarke, who was heavily involved with the Hawk and Owl Trust at the time and also studied harriers. He in turn contacted Donald Watson, whom I had met for the first time six weeks earlier. He had been studying hen harriers for over 40 years and had never encountered tree nesting in his native Dumfries and Galloway. I got the impression that he did not believe my story.

The plan now was for both Colin and Roger to come over to Northern Ireland on Saturday 20 July, hopefully to confirm my findings. No one nearer home showed any interest in doing so.

I collected my distinguished guests from Belfast International Airport at around 10.30 a.m. and drove directly to the forest to verify the find and record all that we could for historical purposes. When we were about 50 metres from the actual nest site, the female and two young harriers were circling in the sky directly above us, indicating that the second chick had now fledged.

The nest was thankfully now vacated. It was 4.5 metres above the ground in the uppermost whorl of branches of a deformed Sitka spruce which had lost its top during the early stages of growth. It was a substantial nest, about 75 centimetres in diameter, built of fine branches, heather twigs and grass, similar in some ways to the make-up of a hen harrier ground nest. It was open to the sky, with the neighbouring trees five metres taller. On the forest floor we found the shell of a hatched hen harrier egg, the outer surface bluish-white, the inner surface blue, and a further large piece of shell a few feet away. The ground below the nest was still heavily soiled with hardened white excreta, consistent with hen harrier droppings. Twenty six pellets, a secondary feather from the male and two primaries from the female also littered the forest floor.

Under a light covering of pine needles we discovered another flight feather from a female. This feather was sodden and discoloured, the shaft was fragile and split in several places and the vane was also incomplete and ragged. We also found the remains of a disintegrated eggshell, both items too badly decomposed to be from this year's nest. It looked as though these birds had used this same site in 1990 as the nest itself was far too solid and substantial to have been used only in 1991.

From our prominent roadside vantage point, Philip and I had watched a pair in 1990 dropping down into what we thought was an open area amongst the trees but we hadn't been sure of the exact location. There was now no doubt about it: a pair of hen harriers had tree nested in County Antrim and the evidence pointed to the same site having been occupied in 1990. This was later confirmed by my friend Larry Toal who had been tracking merlins in the same area in 1990 and had come across two recently fledged harriers, but no ground nest had ever been discovered in the area. This pair of hen harriers was almost certainly tree nesting then as well.

Philip joined us the next day as we examined the site further and photographed the nest and tree for record purposes. We speculated as to whether the harriers had the expertise to have built the nest themselves or whether it had been built by hooded crow, or even sparrowhawk or common buzzard. It would be another couple of years before we could answer that important question.

Donald Watson was next to come and see the tree nest. I met him and his wife Joan at Larne Harbour on 23 July and drove the short distance to the forest. Donald was 73 years of age at that time and dearly wanted to see the nest, probably more for peace of mind than for any other reason

I was immensely pleased to see his face light up as he viewed the nest for the first time. We spent about an hour in the area, enjoying a brief flypast by the female and the two young harriers, discussing the nest site and the surrounding habitat and even speculating as to why they had chosen to nest in a tree in the first place. He was absolutely fascinated by what he observed.

About 500 metres to the rear of the tree nest was an additional small plantation where the conifers were only two or three metres tall, and an extensive patch of reasonably deep heather which appeared to be ideal nesting habitat. The harriers had nonetheless preferred to be arboreal in a 4.5 metre Sitka spruce. Fascinating stuff, given that this species had never before been recorded tree nesting. We would have to wait and see whether these birds would tree nest again in 1992. As a footnote, bi-monthly visits to the Antrim Plateau from October 1991 to February 1992 failed to find any trace of a communal winter roost site, despite the presence of several individual birds in the general area.

There were probably many valid reasons why this pair of harriers had decided to tree nest, especially as a failed traditional ground nest had been found five weeks earlier, less than a kilometre away in the same plantation. There was the ongoing problem of the overgrazed heather moorland and probable depredation by foxes, which were rife in those hills at that time, thanks to hill farming in general and the lambing season in particular.

In 1859, Charles Darwin theorised that survival depends on the ability to change and that humans were living proof of that. I think that this intuitive statement applies to this pair of tree nesting hen harriers, for if they had lacked the ability to change, they may have been lost to this area, always regarded as their main stronghold in Northern Ireland.

1992: another tree nest

In mid January 1992, prior to the start of the breeding season, Philip and I revisited the 1991 tree nest site for old time's sake. On the forest floor we found the shell of a hatched hen harrier egg which appeared to have fallen out of the tree and to be extra to the two eggshells found in the summer. It seemed to indicate that a third chick had hatched, although only two were seen fledged. A small amount of fresh hen harrier excreta was also found beneath the tree, showing that it had been visited at some stage after the breeding season but not necessarily used on a regular basis.

The spring of 1992 was cold and wet and the weather remained so during most of the breeding season. Several ground nests appeared as a result to have failed during the vital incubation period. Of those that were reasonably successful, only one or two young fledged, which was most disappointing. On 17 March, St. Patrick's Day, a male was seen displaying over the tree nest used in 1991. By the 22nd of that month there were two males present and on 5 April three, accompanied by two females.

The three males were last seen together on 21 April and by the end of the month just two pairs remained. Activity above the forest by all four birds continued well into May and nesting was most definitely delayed by the inclement weather. Both pairs were regularly observed throughout June, but by 4 July the birds at site A had disappeared, presumably having failed, leaving only a single pair at site B at the north end of the forest.

From 4 July the remaining pair were regularly watched from a hillside vantage point about 500 metres outside the forest and early indications appeared to show that they were tree nesting. Prey deliveries to the site on the 14th, 18th and 25th July saw both male and female disappearing down into the trees where no clearing was known, a sure sign that arboreal nesting was occurring for the second and probably the third consecutive year.

Both birds were observed lifting their wings up vertically before descending into the tree tops and then ascending in helicopter fashion when leaving the nest site. The bulk of the food was provided by the female while the male was often seen loafing on the nearby moorland. The male was a young bird, as he had a dingy brown mantle and wing coverts and was obviously not experienced in regularly provisioning the female or any chicks that may have been in the nest.

On 29 July, the female was observed looking down into the trees whilst circling and calling from a great height. She subsequently landed at the nest at around 10.40 a.m. and at 11.02 a.m. a young bird flew out of the trees, immediately followed by the female. Philip and I wondered if this was the first time it had taken to the air as it flew in an erratic manner before suddenly plummeting to the ground within feet of the forest edge.

At around noon the male flew in calling loudly and carrying prey and when he was within metres of the nest site, two young birds flew up to greet him. Both fledglings continued to fly around the vicinity of the nest site that day, preferring to perch on the tops of the surrounding conifers rather than on the ground. They were both seen again on the 1st, 5th and 9th August with neither adults nor young observed after that date.

Almost three weeks later, on 29 August, Philip and I eventually found the long-vacated nest using a method devised in the USA by the late great Frances Hamerstrom for locating Northern harrier nests in tall reeds and grasses. Philip carried a long pole bearing a flag as I, using my mobile phone, guided him through the forest until he reached the approximate point where the adults had been disappearing down into the trees. After only one hour of cold-searching, the nest was found, close to a drainage ditch between two blocks of trees, with both banks littered for about 20 metres with harrier excreta, numerous pellets and bones from decaying prey items. Surprisingly, though, there were no hatched eggshells and no moulted feathers.

The nest, to our surprise, was only two metres from the ground in an area of the plantation where the surrounding trees were between five metres and seven metres tall. Radiating in all directions from the top of the deformed trunk were ten mature branches, each about two metres long. The branches were very sturdy and gradually curved upwards, creating what could be described as an inverted umbrella.

On 5 September, Roger Clarke arrived from England and we went with a step ladder to the nest site to record all that we could. The nest had been constructed entirely of grass apart from a few mature heather branches and, surprisingly, a 23 centimetre length of rusty wire. Unfortunately, the nest material had disintegrated and was falling through the branches on one side, probably dislodged by the birds and the heavy rain, so it was not possible to assess the original diameter of the nest.

The materials used appeared to confirm that the nest had been built by the harriers alone and that the substantial nest of fine sticks and heather twigs found in 1991 may have been originally built by another species and subsequently added to by the nesting pair. No eggshells were found in the nest either, but that is not unusual as they are often carried well away from the nest or are broken into small pieces and eaten by the female as a source of calcium. Two primaries from the female and one from the male had been found directly below the nest on 29 August, when it was first discovered, as were 14 freshly deposited pellets, with a further 24 along the banks of the nearby drainage ditch.

Was this the same female that had tree nested the year before? This nest was in fact closer to the site of the ground nest which had failed in 1991 but all three of us believed that the female from the 1991 tree nest had tree nested again in 1992. We based this on a right wing primary feather found below the 1992 nest and similar in size to a left wing primary found beneath the 1991 nest, which appeared to be a perfect match. The bands on both feathers were identical and also matched the surviving vane and banding on the disintegrating feather of a similar size which was also found below the nest in 1991, which indicated that the nest was almost certainly occupied in 1990. Now, after examining the evidence discovered below both nests, we believed quite strongly that the same female hen harrier possibly tree nested in 1990, 1991 and 1992. We also toyed with the idea that young harriers reared in tree nests could be imprinted with this type of behaviour so it was possible that the incidence of tree nesting might increase in future years.

Harriers have often been observed retrieving young who have wandered or been kicked out of ground nests. We wondered whether the impossibility of such retrieval at tree nests contributed to the fledging of only two chicks in 1990, 1991 and 1992. However, if tree nests did indeed suffer from low fledging rates, this could be balanced in the longer term by the prevention of losses of whole nests to ground predators like foxes. Safe nesting could also be improved in future years by the provision of artificial platforms.

If hen harriers were to be encouraged to nest on artificial platforms, possibly during the 1993 breeding season, common sense would dictate that they should not be in very tall trees and be close to an open area so that any mobile young falling from them could be reached by both adults. I hoped that a regular contact of mine in the Forest Service, John McGhie, would allow me to construct several artificial platforms in time for the 1993 breeding season.

Well in advance of the 1992 season I had again applied to the NIEA for a disturbance licence but had received no reply by the time Philip and I set off for another breeding season in the Antrim Plateau. In August, I received a letter from Jim Wells, well known in Northern Ireland raptor circles for his long-term study of peregrine falcons, suggesting a meeting to discuss the formation of a Northern Ireland Raptor Study Group to join the network of similar groups around the UK. The recent upsurge of interest in birds of prey in Northern Ireland meant that this could be an appropriate time to form a similar group in the Province, allowing for better co-ordination of the study and protection of birds of prey and a reduction in duplication and unnecessary visits to vulnerable nest sites. Dave Dick, then Species Protection Officer for the RSPB in Scotland, came to address a meeting in September and outlined the benefits of forming a raptor study group, with Jim Wells elected chairman of our new group in November. I hoped that its formation would help me to obtain a much-needed disturbance licence in time for the 1993 breeding season and by the end of March 1993 it was mine, allowing me to visit their nest sites and study hen harriers in greater and scientific detail.

1993: artificial platforms v. tree nests

Roger Clarke and I had several in-depth discussions, as did Colin Shawyer, with John McGhie from the Forest Service about the possibility of erecting at least three artificial platforms in the forest where tree nesting had first been discovered two years earlier. We were granted permission to erect three platforms and Philip McHaffie, George McGrand, formerly of the Forest Service, and I started work on 6 February 1993.

The platforms were conveniently placed in the vicinity of the previous year's tree nests and were approximately two metres high. It took us most of the day to construct them correctly and securely, clearing several smaller trees from around the base of the platforms to allow the adults to reach any chicks which might fall to the ground. We hoped that prospecting hen harriers looking for a nest site in a tree would use them during the 1993 breeding season.

Two of the platforms were slightly damaged by the weather and the third was unused in 1993 but all were maintained until the end of the 1996 breeding season, although none of them was ever occupied by tree nesting hen harriers. It appeared that there was no shortage of deformed Sitkas for these over-ambitious birds to choose from, even though they were frequently observed quartering over the areas where the platforms had been placed. In light of this, it was decided that, unless they were used in future years, it would be not worthwhile erecting any more in County Antrim.

One day when we were in the area, all three of us paid a brief visit to the 1992 tree nest site. On arrival we discovered an exceptional amount of fresh excreta and a few pellets on the forest floor, which, because of the harsh and wet weather which prevails in our uplands, could not have survived from the previous summer. I therefore paid a return visit on 13 February 1993.

The weather was damp and misty when I got there and as I approached the site, I inadvertently flushed an adult male from the nest. It appeared that this bird had been using the vacated nest as a winter roost site, which explained the fresh excreta and pellets that were littering the ground. A small amount of fresh excreta had been found in mid January 1992 below the 1991 tree nest showing that it had been visited at some stage after the end of the 1991 breeding season – perhaps it too had been used as a roost site.

The 1993 season began with the usual wet, cold and occasionally windy weather typical in Northern Ireland during March and April. A small number of hen harriers were observed in all the known forests from early March, with sky dancing regularly recorded from mid April to surprisingly late in May.

Several pairs throughout the Antrim Plateau had already begun nesting by the first week of May as the weather was exceptionally warm and sunny, but two cold fronts suddenly moved in by the middle of the month, bringing a much colder and wetter spell. It was regarded as the most extreme May weather since 1916, with five centimetres of rain falling in less than two days and, amazingly, a major snowfall in the Antrim Plateau. I remember having to carry my son Douglas, who was almost four years old at the time, because the snow was so deep in one particular forest. Heavy snowfall in the uplands wreaked havoc and destroyed several ground nests which had already been built, causing at least two and possibly three pairs to re-nest.

Despite the poor weather, Philip and I managed to locate 25 territorial pairs, visiting 22 forests and suitable moorland sites in four counties of Northern Ireland. This was the first time we had ever attempted a full-scale survey of hen harriers beyond Antrim, with counties Fermanagh, Londonderry and Tyrone visited at regular intervals throughout the season. Sadly, though, only a small proportion of the birds found displaying and holding territory early in the season stayed on to breed successfully.

These abnormal weather conditions also affected other upland breeding raptors like peregrine falcons and merlin. One raptor which benefited was a wing-tagged red kite, my first in Northern Ireland, which was observed circling on one occasion with two male hen harriers and then being mobbed by a highly agitated female merlin. This bird remained in the same part of south Antrim from 9–23 May and took advantage of the high lamb mortality caused by the out-of-season snow. Thankfully, it survived and was found to have returned safely to its release area on the Black Isle in northern Scotland two weeks later.

In early May a pair of harriers were seen displaying above the 1992 tree nest site, with two food passes noted and both birds observed alighting on the nest. This was still the situation, despite the heavy snow mid-month, when I left for a family holiday on 28 May. When Philip and I returned to the area on 13 June, the pair had moved to a new site at the north west corner of the forest and both were observed that day landing in helicopter fashion amongst a block of tall conifers. From what we had witnessed in previous years, it was now apparent that these birds were again tree nesting, this time at another new site.

For around five weeks a male from a nearby failed ground nest regularly brought food to the nest. This caused a conflict with the resident male but the female readily accepted his offerings, which were occasionally and hastily dropped into the nest as he flew low over it. I am not sure if this was my first case of polyandry or whether the male was simply going through the motions after his own nest had failed. Female hen harriers do occasionally indulge in polyandry, particularly if other nests are close by. The resident male was noted as a good provider for his mate and many of the prey items were personally delivered to the nest when the female failed to appear for a customary food pass. Interaction was observed between both males on many occasions during the remainder of June, with the more mature resident male always seeing off the dingy- plumaged and much younger bird.

This pair were obviously late breeders and so we decided to monitor the site from a discreet distance within the forest instead of searching for the nest, which could have caused them to desert at this late stage of the season. It was not until 3 August that the first fledgling was seen and heard calling, or whistling, from within the block of conifers and was later observed on the wing above the canopy with the female. I visited the area again on 7 August to see if any more young had fledged but none were seen or heard in the vicinity of the nest site.

On 8 August I found the nest, 4.5 metres high in a Sitka spruce which once again was of stunted growth. It was 500 metres from the 1991 site and a similar distance from the 1992 nest. I was also able to view the interior of the nest by climbing an adjacent tree: from my vantage point it appeared very flat but with a slightly depressed centre. Lots of hardened excreta were clinging to the surrounding branches and 11 pellets were found on the ground beneath the tree. The nest contents were mainly mature heather twigs but several strands of grass had also been added.

To my surprise, two unhatched and probably addled eggs lay close together in the centre of the nest. I collected them with the aid of a fisherman's landing net on an extending pole and had them analysed by the Veterinary Sciences Division in Dundonald. They were found to be fertile but the embryos had died at an early stage of growth, probably due to the inclement weather. Only one young had fledged but feathers still partly in pin from another chick were found in the nest and on the ground below, which suggested that it had died and been eaten by the remaining chick, or possibly by the female.

The same female was thought to be responsible for the 1991 and 1992 nest sites, as determined by the band-matching of corresponding primary feathers found below each nest. Unfortunately, no corresponding primary was found in 1993 but a much smaller secondary feather had a band width consistent with those found in previous years. The 1993 female, though, was a very timid individual and after many hours of observation she was thought to be a different bird.

Meanwhile, at the south end of the forest, Philip and I suspected that a second pair was tree nesting, but despite several long searches for the nest in June and July we failed to find it before the end of the breeding season. Once again, only one chick had fledged. It was first seen on the wing on 28 July along with both adults above the plantation This was almost certainly another late nest due to the poor weather, which had delayed the start of a badly interrupted season by at least two or three weeks. All we could hope for now was that both adults would return to the south end of the plantation in 1994 and possibly use the same nest site.

Despite several autumn and winter visits to the now familiar hen harrier haunts in the Antrim Plateau, our luck had not improved since the year before: we still found no trace of a communal roost site. And in the contest between artificial platforms and tree nests, the nests undoubtedly came out the winner.

1994: the breakthrough year

A late February visit with my wife and son to the moorland of the Antrim Plateau revealed how badly the area was suffering. Peat cutting had been rife in certain areas during the previous summer, with many bags left rotting for years on end on the hillside above the Byvore Bridge at Slieveanorra. A pair of hen harriers had nested there for two consecutive years but had soon deserted the area due to continuing disturbance and loss of habitat. So-called agricultural improvement schemes had also removed valuable acres of heather moorland, to be sown with grass to accommodate numerous sheep. Then, of course, there was the overgrazing by the sheep already there. All these factors had clearly reduced the hen harrier's chances of nesting and foraging on open moorland.

When hen harriers turn to tree nesting and ground nesting, preferably in mature conifer plantations, it's the first warning sign that their moorland habitat is unsuitable. Tree roosting recorded during the winter months of 1992 and 1993 had provided further evidence that the moorland was virtually unusable as a traditional ground roost. Poor ground cover does not give nesting or roosting harriers the degree of protection they need. It renders them vulnerable to predators like foxes and people hellbent on deliberately disturbing or persecuting them. Harriers resort to abnormal behaviour in an effort to survive.

The weather in 1994 was much better for hen harriers than the spring and summer of the previous year had been. To my surprise most of the resident males had arrived back on their breeding grounds by the second week of March, followed almost immediately by an unprecedented number of females.

What a difference a good spring made, with displaying harriers guaranteed in almost all of their known haunts. Despite the occasional heavy shower there were at least 13 territorial pairs inhabiting the usual conifer plantations and moorland sites in the Antrim Plateau and by early May most pairs had already nested. During our random travels, we also discovered two territorial pairs in Counties Fermanagh, two in Londonderry and four in Tyrone, bringing the total for the season to 21.

The first signs of tree nesting were observed at the south end of the original forest. The birds appeared to be using the nest that we had failed to find in 1993, from which only one chick was known to have fledged. In early May, further north in the same forest, Philip and I had the unique pleasure of watching a pair of hen harriers constructing their own tree nest. Nest material was gathered by both male and female from the western edge of the adjacent moorland and then deposited in what was probably another deformed Sitka spruce tree. The myth that harriers occupied another bird's nest was completely dispelled.

Further north we observed two ground nests being built, one on 8 May in an unused turbary within the confines of a mature conifer plantation and the other on open moorland the following day. The latter was the only nest on open moorland to be found in 1994, with the rest either on the ground or in trees in mature conifer plantations. When both were visited during the second week of June, the first nest contained five eggs, the second only four, and they fledged four and three chicks respectively. At another forest ground nest in south Antrim, a further three young fledged but two unhatched eggs were also discovered in the nest.

During our forays into the Antrim Plateau in 1994 we made another exciting discovery. In the early 1990s it was assumed that goshawk were breeding in Northern Ireland but there was no firm evidence of it. The occasional male and female had been seen in suitable habitat but their secretive and elusive nature meant that no nests were ever found.

Then on 2 February 1994, on a visit to two conifer forests in north-east and mid Antrim, we observed two male goshawks displaying, although there was no evidence of a female at either location. On 10 April and throughout the remainder of the month, the male was again observed at the plantation in the north east, which led us to believe that a female may also be present. Sure enough, on 3 May, the male and a very large female were seen circling high above a tall stand of European larch.

At around 3.30 p.m. both birds swept down swiftly from a great height into the trees and we briefly lost sight of them both. Minutes later, what we presumed to be the male was seen perching halfway up a tall larch by the forest edge, the tree having lost almost all of its lower foliage. The female had almost certainly returned to her nest, which meant that this pair were definitely breeding.

Both birds were seen several times in April when I visited the area with my wife Linda, the male on one occasion carrying what appeared to be a woodpigeon to the nest site. On 15 May, both birds were again observed drifting close to our observation point, passing overhead at a height of between 75 metres and 100 metres, allowing us clearly to see the sheer size of the female in comparison with the much smaller male.

These birds were occupying a part of the forest usually frequented by a pair of hen harriers and it came as no surprise when the harriers mysteriously disappeared from the area before the end of April. On at least four occasions during June and July, the male goshawk was observed carrying large prey items to the nest, which from their size and overall shape appeared to be rabbits or young hares. Each time the male appeared with prey he was mobbed by a small flock of meadow pipits, which were bold and brave enough to attack his upperparts. Subsequent sightings of both birds continued until at least 31 July when three large fledglings were also seen in flight.

Further proof of breeding at this site was confirmed a short time later when a large nest was found 20 metres up a tall larch. Numerous bird prey remains such as hooded crow and woodpigeon, found in the vicinity of the nest site, provided firm evidence of occupancy by goshawks. This was the first confirmed breeding record for this species in Northern Ireland.

In mid June Philip and I revisited the north end of the forest where we had earlier observed both adults building the second tree nest and encountered both birds in the air high above the canopy. The male was seen again on 1 July but the female was presumably brooding several chicks by this stage. Regular visits after this date drew a complete blank with no sign of either bird.

With again no sightings on 16 July, I decided to look for the nest site and after an hour of cold searching had found it. The nest was six metres from the ground and sadly had collapsed, smashing all five eggs, which littered the ground beneath the tree. There were no pellets, prey items or feathers to be collected for analysis and only slight traces of crystallised excreta were visible on the carpet of fine pine needles. This was my first known failure.

When I looked up to survey the tree chosen by this pair I was not surprised that it had collapsed. There were no strong branches or foliage to support the nest, which, being built mainly of grass and a few heather twigs, had also disintegrated. The weight of the eggs and of the sitting female had made collapse inevitable, and sooner rather than later. As tree nesting was still in its infancy, it seems reasonable to suggest that this pair were experiencing it for the first time.

Roger Clarke arrived on 24 July and, after visiting the failed site, we immediately turned our attention to the tree nest site at the south end of the forest. By this stage of the season two young had already fledged from the nest and from our hillside vantage point we watched them landing and then leaving the site on several occasions. At one point both adults arrived simultaneously with food and all four birds were observed landing on the ground about 200 metres from where we were. Early next morning we began our search for the nest which had eluded Philip and me the year before.

We split up to save time and energy. After about two hours beneath the dark and eerie canopy, I heard Roger calling. 'Look up!' he said. 'I've found the nest!' I could not believe what I was seeing – and I needed binoculars to see it at all. A staggering 12 metres above us was the highest tree nest to date.

The nest was extremely large and resembled a figure eight, sideways on. It was obvious why Philip and I had not found it the previous year. The ground directly below the nest was free of excreta, pellets, eggshells and moulted feathers. We had probably walked past this nest on several occasions in 1993, but there may not have been any clues then either to catch our eye. A short distance from the nest we made another significant find: the badly decomposed but recognisable remains of two fully-feathered chicks. These birds had obviously fallen from the nest the year before, when only one young was known to have fledged.

It was probably inevitable that with this giant leap forward for hen harriers, complete failures and fatalities would eventually occur at these arboreal nest sites. The findings of 1994 reflected for the first time that hen harriers were probably never a tree nesting species. Poor tree selection leading to nest collapse and the loss of the two chicks which fell to their deaths in 1993 showed that new strategies were urgently needed if all known nests and their chicks were to survive in 1995 and beyond.

1994 was a double breakthrough year in terms of tree nesting and of our first hen harrier winter roost site in County Antrim. At 2.40 p.m. on 13 November 1994, parked in a lay-by enjoying a welcome cup of hot coffee, Philip and I noticed a grey male flying low over the south end of Slieveanorra Forest.

When the bird was directly in our line of vision, it made a 180 degree turn and suddenly dropped down into the tree tops in an area where no open spaces were known to be available. By the time we left the area at around 4.00 p.m., no other harriers had been observed. I returned alone to the same area a week later and what may have been the same male tree roosted again, this time at 3.50 p.m. On the afternoon of 27 November, we were surprised to see six harriers – four males, a female and a first winter male – arriving to roost in the trees.

Five further watches, in early December and in February and March 1995 revealed the presence of three grey males, with four watches from mid December to mid January drawing a complete blank. The same area was also used during the winter of 1995–1996 with five harriers – four males and a single female – roosting in the tree tops on 8 October 1995, and possibly the same five birds during November, but with only two males recorded in December. Further visits in January and February 1996 revealed the presence of three grey males, one of which was a very pale individual, with two birds still present on 14 March.

This unique roost was inextricably linked to the winter movements of a large flock of 2,000–3,000 starlings, which also roosted in the same plantation. Although no significant interaction was observed between the species, the starlings could either be regarded as potential prey or simply as a nuisance in mobbing the harriers. Sadly for the starlings they did attract two peregrine falcons, a common kestrel and at least three sparrowhawks with, on one occasion, a male merlin.

On most evenings during our counts at this site, these raptor species could be observed hunting the unfortunate starlings, making winter roost watching even more exciting. The spectacle, though, was not to last and by the time our 1996–1997 winter visits to the area began in October, the harriers, starlings and the other predatory birds had moved on to another undiscovered location, meaning the demise of this highly unusual roost site.

This was to our knowledge the largest number of hen harriers ever recorded at a roost in Northern Ireland and was particularly special for involving the use of trees. It is most unusual for harriers to roost in trees but given the poor ground cover and pressure from ground predators such as red foxes, badgers, stoats and the occasional mink, roosting in trees was probably a much safer option.

An inspection of the old 1992 and 1993 tree nest sites, on 25 and 26 March 1994 respectively, revealed fresh excreta and several pellets below each of the nests, which clearly indicated the further use of both for roosting purposes.

This was another warning from this species, again unheeded by the conservation bodies, that their traditional moorland habitat was unfit for purpose. In these exceptional circumstances it would be unfair to class afforestation as a threat to the hen harrier without qualification. In the absence of better alternatives, the protection from overgrazing and peat cutting offered by plantations can only be seen as a good thing.

1995: a record year

The excellent weather during the spring and summer of 1995, the best for probably a decade, played an important role in the breeding success of hen harriers in County Antrim. Eight forests throughout the county were visited regularly, as were the usual patches of open moorland suitable for the occasional ground nest.

By the end of April, at least 12 territorial pairs had been observed displaying but by the time nesting had started, by the second week of May, a decline in numbers of at least two pairs, possibly three, was immediately noticed at Slieveanorra Forest in north Antrim. The decrease at Slieveanorra was probably due to a combination of factors, including an increase in human disturbance, a rapid loss of vital habitat and depredation by foxes.

The first signs of ground nesting were recorded on 7 May, when a grey male and female were observed carrying nesting material to a disused peat cutter's turbary in a mature conifer forest in the north of the county. On 17 June, I paid my first visit to the nest and found five downy chicks of between seven and ten days old. This was the largest brood of harrier chicks I had ever observed during my 10 year study of the species.

All five chicks were ringed on 1 July by BTO ringer Mervyn Hyndman and were apparently the first hen harrier chicks to be ringed in Northern Ireland for many years. Four of the chicks were female with the fifth positively identified as a male. By 9 July one young had fledged, with three on the wing by the 14th and all five seen together on 17 July.

On 11 May I had taken a brief leave of absence from my harrier duties and jetted out of Belfast, by kind invitation of the Hawk and Owl Trust, to attend the opening of their new conservation and education centre at Chalfont St. Giles in Buckinghamshire by Her Royal Highness the Princess Royal.

I was absolutely thrilled to be one of the lucky few chosen on the day from a guest list of over 200 to meet and chat – about my harrier work, of course – to Her Royal Highness. Being the HOT's local representative and the only Northern Ireland participant, I was really delighted to be given this recognition after only ten years of studying the hen harrier in my native Ulster.

Five days later, I was lucky enough to observe a Western marsh harrier at the Star Bog near Capanagh Forest. I saw this female or immature bird hunting over the rushy sheep-walk as I drove northward towards the forest. When I first caught sight of it, just briefly out of the corner of my eye, I took it to be a female hen harrier. I pulled up immediately and it flew close to where I had stopped, landing on a grassy mound.

The bird's plumage was chocolate brown apart from a rufous crown and throat that showed it to be a relatively young individual. This was the first Western marsh harrier I had ever observed in hen harrier territory, where they apparently bred in the 19th century. Two days earlier, on May 14, a different individual had been seen at the nearby Ballyboley Forest.

Another two hen harrier ground nests were found in June, one among bracken and heather on an open hillside and another in a recently planted conifer plantation. The former had fledged four young by 20 July with the other site fledging three young a few days later. I had never before found three ground nests, one or two being the norm for Antrim.

The highlight of the year was undoubtedly the discovery of a record three tree nests, found in the original plantation where harriers had definitely tree nested in 1991 and almost certainly in 1990.

We needed a new strategy before the 1995 season. We knew that two chicks had fallen to their deaths at the 1993 tree nest before we had discovered it and that chicks on the ground were only saved in 1994 because the site had been reused. Chicks seemed to become very active on these small base nests and die in a fall or due to predation on the ground. We decided to monitor closely all known tree nest sites from at least two or three weeks prior to fledging.

None of the previous year's tree nests had been monitored for fear of causing undue disturbance and the possible abandonment of the sites by the adults. Only when the sites had been vacated had we considered it safe to search for them, as pellets, moulted feathers and dislodged prey items could be gathered for analysis and record purposes. This meant that tree nests discovered in 1995 would hopefully not be visited again until after the chicks had hatched. We would only visit if the weather was exceptionally wet and windy, as the first nest to be found in 1994 had collapsed due to its flimsy construction and a poorly chosen site. The spotted harrier from Australia which habitually nests in trees is also known to build flimsy nests which have occasionally been found on the ground after a storm, complete with eggs and even chicks of all ages. I was nonetheless extremely apprehensive about even a single visit to these nests during the incubation period and more regular ones later in the season.

Observations during the first half of June suggested that there were at least three pairs tree nesting but this would only be confirmed when the sites were discovered. The first tree nest was found on 27 June, halfway between the south and north end of the forest. It was at a height of ten metres, close to the forest edge, and could be viewed clearly from an observation point on the main road.

An evening visit to the nest on 18 July proved to be well worth the time and effort as two fully feathered chicks were found huddled together beneath the tree. Neither could fly and they had either fallen or been accidentally dislodged by their elder siblings. As both adults were incapable of reaching the forest floor to feed them they would surely die of starvation or hypothermia, or were very likely to fall prey to a fox or even a browsing badger.

A survey of the nest from below showed that it was virtually impossible to climb the tree to return them to the nest, so I had to decide what to do with them. I walked the short distance back to my car and explained the situation to my wife. After some deliberation, I returned to the nest with a car rug, cautiously wrapped both the chicks in it and returned home, with Linda carefully nursing them on her lap. We diligently and regularly handfed them with small slivers of raw meat, as both were extremely hungry, before I rang the Wildlife Inspector from the NIEA, who kindly took them to an experienced falconer for care overnight. The birds were later transferred to a hacking pen in County Tyrone and successfully released in the Sperrins in early August.

On 29 July a fledgling was found below the same nest but this time my colleague Philip and I managed to guide the bird to safety via a small open area some 20 rows to the rear of the nest site. A fourth chick thankfully remained in the nest and fledged successfully two days later. Our new strategy of monitoring tree nests prior to fledging was paying off, with three chicks already safely returned to the wild.

The second nest, found on 1 July, was 12 metres above the ground at the south end of the forest and an incredible 60 rows in from the main firebreak. By 26 and 28 July respectively, two young had fledged successfully from the nest, thankfully without needing our help. The third nest, only five metres high, was eventually found on 13 July towards the north end of the plantation.

Roger Clarke arrived from England on the evening of that final find, unaware that he was coming to study a record three tree nest sites. 14 July 1995 was the fourth anniversary of the discovery of the first tree nest in that forest and we spent it visiting the first two nests, found much earlier in the season, and the third nest that Philip and I had discovered the previous day.

On arrival below the five metre high nest, which appeared to be a superb construction containing three chicks, Roger and I had wonderful views of the female mantling over her brood to protect them from the hot sun. Thanks to the bright sunshine the female could clearly be seen as she lay prone, her body and long wings fully extended against the surrounding foliage.

So good was the light that penetrated to the forest floor that we were able to take pictures of the female in that position without causing her undue alarm. For the first time ever, I was able to climb a nearby tree and successfully photograph a tree nest containing live chicks. All three chicks had fledged unaided by 12 August, two weeks later than the two previous nests. It would appear that fledging from tree nests tends to be one or two weeks later than from traditional ground nests, perhaps due more to tree selection than to the weather.

Polyandry, a strange and previously unrecorded behaviour, was observed, probably for the first time, by both Philip and me at this site. In the vast amount of hen harrier literature, this behaviour, by which one female breeds with several males, has only recently been documented (Hesketh and Murphy 2004, Scott and Hipkiss 2006) whereas polygyny, by which one male breeds with several females, has been documented and recorded regularly on Orkney and elsewhere in the UK, although hardly ever in Northern Ireland.

Polyandry appeared to occur when a male, whose own ground nesting attempt within the same forest had failed early on, joined forces with this tree nesting pair for well over seven weeks before suddenly disappearing prior to fledging. Not surprisingly, all three chicks fledged successfully due to the vast amounts of prey brought to the nest by the two males and subsequently by the female. Although several acts of aggression and regular interaction were noted on many occasions between the males, the female readily accepted the intruding male's offers of food.

For the record, polyandry was first recorded in Northern Ireland in 1978, by Fred Quinn of the Forest Service at Ballypatrick Forest in north Antrim. This case involved a polyandrous female who had not two but three grey males attending her at a ground nest. At one stage the nest contained five small chicks, of which two regrettably died, with the remaining three fledging successfully.

A record three tree nests in 1995 fledged a total of nine chicks, making an average of 3.0 young per nest, with no fatalities at any of the known nest sites. The excellent weather played its part: broods were larger than normal, no addled eggs were found either at ground or tree nest sites and avian prey was abundant. For proof, we needed to look no further than the third tree nest site, where three headless juvenile starlings were found in the base of the nest.

1996: a new tree nesting record

I specifically made a pre-breeding season visit to the Antrim Plateau on Sunday, 3 March 1996 accompanied by my wife Linda and son Douglas. It was a glorious day for the time of year and we went to our usual lay-by, conveniently overlooking Slieveanorra Forest. At around 1.40 p.m. our attention was drawn to a large bird of prey circling high above Altnahinch Reservoir to the west of the summit of Slieveanorra.

A couple of minutes earlier this same bird had been seen gliding towards the reservoir from the direction of the wind farm on nearby Slievenashanaghan Hill. The huge profile of this bird immediately ruled out common buzzard and when it flew to within 200 metres of our observation point, I could clearly see that we were viewing a sub-adult golden eagle.

The bird was by this stage high in the sky as it flew over the forest and past our viewpoint. Flying back towards Slievenashanaghan Hill, about 500 metres to our left, it circled high above the site for several minutes and then obligingly soared across the forest once again. After spending about 15 minutes in the area it drifted away to the north west and, amazingly, was seen 30 minutes later by another eagle-eyed observer near the village of Armoy. This was only my second golden eagle in Northern Ireland, the first having also been in County Antrim in 1987, more than eight years before. It made a magnificent start to my 11th season in this area.

During this remarkable sighting, two grey male hen harriers had arrived simultaneously and pre-roosted in the tall conifers directly in front of our car. I admit they barely got a second glance.

The weather during the spring of 1996 was particularly wet and windy but conditions had improved slightly by the start of June and we expected a reasonable breeding season for Antrim's hen harriers. A total of seven forests, usually eight, were regularly visited, with a maximum of 14 pairs known to be holding territory during our spring visits. For the first time in several years, no visits were paid to Ballycastle Forest: no harriers had ever been observed there and it was difficult to get a decent vantage point to view the surrounding area.

When the breeding season finally got underway, only nine pairs appeared to have stayed on to breed, possibly due to a sudden cold spell during the early stages of incubation, which may have caused an early abandonment of at least two ground nests.

An adult male and female were present throughout most of May at the non-forest site on an open hillside that had been successful in 1995. By 10 June, though, no birds remained in the area and I believe that this third ground nest site may have been depredated by a passing fox. For the second year in succession a closely monitored ground nest in a north Antrim forest fledged five young. All five fledglings and both adults were seen at the site on 27 July and again on 3 August.

A record four of the nine pairs that remained in the Antrim Plateau were discovered tree nesting. Two nests were in the original forest and another two were, amazingly, at a new plantation some 20 miles away. Remarkably, the first nest, found on 27 May, was ten metres from the ground on the same site that had been occupied the year before.

This nest would have to be watched closely as three of the four chicks in 1995 had fallen to the ground and had needed to be rescued. Three weeks after hatching, at least four chicks were observed scuffling and calling on the nest. Then, on two consecutive evenings in early July, two fully-feathered chicks were found below the tree. I delivered them to hacking facilities owned by Tom Scott in Coagh, County Tyrone, while thankfully, the two remaining chicks fledged unaided later in the month.

Within hours of those two remaining chicks fledging, Roger Clarke and I witnessed an event previously unrecorded at this nest. The female arrived above the nest carrying a small item of prey in her talons which she proceeded to drop into the nest, but it fell through a gap in the surrounding branches and landed at my feet. It was a live and partially plucked meadow pipit which sadly died ten minutes later, probably of shock. On reflection, I believe that this live prey item was delivered to the site deliberately to teach the two would-be fledglings, and most likely the eldest too, the art of pouncing and making their first kill before they left the nest. They would need this important skill within a few days of becoming totally independent of both adults. To my surprise this behaviour has never been recorded at ground nests although several well-known harrier researchers have studied many of them over decades.

The second tree nest at the north end of the forest, six metres up, was not found until 6 July. By the time Philip and I did find it, a fully grown chick had fallen to the ground and had presumably been eaten by a marauding fox, as a considerable number of chewed feathers and telltale fox droppings were discovered nearby.

The remaining single chick fledged successfully a week later and was seen in the company of both adults on several occasions but suddenly disappeared before the end of July. Both these nests were flimsily built, the first one particularly so, as five chicks out of eight had fallen from it over the past two seasons. The base of the second nest was relatively small in comparison with the first, so when both chicks became active it was inevitable that one or both of them would become a potential casualty.

At the newly discovered tree nesting forest, the first nest, at least 12 metres high, was found on 1 June. Shortly after an unknown number of chicks had hatched, one chick in down, around ten days old, was found directly below the tree. Once again I drove the considerable distance to the hacking pen in County Tyrone. To save time and money getting to and from this facility, I hoped in future years to be able to rehabilitate these dislodged chicks at my home in Dundonald, once I had been given permission by the NIEA Wildlife Inspector to do so.

This extremely large nest was almost certainly overlooked in 1995, as a pair of hen harriers were regularly observed in this area but were not thought to be tree nesting. When the male arrived with food for the female, she would fly only a few metres to the forest edge and eat it on the stump of one of several recently felled Sitka spruce trees. It was possible to park our car on the forest road within metres of where she would consume the prey without disturbing her. It was here that Philip, Linda and I would enjoy close-up views and collect moulted feathers from both male and female as well as numerous pellets and prey remains.

As the chicks grew stronger and became more active, especially when both adults arrived with food, I could see that there were a further three on the nest. Jostling and squabbling was common and I wondered if these well-grown chicks would survive until fledging. To my amazement they did, with all three seen in a nearby firebreak to the rear of the nest from mid July until at least the end of the month. The chick that I had earlier rescued was later released in the Sperrins, sadly not in its natal area of County Antrim. It was important that any future releases occurred in Antrim and I hoped to discuss this with the NIEA before the start of the 1997 season.

The second nest at the new forest was not discovered until 27 July. This discovery was made more by luck than judgment, for when I was driving out of the forest I noticed a male and female make a food pass above a block of tall conifers to my left. The female immediately dropped down with the prey into the centre of the block, suggesting that there was another tree nest in the area. The male retreated to a nearby grassy area close to the forest edge and was rejoined five minutes later by his mate. Both birds then took to the air and flew off in different directions, presumably to resume hunting.

It was now 3.30 p.m. I set off to find the nest, knowing that if I did not do so quickly I would have to return the next day, another round trip of 150 miles. Just before 4.45 p.m. I found the nest, seven metres from the ground and this time placed on the side branches of another slightly deformed Sitka spruce tree.

On the ground lay the usual telltale signs of occupancy: fresh excreta, numerous prey remains and three hatched eggshells. Approximately ten metres to the right of the nest lay the fresh carcass of a fully feathered chick, which had fallen and then strayed a short distance from below the tree. Unlike the chick found dead in the original forest, this one had not been eaten by a fox but had probably died of starvation or hypothermia.

When I eventually got the time to study the nest site properly, I could see two large chicks wing-flapping and making begging calls until, out of the blue, the female appeared with food. Total mayhem ensued as the chicks took to the air to greet her. Experience told me that both these birds had fledged several days earlier and had only returned to the nest to be fed. When I left the nest at around 5.30 p.m. to make my way out to the forest road, both fledglings were competently circling above the site with the female.

From a record four tree nests in 1996, 11 chicks eventually fledged, making an average of 2.75 young per nest. This figure would have increased to 3.25 young per nest had all 13 chicks survived. Although the weather was not great by 1995 standards, fledging success was on a par with that year, which can only be good for the species. Once again the regular monitoring of tree nests from shortly after the chicks had hatched paid off handsomely, with another three would-be fledglings saved and successfully hacked back to the wild.

1997: a nap hand of tree nests

Prior to the start of another season, a raptor group meeting was held in early March, discussing among other things how we should deal with chicks dislodged from tree nests, their delivery to hacking pens in far-off County Tyrone and their subsequent release back into the wild. I was in full-time work at the time, working late at least two and sometimes three evenings per week, so I had just enough time to check all the known tree nest sites without having to deliver any fallen chicks to Tom Scott in Coagh. He was a great help but lived a considerable distance both from my home and my study area.

It was eventually agreed that from 1997 onwards I would be allowed to care for any fallen chicks at my home, provided that I gave notice that I had these birds in my possession to the NIEA Wildlife Inspector. This meant not only an end to long journeys but also that the birds would be released in Antrim, their proper natal area. The fact that I had my own captive-bred owls at home and spare facilities in which to rehabilitate hen harrier chicks prior to their release was probably crucial to this common sense decision.

At the start of the 1997 season we also adopted new strategies on prey items that had fallen to the ground directly below tree nests. These would be collected and placed where possible on mounds, tree stumps and fence posts close to the nest site, the only exception being where nests were not situated close to the forest edge or to an adjacent firebreak. In this case, prey items would be completely removed. The smell given off by rotten remains would almost certainly attract unwelcome visitors and leave any fallen chicks vulnerable to depredation so their total removal would deter foxes and other ground predators. This idea had been tried, tested and proven at two suitably located tree nest sites in 1996 when, to our amazement, all the misplaced prey items – in this case small birds – were used again when left close to the nest sites.

The season again started with the cold and wet conditions usual for March and April but this did not seem to deter hen harriers from returning to their traditional breeding grounds in Antrim. A pre-season visit on 30 March to the first tree nest in the new plantation revealed lots of fresh excreta and several pellets below the tree, showing that a harrier had occupied the site during the winter months.

The on-high bouts of sky dancing between the so-called April showers were a feature in many areas but especially at Capanagh Forest, where three pairs were holding territory by the end of the month. By early May, Philip and I had identified at least 13 and possibly 14 pairs in the Antrim Plateau and our observations now showed that five pairs, 36% of the population there, appeared to have tree nested.

Late in the afternoon of Sunday, 6 April, Linda and I had just left Ballypatrick Forest to return home when we observed a short-eared owl flying along a grassy verge close to the main road. The bird seemed to have emerged from over a high bank to our right and continued flying north along the busy left-hand side of the road.

On 11 May I observed what I presumed to be the same bird as I walked in search of a pair of nesting hen harriers on moorland two kilometres south of the forest. From a distance of 75 metres, my first thought was that it was a female hen harrier, as it quartered very low to the ground and flew in a similar fashion. Within seconds I realised what it was, the foraging owl's long wings almost beating the heather-covered moorland. I expected to see a second bird or perhaps this individual eventually carrying prey to a nest site but I saw nothing of that nature that afternoon.

On 21 June, while in the same area, I observed two short-eared owls. One was perching on a fencepost about 100 metres away from where I was standing on the main road, the second casually appeared above me, its piercing lemon-yellow eyes clearly visible as I stared up at it through my binoculars.

When that bird suddenly landed in rank vegetation directly below my observation point, I suspected that there was a nest nearby. I later went down to the bottom of the steep and slippery hill where I immediately found fresh excreta, a moulted feather and, finally, a single downy chick huddled on a grassy bank, surrounded by deep heather and rushes (juncus). A small flock of sheep were grazing nearby but did not appear to be a threat to the chick or the adults.

The very downy and robust chick was probably seven days old and lay motionless with its head resting firmly on the ground, seemingly unable to move. There was no nest as such, just a slight depression in the ground, and only some traces of down clinging to the nearby heather with no pellets or discarded prey remains nearby. I briefly searched the area for other chicks but found none. Older chicks apparently disperse quickly from the nest into the surrounding heather for fear of depredation so I gave up the search rather than risk treading on one. Before leaving I took a single photograph of the chick for record purposes.

Prior to this discovery, I had observed an occasional short-eared owl in Antrim during the months of May, June and July but these records were only of single birds. On 1 December 1991, I inadvertently flushed two within metres of each other from the heather at Slieveanorra when searching for wintering hen harriers. This was an incredible find and as exciting as discovering tree nesting hen harriers in 1991 and breeding goshawks in 1994. In the past, the breeding of short-eared owls in Northern Ireland had been always suspected but never proven, so this was undoubtedly the first such record for the Province. Historically, the only recorded instances of breeding in Ireland have occurred in the Republic so it was a pleasure to add this species, missing for far too long, to the Northern Ireland Breeding List. Hopefully, despite the absence of voles, the short-eared owl can adapt to the unique circumstances we have here in Northern Ireland and will breed again very soon. Had it not been for a chance sighting of a single bird on 6 April, this unique record may never have been made.

By the end of May hen harrier nesting was well under way and there were definitely five pairs tree nesting, but the poor weather up till then had caused a ten metre nest to collapse, smashing all four eggs. This nest was one of three in the original forest of 1991 while the fourth nest was in the second forest, discovered in 1996. Remarkably, a third forest was now added to that list. Thankfully, warm and sunny weather by the start of June and throughout July came to the rescue of those nests which had survived.

The fourth nest in the second forest was believed to have failed midway through the incubation period, as no sightings of either male or female were made during the first two weeks of June or thereafter. This was a completely new site, added to the two that were found the year before, and because the birds deserted the area prematurely we did not find the nest.

Sadly, we also failed to find the nest in the new, third forest, despite several exhausting searches by Philip and myself with extra help from Linda in June. Two fledglings were seen in the vicinity of the nest on 10 July but they may have been from an undiscovered ground nest elsewhere in the forest. The amount of time required to find an individual site can be soul destroying, especially when they, like these last two nests, are located in very large and dense conifer plantations.

Two ground nests had in the meantime been found on 10 June, one again in the unused turbary within a mature conifer plantation, the other in a recently planted forest in mid Antrim. The first nest contained a single chick of about a week old and three unhatched eggs, the second held four chicks aged between one and seven days old. The smallest of the brood was barely hours old, its eyes not fully open. We left the area quickly, reflecting on what a beautiful sight we'd seen.

The first tree nest in the original forest was eventually found on 14 June and was over 12 metres high. Due to the sheer height and size of this nest it was difficult to surmise how many chicks it held, even four weeks after hatching had taken place. By the end of the fifth week the chicks had become more active and Philip and I eventually agreed that there were at least three in the nest. Three it was, and all fledged successfully during the third week of July.

Incredibly, the second tree nest in this same forest was found the following day, 15 June. It was well over seven metres high, probably eight if we could have measured it precisely. It was poorly constructed, though, and one downy chick had already perished when Roger Clarke and I arrived below the nest. I returned two days later and found another downy chick, probably two weeks old, huddled below the tree and then, to my surprise, on 19 June, found another chick of approximately the same age on the forest floor. Both birds were hastily dispatched to my home to be rehabilitated and, as they were so small, had to be hand-fed several times over the course of a day.

I informed the NIEA that I had both chicks in my possession and that they were being well cared for but that they could not be released until they could fly and fend for themselves. I then remembered a conversation I had had with Brian Etheridge (RSPB Highland) during a visit to Scotland in 1996. We had discussed what to do with chicks which had fallen from tree nests and Brian had advised me always to find a couple of ground nests at the start of each season and to monitor their progress over the following months. Then, if the nests did not have large broods, fallen harrier chicks could be fostered into the ground nests, along with additional food for the female to feed them.

This technique would only apply if the chicks to be fostered were of a similar age to the chicks in the ground nests.

I had the very nest into which to foster these two chicks: the first one to be found in north Antrim on 10 June, which held only one small chick and three unhatched eggs. This chick would now be of a similar age to the two that I had at home but if the three unhatched eggs had now produced further young, I would have a problem.

Roger, Philip and I, with the two chicks and a supply of food, set off to visit the nest in question on 20 June. On arrival, the nest still only contained one chick plus the three unhatched eggs and so we immediately left the two chicks by the edge of the nest along with a quantity of dead day-old chicks which I use to feed my owls. We could now only hope that this nest would be successful. It would have to be closely monitored until the end of the season.

When I returned to the tree nest a few days later, I could see that there were another two chicks still in the nest. It had actually contained five chicks, a record for a tree nest in Northern Ireland. Overcrowding was obviously the reason why so many casualties had occurred at this site. Thankfully, the two remaining chicks fledged unaided as they obviously had more space to move around on what was again a relatively small nest. As for the fostered chicks, all three birds in the nest had fledged successfully by 20 July, which was a relief to everyone involved. In future years this will be a useful technique to have at my disposal, as I am sure other casualties and fatalities will occur at these unpredictable nest sites.

With the 1997 season in Antrim now officially over for another year, I received an unexpected telephone call on the evening of Friday, 1 August 1997. Basil Lenaghan from the Forest Service in County Fermanagh kindly rang to inform me of an albino hen harrier that had fledged from a ground nest in Lisnaskea Forest. The nest, in a clear felled and restocked part of the forest, had originally contained five eggs of which four had hatched, producing the albino and three normal-plumaged chicks (ringtails).

Roger Clarke from Cambridge had arrived to see me earlier that afternoon as he had been working in the Province during the week with Raptor Group chairman Jim Wells, looking at the effects of peregrine falcons on racing pigeons. The next morning we set off early to meet up with Basil, who then took us to Lisnaskea Forest to view this unique bird. Within seconds of our arrival in the forest at around 10.30 a.m. we observed it quartering over a recently planted area of young conifers. It was a truly beautiful sight and, as far as I am aware, the first ever albino hen harrier to be recorded in Northern Ireland.

During our four hour visit we observed the bird in flight and also perching on several tree stumps in a clear felled area within this large forest. We watched in awe as the female made a spectacular aerial food pass to the young albino, an absolute treat to watch. As for plumage details, we noticed a small dark mark on the crown with other prominent markings on the nuchal patch at the back of the neck. In flight, at least two or three secondary feathers on each wing showed dark shading which appeared greyish in colour when the bird was at rest.

This bird was very timid and during most of our observations we used the car as a hide. The previous week, Basil had watched the young harrier being attacked by a peregrine falcon, which did not bode well for its long-term future in this area. We also observed the three young ringtails and the female, but there was no sign of the grey male.

As Roger had gone back home to Cambridge late on Saturday night, Douglas and I returned to the area with Linda the following day. The bird was conveniently perching on a pile of old brash as we entered the forest. It obligingly remained there for almost ten minutes and so with the aid of a telescope I was able to obtain a more detailed and personal view of its plumage.

The dark shading on the head, neck and secondaries, which on the previous day we had thought to be greyish in colour, was actually dark brown. I also noticed that the eyes appeared to be dark red, with the cere and tarsi yellow, but strong sunshine meant that I could not determine if the bill and talons were pink.

This bird, to our great surprise, survived the rigours of its first winter and even returned to its natal area during the spring of 1998, but was not known to breed. Regrettably, it was not observed again after 1998 and may have fallen victim to a much larger avian predator, due to its very conspicuous plumage. I must admit that this was the first time that either Roger or I had ever twitched a hen harrier, but this one was extra special and well worth the effort. There are not enough superlatives to describe this exquisite bird, but to see it at the end of another hard season boosted everyone's flagging spirits and made the long hours in the field seem worthwhile. We were looking forward to 1998.

1998: eight tree nests

The 1998 Hen Harrier Survey, the first for a decade and also the first to include Northern Ireland, was organised by RSPB and Raptor Study Groups throughout the UK. Coverage by entirely local fieldworkers was comprehensive in Counties Antrim, Fermanagh, Londonderry and Tyrone, as no breeding records are known from Down or Armagh.

Prior to this survey the Northern Ireland population was estimated to be in the order of between 25 and 30 pairs (D. Scott in Lit.). Subsequently, 39 pairs were confirmed breeding, with a further 13 possibles, giving an overall estimated breeding population of some 40 or 50 pairs. The survey was generally recognised in Northern Ireland as a success, due mainly to local involvement and knowledgeable field staff.

Once again Antrim was the stronghold with around 15 territorial pairs, of which an unprecedented eight, or 53% of the population, were known to have attempted tree nesting in three County Antrim forests.

Despite March being exceptionally mild and mainly dry for the return of the harriers to their breeding grounds, this weather was not to last beyond the end of the month. April brought a total contrast, with incessant heavy rain throughout except for Easter Tuesday (March 14) when 10 centimetres of snow fell in the Antrim Plateau and elsewhere in the Province. Due to the poor conditions, sky dancing and courtship flights were greatly curtailed, with birds mainly remaining static in the tops of tall conifers, seemingly mystified by the sudden change in the weather.

Unbelievably, May was exceptionally warm and balmy for most of the month with the temperature soaring to over 20 degrees on most days. These conditions were obviously to the liking of the harriers, with a female in north Antrim observed building a ground nest on 2 May, a week earlier than normal. We do not know the reason for this early nest building behaviour, but it may be linked to the milder and drier conditions in the northern part of the county. It was not until 16 and 17 May that two females were seen constructing their intricate but vulnerable tree nests in south Antrim.

Regrettably, May ended with many heavy showers and cooler temperatures which carried on into June, with no more than a handful of dry days all month. The weather during July was similar to that of the previous month, with the spring and summer turning out to be among the wettest on record, including the wettest eight week period for 40 years and the wettest July for over a decade.

In light of the poor weather, fledging success was extremely low at known ground and tree nest sites. Mortality and complete failures were also particularly high, especially at tree nest sites, with probably five nests being washed or blown out of their Sitka spruce foundations at both the egg and chick stages. Sadly, we found only three of the eight tree nests, due to the severe weather conditions that prevailed all summer.

The first tree nest that Philip and I found was on 6 June, ten metres high, in the second forest in north Antrim. Below the tree lay two unbroken eggs which had either been ejected from the nest by the female or had accidentally fallen through the surrounding branches. It is highly unusual to find hen harrier eggs unbroken after a fall from a tree nest. When we visited the site again on 20 June, two sprightly chicks were clearly seen standing on the nest, rain-soaked nesting material having slipped through the side and upper branches.

The prevailing conditions and the poor state of the nest site meant that it would now have to be monitored more closely. On two occasions, eight and ten days later, a chick fell to the ground and was transferred to my home for rehabilitation. Both were fully feathered, completely sodden, and made feeble attempts to fly when I approached them. Within four or five days they had revived sufficiently to be released back into the wild, which was of course in their proper natal area. Both were competent flyers when finally I liberated them in Ballypatrick Forest on 7 July.

A second tree nest, also ten metres high, was discovered on 20 June, this time in the original forest in south Antrim. This was another flimsily built nest, mainly of grass, so it would have to be closely watched for fear it too should collapse. When I returned from holiday on 13 July, I hastily made my way to the nest site as there had been persistent heavy rain and strong winds during my absence.

On arrival at the site, I was absolutely dismayed to find that the nest had been completely washed out of the tree, with three fully-feathered and sodden chicks lying dead on the forest floor. The smallest of the three chicks, probably a male, had actually drowned in a deep pool of water directly below the nest with two much larger chicks, almost certainly females, found a short distance away.

The final tree nest, at least 11 metres high, was eventually found on 26 June in the third forest, also in north Antrim. Although this nest had been built on the side branches rather than the bole of a deformed Sitka spruce, it appeared to be in no danger of collapsing.

How wrong I was, for when Philip and I returned to the site on the evening of 4 July, three fully-grown chicks, which were capable of flying, were huddled together beneath the tree. We immediately carried them to a nearby open area and fed them with avian prey, which had fallen through the collapsed nest, before releasing them. In a year renowned for its poor weather and low fledging success, to save a further five chicks from certain death was very important for the species.

I only managed to find and monitor a single ground nest in 1998, the one I had observed being constructed as early as 2 May. When Philip and I first visited it on 14 June, there were three recently-hatched chicks and three unhatched eggs. The chicks ranged in age from three to eight days old and lay close together, looking directly up and taking advantage of the blazing hot sun. This was one of the very few exceptionally good days we had in Northern Ireland that summer.

I returned to the site near the end of June expecting a full complement of six chicks, which would have been a record for me at a ground nest in Antrim. Instead, I found the nest completely empty of chicks and eggs, but the nesting material was surprisingly intact, if extremely wet. If a predator had got to the nest it would have been completely destroyed and pieces of eggshell and traces of the chicks would have been found nearby. It was as if someone had cleanly lifted the occupants and the contents without damaging the nest, which made me angry and very suspicious. It was more likely to be a two-legged persecutor than a four-legged predator that was responsible for the unnecessary failure of this nest.

Persecution was not a severe problem in Antrim at that time but hen harriers had recently acquired an unwelcome high profile, due to local press coverage fuelled, of course, by the local shooting fraternity. A few of them might have the audacity to consider themselves conservationists, but they are anything but, as far as I and others in Northern Ireland are concerned. Sadly, inaccurate statements about hen harriers go unchallenged by our statutory conservation organisations when they could so easily put the record straight. One of these so-called sportsmen is even employed to write a column in a local newspaper in which he regularly castigates hen harriers in particular for the decrease in red grouse before swiftly turning his attention to any other raptor in the Antrim Plateau which might be annoying him His ill-founded remarks about harriers and other raptor species could easily be picked up by rogue elements and possibly incite them to commit a crime against these Schedule 1 birds. I doubt he has read my paper on the diet of hen harriers in County Antrim, for if he had, he would not be blaming them for the exceptionally low numbers of red grouse. I can see a day in the foreseeable future when some other unfortunate raptor species has to shoulder the blame for their decline because there will be very few, if any hen harriers left in the Antrim Plateau.

These so-called conservationists claim that there are too many ravens, buzzards and hen harriers in the hills. I've even heard hen harriers described as vermin. To me, this can mean only one thing: persecution. It's tragic that, in Northern Ireland as in other parts of the UK, harriers and other beautiful and rare raptors are persecuted on an almost daily basis with no threat of prosecution for their killers.

1999: an exceptional harrier year

1999 was probably the most successful year since the early 1970s for hen harriers in the Antrim Plateau with around 20 pairs known to have bred successfully. The Antrim population since 1986 had generally remained relatively stable with around 12 to 15 pairs annually, but a phenomenal 24 pairs held territory during late March and throughout April. These numbers were obviously due to a remarkable influx of the species from elsewhere rather than an overabundance of local birds from the previous breeding season, which had been disastrous due to poor weather.

At the time, these extraordinary figures raised quite a few eyebrows, including my own. They could not be rationally explained as there was no previous history from 1986 onwards to account for such incredible numbers. Fledging rates in previous years had been low due to very poor weather conditions and only several exceptional breeding seasons in a row could account for such numbers, so where had all these birds come from?

From towards the end of March until at least the first week of May, Philip and I had gradually watched numbers of hen harriers in the Antrim Plateau build up to these unprecedented numbers. When breeding finally got under way a week or so later, though, some of the birds had moved on to other locations and numbers were now a more realistic 18 pairs, of which six were known to have attempted tree nesting.

The arrival of such large numbers of hen harriers also coincided with a similar and again unprecedented influx of short-eared owls, with up to 12 observed between April and July and a record three pairs found breeding in Antrim. Amazingly, one of the three pairs was discovered holding territory in the same area where I had found the first successful nest back in 1997. The prospect of an exciting year lay ahead for both these species.

The reason for this sudden influx of hen harriers and short-eared owls into Northern Ireland was a sudden and dramatic crash in the short-tailed vole population in south west Scotland which badly affected both species in south and east Ayrshire (R. Gladwell, pers. comm.) with the Dumfries and Galloway breeding populations dispersing within days of their arrival (G. Shaw, pers. comm.). At Langholm in southern Scotland, hen harrier numbers had declined by around 50% from 1998, to ten pairs (R. Clarke, pers. comm.).

In contrast, in Argyll and the Highland regions of Scotland, well away from the crisis areas, short-tailed voles were said to be plentiful (Mike Gregory and Roy Dennis pers.comm) but short-eared owl numbers were much lower than in previous years. An influx of "shorties" was also noticed on the nearby Isle of Man (A. Moore, pers. comm.) with up to six birds recorded away from the main breeding areas but hen harrier numbers described as stable.

Thankfully the spring of 1999 was mainly dry but was occasionally interrupted by the odd heavy shower and a biting northeasterly wind. Fledging success was reasonably high and mortalities and complete failures were low in comparison with 1998, thanks mainly to excellent weather during June and July. Having said that, two known ground nests in north and south Antrim were found to be deserted by the end of May with this more likely to be due to depredation rather than persecution.

Not surprisingly, more pairs than normal were located ground nesting on selected areas of open moorland and also in relatively young conifer forests. These birds were almost certainly migrants from Scotland, as very few of our local hen harriers, especially in County Antrim, are known to nest consistently on heather moorland because of its poor quality.

After several weeks of dogged persistence, we eventually found and closely monitored three of the six tree nests in the original forest. Of the remaining three in the more northerly plantations, only one of the two in the second forest appeared to be successful, fledging three chicks, despite the nest not being found. The second nest there appeared to have failed early in the season, as had the single tree nest in the third forest. No activity was observed at either of these sites from the end of May onwards.

The first tree nest was found on 26 June near the south end of the forest and was a staggering 13 metres high or more, the tallest site recorded so far. This was a well-built and sturdy nest and it needed to be, to withstand the poor weather and high winds which badly disrupt life in our uplands each year. Its considerable height from the ground was not in its favour so it was definitely another case of hoping for the best. As the season progressed, this skyscraper of a nest held firm and in late June two almost fully-feathered chicks could be seen scuffling towards its outer branches.

Unfortunately for the harriers, a pair of common buzzard had also nested nearby and interaction between the two species was recorded several times during June and on a visit on 4 July. On that occasion I noticed the male buzzard flying low and circling above the nest as if he were going to land and attack the chicks.

Despite the gallant efforts of the female to protect her brood and the male's occasional weak defence of the nest against the much larger predatory bird, this constant harassment appeared to continue unabated. When I returned to the nest on 17 July after a short break, I found it deserted, with several plucked feathers from the two chicks strewn over the forest floor: sadly, both had been depredated by the buzzards.

The second tree nest was found on 28 June, halfway between the south and the north end of the forest. It was a respectable ten metres high, precariously built on the side branches of a deformed Sitka spruce. Thankfully, there were no problems at this site, although one broken egg was found below the tree when we got there. Two chicks fledged here around 16 and 18 July, with both seen in the immediate vicinity of the nest on those dates but not after 26 July.

Luckily for Philip and me, the third and final tree nest was also found on 28 June at the north west corner of the forest, less than 500 metres from the second nest site. It was at least 12 metres high and similar to the first nest but firmly constructed on the bole of the badly deformed trunk. Directly below and a short distance from the nest lay three hatched eggshells and two moulted primaries from the female but to my surprise only two chicks ever fledged from this nest. One of the chicks, quite possibly the youngest, had probably died earlier and had been eaten either by the female or its elder siblings, normal practice for harriers and most other species of raptor.

Although there were no cases of persecution to report in 1999, a local farmer in mid Antrim did decide to illegally burn a large patch of heather moorland in early May, at the peak of the breeding season, to allow his sheep more grazing space in future. Single pairs of hen harrier and short-eared owl were present at the time and although it did not have an adverse affect on the owls, the harriers had deserted the area by the end of the month.

This was an exceptional year for raptors in the Antrim Plateau with three pairs of short-eared owls and one pair of goshawk breeding successfully. I just adore seeing 'shorties' which have been missing for far too long as a breeding species in Northern Ireland. I should probably say the same of goshawk, but they pose a real threat to my beloved hen harriers and other vulnerable species in this area

The first pair of short-eared owls was discovered nesting in a young conifer plantation in south Antrim where the trees were approximately two metres high. The wider-than-normal rides on a gently sloping hillside were abundantly covered with long grass and rushes, which afforded the birds good all-round cover. The first sighting was on 22 May followed by views of both birds on 26 and 28 May. Then, on 18 June, one of the owls was found dead in the middle of the road by my colleagues Philip McHaffie and David Nixon.

After informing the NIEA, I forwarded the bird for post mortem to the Department of Agriculture's Veterinary Sciences Division near my home in Dundonald. Within days I was informed that the bird had suffered traumatic and serious internal injuries, consistent with having been hit by a passing vehicle. More importantly, the bird was identified as an adult female and was probably killed while flying low across the road to hunt over the adjacent moorland.

On 26 June, as I approached the forest, the male rose from a fence post close to the main road. I was absolutely delighted that he had not deserted the area following the death of his mate. As he was now probably feeding young, I immediately decided not to search for the nest in case he abandoned it and any chicks that might be in it.

On 10 July at exactly 11.30 a.m., the male flew low across the main road from the nearby moorland, carrying prey. When he entered the forest, two young owlets briefly rose from the long grass to greet him. Unlike young hen harriers, which, when adult birds arrive at the nest, instantly take to the air and proceed to cause a needless fuss, these young owlets barely lifted from the ground. I would probably have missed seeing them altogether had I not been standing where I was on the road.

It was surely a tremendous feat for this male 'shortie' to remain loyal to this nest and his brood of two, successfully rearing them on his own and making the second proven breeding record for Northern Ireland.

The second pair was located in mid Antrim, living on a large and undulating area of open moorland which was completely devoid of trees. The first two birds seen here, by Linda, myself and Brian Nelson, were hunting in tandem at 4.25 p.m.

and 4.50 p.m. on 27 June. Sightings of either the male or female were noted on 3 and 10 July, with both adults and three recently fledged young seen on 17 July. As I had not found the exact location of the nest, I returned to the area the following day to mount a search for it.

At 8.00 a.m. the next day, I saw all five birds again, conveniently perching and flying to and from a copse of gorse bushes which I suspected was the nest site. I found no evidence of nesting amongst the nearby heather but close to the gorse bushes were several breast feathers, small amounts of fresh excreta and down clinging to a substantial stand of rushes. There were also the legs and flight feathers of freshly plucked meadow pipits and skylarks but, surprisingly, no pellets or hatched eggshells.

Short-eared owls do not build a nest, a mere scrape on the ground usually being enough for them, and we know that cleaning duties by both adults is a priority during incubation and after hatching. This immediately led me to favour the superb all-round cover and shelter provided by these gorse bushes as the most likely nest site. If this were the case, I could only admire the site's cleanliness in comparison with that of most hen harrier ground nests. Sanitation does not appear to be high on their list of priorities, which probably explains why so many broods are lost to foxes and other predators.

As at the previous site, cold-searching was ruled out early on for fear of endangering the nest site and any chicks that may have been present. Having a record two successful nests in one season was the main priority and we hoped for a third before too long.

The third and final nest was over 20 miles from the first two and, amazingly, was in the area where the first proven breeding of short-eared owl in Northern Ireland took place in 1997. Late in the season, I was informed by my good friend Larry Toal that at least one bird was holding territory on 11 July. During several visits to this area in April, May, June and early July while searching for displaying and nesting hen harriers, no short-eared owls had been observed. They could quite possibly have been overlooked or they could simply have been late arrivals to the area. The latter was more likely as one or both adults would have surely been observed at some stage during the season.

It was not until 17 July that two birds were seen together for the first time. The other two nests had fledged young by 10 and 17 July respectively but early observations at this site suggested that the female was possibly still incubating or that she was brooding small chicks, as only one bird, presumably the male, was regularly observed hunting and then perching on a line of fence posts close to the nest. This was another good reason to believe that this was a late nesting attempt.

The chosen site was only a short distance from a mature conifer plantation, with the nest itself located among a tall stand of rushes and dried grass at the bottom of a steep-sided valley to the west of the main road. As in 1997, a large flock of sheep could be seen grazing close to the sitting female but neither of the owls appeared to be concerned by their presence. On the odd occasion when the male landed on a well-used mound close to the nest, his plumage blended in so well with the surrounding vegetation that he was almost invisible, even with the aid of a pair of binoculars. The nesting female was even more inconspicuous and could only be observed occasionally with the aid of a telescope.

Intrusions by pairs of hunting kestrels, buzzards and a pair of nesting hen harriers were common in the area – I myself saw harriers 15 times – yet no interaction with the owls was ever recorded. A sighting of both owls was noted on 25 July and, on 31 July, both birds were seen together in flight for the first time since 17 July. I soon discovered that the best time to observe these birds was very early in the morning, from around 7.30 a.m. to about 9.00 a.m. and then from 4.30 p.m. each evening until dusk.

During the late afternoon of 5 August, I arrived at the site to try to find the nest as a week-long family visit to Scotland would begin on the 7th and I would probably miss the chicks fledging. At 5.20 p.m. both adults were seen carrying prey and as they approached the nest, two young owlets rose briefly from a nearby patch of heather and were simultaneously fed on the ground.

Minutes later, I had left my roadside vantage point and made my way to the nest where I immediately found a slight depression amongst a tall clump of rushes, with two moulted feathers lying nearby. There were also slight traces of down, fresh excreta and a freshly caught pygmy shrew but no hatched eggshells or pellets.

From a record three nests in 1999 there fledged a total of 7 chicks, equivalent to 2.3 fledged young per nest. This was an incredible year for both short-eared owls and hen harriers in the Antrim Plateau, where so many of both species had gathered together to breed successfully, but we knew that these unprecedented numbers might never again be equalled in Northern Ireland.

During the spring and for most of the summer of 1999, Philip, Linda and I did not, for some unknown reason, observe a single goshawk in County Antrim nor for that matter anywhere in Northern Ireland. Then, on 31 July, when travelling south through the Antrim Plateau, I fortunately came upon a family party of three. I had just left Slieveanorra and had only driven about one kilometre when I heard a crescendo of calls coming from the moorland to my right. Without the aid of binoculars at that particular moment, I could clearly make out the large brown forms of two raptors perching on fence posts, with another much paler bird squatting on a mound of heather.

I at first stupidly dismissed them as young buzzards but after hastily viewing them with my binoculars (9×63) I soon changed my mind. These were two recently fledged juvenile goshawks and an adult male, which was furiously tearing pieces from an extremely large rabbit. When a piece of the rabbit became available, one and sometimes both of the juveniles would drop to the ground and start to squabble over the food, hence the loud and raucous calls I had heard earlier. Within the space of 20 minutes, the rabbit had been totally devoured by all three birds.

Being in the right place at the right time on so many occasions in 1999 proved conclusively that both goshawk and short-eared owl are breeding successfully, if sporadically, in Northern Ireland and perhaps more widely than we first thought. I certainly know from 14 years of regular raptor watching in the Antrim Plateau that you can find a lot more than you hope for on a day in the field.

2000: the new millennium

Up to and including 1998, as discussed in the previous chapter, the population of hen harriers in the Antrim Plateau fluctuated annually between 12 and 15 pairs but in 1999 a sudden and dramatic increase, due almost certainly to an influx of birds from mainland Scotland, unexpectedly boosted our relatively stable population.

There were probably 24 territorial pairs early in the 1999 season and around 18 pairs when the breeding season finally started in May, but these figures were not a true reflection of the Antrim population. Until then, hen harriers had struggled to produce large broods and reliably maintain a firm and secure foothold in Antrim, always regarded as their stronghold in Northern Ireland. We wondered if these figures would be sustained in 2000 and whether this upward trend might continue into the new millennium, but only time and continuing study would provide the answers to those crucial questions.

The year 2000 started with the usual exuberance at the end of March and both Philip and I were hoping for another successful season. The weather in April and May was unimpressive, to say the least, with wet and cold conditions prevailing for several weeks of both months. During the infrequent dry and sunny spells, though, harriers were observed displaying in their usual haunts and by the time both tree and ground nesting had got under way there appeared to be a minimum of 16 and a maximum of 18 territorial pairs, with five of these known to have attempted tree nesting.

With excellent weather from mid June and through most of July, there were probably ten successful pairs, mainly in conifer plantations, raising a minimum of 27 young. Three ground nests and two tree nests appeared to fail at the egg stage, while three other nests were found deserted before the end of the season.

Human disturbance was believed to have been responsible for the demise of one of the ground nests in mid Antrim while in the north of the county, controlled burning of moorland by the conservation-minded shooting fraternity, to accommodate red grouse, was definitely to blame for a second complete failure. On the positive side, Philip and I did manage to find and monitor two of the three remaining tree nests. The year 2000 was the tenth anniversary of tree nesting in Northern Ireland, a trait that looked likely to continue in the near future, given the poor ground conditions and other ongoing problems that were still allowed to prevail in the uplands of County Antrim. It was therefore appropriate that one of the two tree nests we found was in the original forest where this unique form of nesting was first discovered in 1991, with firm evidence pointing to use of the same nest in 1990.

We did not visit the first tree nest until 13 June as it appeared to be the same site that had been occupied in 1999, indiscriminately depredated by a pair of common buzzard. When we arrived below the tree, we confirmed that the same 13 metre nest had once again been occupied, despite the close attendance of probably the same pair of buzzards. They are our largest predatory raptor and, given that this pair had caused havoc at the site the previous year, it was going to be interesting to see if the harriers were successful the second time around. We could only keep our fingers crossed for a satisfactory outcome.

By early July the site was still active and two large chicks could be seen moving about on the nest, which had undoubtedly increased in size from 1999. Thankfully, no chicks had fallen from the nest and perished below the tree, so everything so far appeared to be fine. For the second year in a row we confirmed that the buzzards were also nesting nearby, but neither of us noted any aggressive interaction on visits to the area. Had their much larger neighbours accepted the harriers' presence or called an uneasy truce? Somehow that seemed too simple.

Although the weather began to deteriorate again by mid July, the two chicks in this high-rise nest did manage to fledge successfully by the 17th of the month. On that day, the two young were observed on at least two occasions above the forest canopy in the company of both adults The buzzards also fledged two young a few days later, so overall I was extremely pleased with this score draw as the final result.

The second tree nest, around ten metres high, had been found a week earlier, on 6 June, in the second forest. It was haphazardly constructed on the side branches of a deformed Sitka and we doubted if it would survive until fledging had been completed – yet, lo and behold, two young fledged successfully around 16 July. We looked for the third tree nest on at least three occasions in the third of the known forests where the trees were at least 15 or 20 metres high. We did not find it before the end of the season and the outcome there was not known but our instincts told us that it had probably failed prior to fledging.

The sudden expansion of goshawks into Antrim's mature conifer plantations had now to be considered a real threat to tree nesting hen harriers and other raptor species that also lived there. During the 2000 breeding season, while searching in the original forest for what I thought was another harrier tree nest, I discovered a huge stick nest built on the crown of a deformed Sitka spruce. The nest was at least 12 metres high and the ground below was littered with feathers and fresh remains of magpie, hooded crow, rook and woodpigeon.

As I looked up and viewed the nest in good light with my binoculars, I was astonished to find the carcass of a very small fox cub draped over the lower branches of an adjacent Sitka. Goshawks are known to be vicious and powerful predatory birds, but for one to be able to carry and deposit a prey item as large as this 40 feet up a tree takes some strength and deserves a fair bit of admiration. A single bird, a male, had been seen earlier in the season in this particular part of the forest. Due to their secretive nature, particularly during the breeding season, a female was never observed but they had probably bred.

For the last three or four years, Philip, Linda and I have consistently observed goshawks in almost all of Antrim's mature conifer plantations and would now confidently estimate the population at between one and four pairs, maybe more. This species, above all others, seems to turn up unexpectedly, absent one day, present the next, but they could of course have been there all the time. They are certainly worth looking out for, as their continued presence may govern future numbers of both ground and tree nesting hen harriers and other species within the confines of these forests.

The same can be said of the common buzzard, as their numbers in Northern Ireland are now at saturation point and they have quickly spread within the past decade into several counties in the neighbouring Republic of Ireland. It's amazing to think that in 1953 there were only four pairs breeding in Antrim, three of them on Rathlin Island. The dramatic increase in their numbers in recent years has seen their numbers more than double in all our large conifer and deciduous plantations, whereas in the past only a single pair might have been found in each. Their intimidating presence has already brought about the demise of one hen harrier tree nest in 1999, with both buzzard and goshawk likely to be responsible for other, unknown failures and desertions at these unique nest sites.

To add to the excitement of the new millennium, a pair of short-eared owls bred successfully in a young conifer plantation in mid Antrim. Sightings of a single bird, presumably the male, were regularly made throughout most of May, with two recorded for the first time on the 27th and then again on 3 June. Observations of two together after that were minimal until the first week of July when both were regularly observed as an abundance of apparently avian prey was brought to the nest by both birds. On 9 July, three fledglings were seen close to the forest path within metres of their nest which was in a wide margin of heather by the forest edge.

Interestingly, a recently fledged short-eared owl was observed on 24 June in the Sperrins at Glenlark, County Tyrone by Cliff Dawson (pers.comm) during his peregrine falcon studies. A brief search of the surrounding area revealed no adults or other young and this was probably the first proven breeding record for the county.

2001: foot and mouth

The 16th year of my ongoing hen harrier studies in the Antrim Plateau was badly disrupted by the temporary closure of all forests and adjacent uplands by a severe and unexpected outbreak of foot and mouth disease.

The outbreak occurred early in the breeding season and, as the majority of hen harriers in County Antrim are confined to young and mature conifer plantations, it was possible, but probably not one hundred per cent successful, to monitor numbers from the main roads and prominent vantage points adjacent to the forests. Observations eventually appeared to show that there were possibly no more than 12 or 14 pairs holding territory compared with around 16 or 18 in 2000 and an unexpected 24 in 1999. One could say with a degree of confidence that normal service had resumed in this area.

The weather during the spring was for once in favour of the returning harriers but their pre-nuptial displays were for some reason not as prolonged as usual. We did though notice two males sky dancing at Slieveanorra in north Antrim on at least three different occasions but they were never joined by a female. Despite this, nesting did appear to get underway on time.

During the latter half of the season, particularly in June and July, there was a sudden drop in temperature with prolonged periods of rain which appeared to affect the crucial nestling stage. This was later reflected in poor breeding success and ultimately in low numbers fledging.

In comparison, the sudden change in the weather had also affected breeding numbers in the north end of the Sperrins in County Tyrone, with a dramatic decrease recorded later in the year at the usually reliable winter roost site. Only a single grey male was observed, whereas in previous years it was not uncommon for three, four or even five birds to be regularly present. Winter roost sites act as useful barometers once breeding has ended, for if the birds have been successful, the young of the year tend to arrive with the adult birds. A drop in numbers at the roost in 2001 was the telltale sign of a poor breeding season in that area.

Due to the closure of the forests, we found only one arboreal nest, the lowest number since the first and second tree nests were discovered in 1991 and 1992 respectively. Luckily, it was the same site that had been occupied for the previous two years – the first time that the same tree nest had ever been occupied for three consecutive years – so there was no need to visit it early in the season. When we did eventually visit it towards the end of June, a single chick, feathers still in pin, was found on the forest floor. It had been partially eaten, probably by a marauding fox. It was not until the last week of July that a further two young successfully fledged.

The unique circumstances of 2001 meant that other tree nest sites may have been overlooked but even allowing for that, our overall observations showed there to have been fewer attempts at tree nesting than in previous years. We hoped that our conclusions were incorrect but we would have to wait until 2002 to find out.

Despite the restrictions that season, a glimmer of hope came in the form of a successful pair of short-eared owls which bred at a moorland site in mid Antrim. Birds were first observed there on 13 May with subsequent sightings throughout most of June. Three young were regularly observed between 10 and 13 July. It is possible that this may have been the same pair which bred nearby in 1999, as their nest was within 20 metres of the previous site. Two pairs of curlew which were also breeding close by harassed the pair at every available opportunity and their shrilling alarm calls were a sure sign that the owls were active in the area.

2002: poor weather and a poor breeding season

In Antrim and across Northern Ireland, inclement weather for the second consecutive year was largely to blame for another extremely poor breeding season. Continuous heavy rain, frequent hail showers and unseasonable cold spells dominated throughout and the summer of 2002 was regarded as the wettest on record.

The season was a complete disaster, surpassing even the 1998 breeding year. The effects of global warming were clearly at last being felt in Northern Ireland. Ballypatrick Forest in north Antrim was confirmed as the wettest area in the Province with 74 mm of rain recorded. Disturbance in the form of car rallying and ongoing forestry operations in several plantations added to the season's woes.

As in 2001, breeding and roosting numbers in the Sperrins (County Tyrone) were also affected by the prevailing weather conditions. In these remote upland areas, it was not uncommon to encounter all four seasons in one day. During eight visits to the roost site, only a single grey male, as in 2001, was present on four occasions. The decrease in this area tied in with that already noted in Antrim and was most worrying. Hen harrier numbers in Antrim in particular were well down on those of previous years, a trend first noticed in 2001 and now fully confirmed in 2002. Records also show that it was a poor breeding season for our forest dwelling merlins (L.Toal, pers. comm.)

In the Antrim Plateau only between around 11 and 13 pairs of hen harriers held territory early in the season with probably fewer than eight pairs being successful. Only four pairs attempted tree nesting, the lowest number since 1996, with two nests failing before fledging was completed, due to the extremely wet weather. Our observations also showed that tree nesting harriers nested two weeks earlier than those birds that preferred to use ground nests, almost certainly due to the waterlogged ground conditions. These harriers had probably delayed their nesting attempts until the last minute in the hope that the weather and the poor ground conditions would improve to their satisfaction, but sadly they did not.

Two ground nests that were monitored in mid and north Antrim originally contained five and four eggs respectively when visited for the first time on 31 May. These two nests were given preferential treatment, as our instinct and previous experience told us that there would possibly be problems at the known tree nest sites, liable as they were to collapse during prolonged periods of heavy rain and strong winds. When both nests were visited again towards the end of June to find out how many eggs had hatched, we discovered only two chicks in each nest and a total of five unhatched eggs. By this stage of the season they were probably addled or perhaps had never been fertile in the first place.

The first tree nest to be visited was again the same 13 metre high site that was now occupied for an unbelievable fourth consecutive season. This now famous nest had stood the test of time admirably and weathered the harsh conditions associated with upland areas. It appeared from below that more material had been added to it so I was confident that, despite the miserable weather, it would survive until the end of the season.

On 20 July, all three young from the nest had fledged successfully and were observed on the forest path at the south end of the plantation where they had just been fed by both adults. My unexpected arrival forced them to fly a few metres to the forest edge where they conveniently perched halfway up two tall Sitka spruce trees.

At a second site in the same forest, a 12 metre high nest was not as substantially built as the unique four-in-a-row nest. It was flimsily constructed, mainly of grass and a few mature heather twigs, on the side branches of a partially deformed Sitka. It was doubtful, given the weather conditions, that this nest would remain intact until fledging took place.

On 15 June a brief visit to the nest revealed two broken eggs on the forest floor but the site was still active, as the female conveniently arrived to feed an unknown number of chicks during my brief stay. By 16 July two chicks had already fledged from the nest which had by this time completely collapsed and lay strewn on a rain-soaked carpet of pine needles. Both chicks obligingly perched and remained on an adjacent Sitka during my visit.

The third tree nest in the second forest in north Antrim was not as lucky, as it was completely devoid both of nesting material and chicks when visited on 4 July. It was around 11 metres from the ground and, surprisingly, no broken eggs were ever found amongst the debris directly below the tree. They could have been eaten by a passing predator but we had no way of telling. The fourth tree nest in the same forest was never found but observations from 4 July onwards sadly proved to be negative. The harsh conditions had obviously taken their toll in this part of the Antrim Plateau.

Despite the atrocious conditions it was not all doom and gloom in Antrim during 2002. On 1 June, I excitedly watched a hunting short-eared owl at the Star Bog close to Capanagh Forest although sadly there was no evidence of breeding as a second bird was never observed. Then, in north Antrim, a pair of goshawk successfully fledged two young in a forest where they had previously bred. They say the best is always saved till last.

Were it not for my annual visits to a relatively young conifer plantation in mid Antrim in search of displaying hen harriers, I would probably never have known about the existence of my next pair of raptors. It was 6 April and I was about to visit my fourth forest of the day. As I had to drive through a private estate to reach the forest, I was met by the estate manager, who asked if I had seen 'the big birds?' 'You mean the buzzards,' I replied. 'No, much bigger than that, with very long wings.' He turned out to be talking about red kites which he said had been on the estate since 17 March at least, and possibly longer.

As I approached a large stand of coniferous and deciduous trees conveniently situated towards the bottom of a steep hillside to the south east of the forest, a large bird of prey flew from a tall larch. A red kite, sure enough, but only one, and untagged. Only single birds were seen on 13 and 14 April with two together for the first time on 19 April, both untagged, which meant that they were probably adults.

On the morning of 26 April Philip and I observed both birds in the air together above the mixed plantation as we slowly made our way along the narrow drive. One bird continued to circle above the trees in typical kite fashion while the second individual appeared to land amongst a copse of tall larch trees.

When we investigated, we became aware that the bird was perching beside a large nest which was simply placed against the robust trunk and seemingly supported on the base by an L-shaped outer branch. The tree was over 15 metres high with the nest approximately 9 metres from the ground. We immediately withdrew from the area for fear of causing undue disturbance and possible desertion. Surely red kites were not attempting to nest in Northern Ireland? If they were, they had certainly chosen a private and secluded area in which to do it.

During the first half of May, sightings of both birds were minimal but one was seen soaring with a pair of common buzzard on 10 May. Two days later, what we took to be the second bird was seen enjoying the obliging thermals above the woodland.

The week beginning 13 May brought an unexpected change of weather to the whole of Northern Ireland. Out went the dry and sunny spells, in came persistent heavy rain, torrential at times. It became noticeably cooler and windier with an unbelievably heavy hail shower recorded on 28 May. Visits to the area on 19, 25 and 26 May produced no sightings of either bird but the kites could have been sheltering from the heavy rain. We now feared that both birds had left the area but could not think why.

On 1 June we arrived at the woodland hoping to locate both birds and to view the nest site at close quarters. At noon we were sure no red kites were still present but found it difficult to pinpoint the exact location of the nest site. The nest seemed to have disappeared and as we had only viewed the site from a distance with our binoculars, we could not at first find the exact tree. When we did eventually locate it, we were astonished to find that the nest had collapsed, leaving only a few branches which still lay close to the trunk.

Arriving below the tree, we found the contents of the nest strewn all over the ground: a considerable amount of sheep's wool, larch and Sitka branches and small amounts of grass and heather twigs. As they had fallen over 9 metres, there were thankfully no unhatched eggs amongst the waterlogged debris. Sheep are an all-too-common sight in County Antrim and their wool, along with more unusual items such as plastic bags, old rags and paper, is regularly used to adorn the nests of red kites in Scotland, just as black kites do in India.

Looking up to where the nest had been precariously placed seemed to show that it had either been blown or washed out of the tree during the poor conditions that had prevailed in May. We both felt that the latter was more likely as a hen harrier tree nest had been completely washed out of a Sitka spruce during similar weather in 1998. Other items discovered beneath the tree included one of the moulted secondary feathers, which tend to be the first moulted at the start of each breeding season (L. O'Toole pers. comm.), three large black pellets, rabbit remains and feathers from corvids, magpie and woodpigeon. The pellets when dissected contained the fur and bones of rabbit only.

And so failed what was probably the first breeding attempt by red kite in any part of Ireland for over two centuries, but this brave move by one of our most beautiful raptors is likely to be repeated. They may soon have more success due to the continual arrival of adults and young birds from various parts of Scotland and, as no wing tags were ever noted, it would seem reasonable to suggest that both these birds were adults, which may bode well for any future breeding attempts.

More interestingly, these rare birds were probably observed many times by local residents and farmers who did not realise their ornithological importance to Northern Ireland and to Ireland as a whole. Had it not been for our regular visits to the nearby conifer forest and the vigilance of the estate manager, this pair of red kites may have gone unrecorded. And while this historic breeding attempt ended in failure like so many others in 2002, it briefly brightened up what was otherwise another poor raptor season in the Antrim Plateau and Northern Ireland in general.

2003: disturbance and persecution

2003 was regarded as another poor breeding season in the Antrim Plateau and elsewhere in Northern Ireland, the third in succession since the foot and mouth year of 2001. This time it was again due to inclement weather during April and May, a critical time for nesting hen harriers. After that, the weather was exceptionally good and with no more than 13 pairs holding territory, a reasonable breeding season was expected and badly needed.

Unfortunately, it didn't materialise, with possibly only a 50% success rate for those pairs that did breed successfully. The decisive damage had been done during the wet and extremely cold spring and there were subsequently too many failed nests for my liking and only small broods produced by those pairs that were successful.

To add further misery to another disastrous season, there were no successful tree nests at the three known forests for the first time in 13 years. Only one pair was discovered tree nesting, the lowest number of breeding attempts since 1992. There was also only one ground nest found on open moorland, the remainder being in young or mature conifer forests.

The lack of successful tree nests in Antrim was simply and disgracefully down to harvesting and improper disturbance by the Forest Service, which had extended quite inappropriately to five plantations by the height of the 2003 breeding season. In the original tree nesting forest, at least six previously used arboreal nests of hen harriers were indiscriminately felled, despite my loudest protests. These unique nests would probably have been used again. And, at a relatively young plantation in mid Antrim, low level helicopter spraying of fertiliser took place on 7 and 8 June with two ground nesting pairs subsequently deserting their nests midway through the season.

I remember a family holiday in the Highlands of Scotland towards the end of August 2003 when I came upon a Forestry Commission lorry being unloaded by three of their workers. The lorry contained a considerable number of large satchels of fertiliser for the purposes of helicopter spraying over an adjacent young conifer plantation the following day.

I asked whether the Forestry Commission fertilised their plantations earlier in the year and was told that they would not be allowed to, particularly by Scottish Natural Heritage (SNH) and RSPB for fear of causing undue disturbance to nesting birds – and that at any rate it would be against the law to do so. If the fertilisation of plantations during the breeding season is against the law in other parts of the UK, why is this behaviour allowed in Northern Ireland?

The answer is simple: the Forest Service here appears to have neither any interest in nor any respect for nesting Schedule 1 birds during the breeding season. Our so-called conservation bodies are miserably failing these rare and vulnerable species by not offering them full protection and by not ordering the Forest Service to get its house in order.

The only tree nest to be monitored was, incredibly, the same site that had been occupied for the previous four years, three of them successfully. It is possible that the same female was involved in all five years but probably not with the same male, as female hen harriers are more likely to acquire a new partner each spring. The repeated use of this nest suggested to me either that there may now be a dearth of deformed Sitkas for these birds to use, or that this was a really special nest site. The felling of existing sites in this plantation certainly did nothing to enhance the overall situation and the pair's eagerness to occupy the site for the fifth consecutive year was sadly thwarted during the egg laying stage by tree felling nearby. This five-times occupied tree nest was never again to be used by a pair of hen harriers. During a second and final visit to the site on 1 June, two broken eggs were found below the tree, several others possibly remaining in the nest. The pair of buzzards that had plagued these tree nesting hen harriers for at least three of the previous four years had also disappeared from the scene, as their tree nest had been felled.

In the recognised literature, it is uncommon for hen harriers to use the same ground nest in consecutive years but it is known that the species will return to nest in the vicinity, on occasions quite close to where the previous year's nest was located. The repeated use of tree nests by hen harriers is therefore a relatively new phenomenon and prior to 1990 had never been recorded.

Since 1990, there have been at least six recorded instances of repeated nesting for two years in the same tree nest. There is also one record of a tree nest being occupied on three occasions, in 1995, 1996 and, amazingly, eight years later in 2004.

The instance of hen harriers occupying the same arboreal nest for five consecutive breeding seasons (1999–2003) at this mature conifer plantation in south Antrim therefore surpasses these records by a considerable margin.

For me, tree nesting was the first significant warning sign that hen harriers were in trouble in the Antrim Plateau. During my initial visits to the area in 1986, I was intrigued as to why the majority of my harrier sightings were made at conifer plantations and rarely over open moorland as I had been led to expect by several published papers and by Donald Watson's fine book on the species.

A few years of diligent study led me to realise why this elegant raptor was so dependent on coniferous forests for nesting and roosting, which occur on prime tracts of heather moorland in other parts of Northern Ireland, the neighbouring Republic of Ireland, the UK and Europe, The answer was there for all to see: the moorland was totally unsuitable for the purpose.

Nineteen years later, in 2009, those first early warning signs have still not been heeded, despite the fact that our conservation bodies know of the difficulties facing the harrier. In recent years, two conservation bodies in particular have seemed hell-bent on surveys and counts but nothing positive, such as the restoration of moorland, ever comes of them. I would even question their dubious findings. You can count harriers or any other species until the cows come home: it is what you do to protect those species and their habitat that matters, especially if you have already been made aware that they are probably in serious trouble. Getting the counts right is also important and conservation bodies have not shown themselves capable of doing so, especially in the Antrim Plateau. Both Philip and I have counted harriers for over 20 years and have reported our findings annually to those responsible for their overall conservation. We have also published several important papers to highlight the continuing problems in the Antrim Plateau. Sadly all this has fallen on deaf ears.

This disappointing season was further blighted by three known cases of persecution in Antrim resulting in the deaths of an incubating female and then three and five chicks at separate ground nests.

The only ground nest to be found on open moorland during 2003 was monitored in north Antrim, about three kilometres south of Ballypatrick Forest. When little or no activity was observed from early June onwards, Philip and I decided to visit the nest for the first time on 22 June. On arrival, and to our amazement, the male was still vigorously defending the nest despite its containing two addled eggs. The female had mysteriously disappeared about two weeks before and we were suspicious about what exactly had happened to her.

It was not long before we solved the crime and it didn't take much detective work to do so. The nest was in a small patch of deep heather and directly below a

Sitka of stunted growth, less than a metre high. The moorland surrounding the nest had been managed and burnt over a wide area for the purpose of accommodating red grouse.

In the vicinity of the nest we found two recently spent cartridges: this bird had been shot during the incubation period. In times of bad weather females rarely leave the nest so she would have been vulnerable to both two and four-legged predators. You're allowed just one guess: who do you think did it?

A week later Fred Quinn from the Forest Service brought me more distressing news about two other ground nests which had met their end in bestial circumstances. At the nearby Ballypatrick Forest three downy chicks had been cruelly killed and purposely left lying in the nest for him to find. Dogs were thought to be the culprits as the chicks' bodies showed signs of savage mauling. Fred believed that the dogs had been deliberately guided to the nest and then let loose by some inhuman individual.

At another ground nest which he had been monitoring, five partially-feathered chicks were presumably beaten to death and left in the nest on a large patch of heather moorland managed specifically for red grouse. This nest site was less than ten miles from the previous location and was conveniently adjacent to Slieveanorra Forest. All three attacks took place during June when the lowlife responsible probably knew that the chicks and the female would be at their most vulnerable.

The overall number of successful nesting pairs in this county has been gradually decreasing since at least 2001, in parallel with the continual loss of the bird's moorland habitat, and disturbance by car rallying, ongoing forestry operations and now persecution have only exacerbated the problem. There is serious cause for concern and yet nothing is being done to put things right by the people with the power to do so.

As my 17th season drew to a close, tree nesting had persisted in the Antrim population for at least 14 years and gave no sign of diminishing but conservation measures had to be implemented as quickly as possible if the long term future of this unique population was to be protected. The problems facing the hen harrier still needed to be addressed and resolved if this species was not once more to disappear gradually from our uplands. What are called the 'evolutionary' achievements of these birds had sadly been overshadowed by persecution, neglect and undeniably poor habitat management. The 2003 breeding season was disastrous for hen harriers in the Antrim Plateau, one of the worst I have witnessed since my studies began back in 1986.

Like the hen harriers in Antrim, the small and vulnerable breeding population in the Sperrins (Tyrone) was also badly affected by the inclement weather early in the season. There were also unconfirmed reports of a grey male being shot in the south of the county, the fourth probable case of persecution that year. Despite these problems, numbers at the forest roost site in north west Tyrone showed a slight improvement on previous years. Out of six visits, birds were present on only two occasions. In total, three males and a female were seen which probably meant that the whole breeding population for this particular part of the Sperrins consisted of no more than two pairs.

There was some good news to briefly hearten the weary and frustrated raptor worker during 2003. Firstly, a single untagged red kite was present from at least 8 June to 6 July at a large mixed stand of coniferous and deciduous woodland in mid Antrim. This was the same plantation where a pair had attempted to breed in 2002 but sadly there was no evidence of a second bird being present. It is possible that this bird may have been one of the two observed there the previous year, waiting for the return of his or her mate.

Finally, one of my favourite owl species, the short-eared owl, bred successfully for only the eighth time in Northern Ireland. On 30 March a single bird was flushed from the edge of a forest drive in a north Antrim conifer plantation. It had been eating a young rat and immediately flew to a clear-felled area where a considerable amount of brash was strewn over the ground.

Subsequent sightings in the same area during April and May revealed the presence of a second bird and later a nest which contained three healthy young. Two recently caught pygmy shrews and another young rat lay close to their scrape on the ground. All three chicks had fledged successfully by mid June and regularly perched on the stacks of brash until at least the end of the month. Observations and previous records show that this was an earlier than normal breeding attempt for this species in Antrim.

2004: inflation and polyandry

My 19th year studying hen harriers in the Antrim Plateau coincided with the RSPB's second Northern Ireland Breeding Hen Harrier Survey, in which neither Philip nor I chose to participate. One of the RSPB's UK organisers had contacted me to say that they would be sending some young fellow over from the mainland to carry out the work and asking if I would show him around my study area. I asked if I would be paid and on being given a categorical 'no', immediately refused to show him or anyone else around my known harrier haunts in Northern Ireland. Neither I nor Philip McHaffie would be taking part.

I was not given a straight answer as to why I, with my vast experience and local knowledge, had not been asked to carry out the survey. I told the RSPB organiser that Philip and I would be carrying out our own independent annual survey as usual, irrespective of their arrangements. This proved to be one of the best decisions we ever made.

The young man contracted to do the work had no previous experience of hen harriers and was unfamiliar with the upland areas of Antrim and other parts of the Province where birds would not be easy to find. His inexperience of this species in Antrim, never mind the rest of Northern Ireland, was evident in the figures he came up with which I eventually saw at the end of the season and which will be discussed later in this chapter.

Our harrier season had not even begun when news filtered through of not one but an unprecedented two golden eagles in the Antrim Plateau. On 15 March, two were seen together for the first time by Fred Quinn from the Forest Service and were believed to have been a male and a female, to judge by the noticeable difference in size.

One was apparently seen on 24 March by an RSPB fieldworker near Slieveanorra and identified as a sub-adult bird. Then, on 30 March, the sub-adult was photographed by Fred Quinn when he was lucky enough to discover it perching on a fence post in Ballypatrick Forest Park and then observe it flying to the upper branches of a tall conifer.

I was extremely fortunate to see both together for the first time on 3 April in Glendun at around 11.30 a.m. One was the sub-adult, the other a full adult bird. As the birds obligingly flew close together on at least two occasions, I was able to compare the size differences and sexes of these birds and judged the adult bird to be a male and the sub-adult a female. My next sighting of both individuals was not until 1 May, when both were briefly seen in flight between the summit of Slieveanorra and Glendun. My final sighting of either bird was of the sub-adult as it flew over Craigagh Wood at the eastern end of Glendun at 9.15 a.m. on 5 June.

These two golden eagles had frequented suitable breeding habitat between Slieveanorra and Ballypatrick Forest for almost three months and were apparently seen nowhere else on the Antrim Plateau. This was the first time for over 40 years that a pair had been seen together in Antrim, which certainly augurs well for the future. As no wing tags were observed on either bird, it is possible that these unexpected but very welcome birds were from Scotland rather than County Donegal.

After all the early excitement Philip and I expected no further distractions and concentrated fully on hen harriers for the remainder of the season. For once, the weather towards the end of March and for most of April was generally favourable but a lack of prolonged displaying by the males was giving us cause for concern. One could normally expect lengthy bouts of sky dancing at this stage of the season when the males had returned to their breeding grounds but this had not been a feature in recent years. We had first noticed this perplexing change in 2001 and it had continued every year since, almost certainly due to a lack of females in the area. History tells us that when good numbers of females are present, the males continuously vie for their attention with frenzied and long-lasting pre-nuptial displays. When there is a shortage of females, males do not need to display vigorously and immediately join forces with probably the only female available to them in that specific area. Here was the third warning sign, along with tree nesting and tree roosting, that all was not well with the hen harrier population.

When we had managed to account for what we thought was probably all the territorial birds prior to nesting there were around 14 to 16 pairs, with at least three floating males, two of which would later be accounted for under strange and unique circumstances. At least four pairs appeared to have attempted tree nesting but we found only three sites, two of which were in the same forest.

The RSPB survey figures for Antrim quoted an unbelievable 22+ pairs for the area. This meant that their figures were out not by 1% or 2% either way, an acceptable margin during breeding bird surveys, but by as much as 30%. This just could not have been right. Philip and I were absolutely flabbergasted as were others who regularly birdwatch in the Antrim Plateau. We have carried out accurate annual surveys of hen harriers in this county for the previous 18 years and everyone, even the dogs in the street, knew that harriers in Antrim were more likely to be decreasing or reasonably stable rather than increasing by an astonishing 30%.

To add insult to injury and state that the overall population in Northern Ireland had increased by 66% from 1998 to 2004 was not only a shock – it was totally unbelievable. If the Antrim figures could be so wrong, we dreaded to think what that said for the survey figures from the other three counties in Northern Ireland.

Harriers have been having a lean time in Antrim and elsewhere in the UK in recent years so we dismissed these figures as totally inaccurate. But as we'll see, the accuracy or lack of it of the RSPB figures would have serious implications for local surveys in which I was asked to participate during the 2006 and 2007 breeding seasons by an environmental body attached to Queen's University Belfast.

When I contacted one of the authors of the paper produced by the RSPB in 2007 regarding the 2004 survey, I was told that he 'agreed to disagree' with me. I take that to mean that my figures were probably correct and that theirs were definitely wrong. I did not even have the courtesy of a reply when I tried on several occasions to contact the main author. This summed up, for me and for others in Northern Ireland, the 2004 survey as a whole: a total shambles and a complete waste of time and money which would have been better spent doing something positive for hen harriers.

There could of course have been an ulterior motive for purposely inflating the figures, to make it appear that the species was not in trouble in Antrim or elsewhere in Northern Ireland. Local raptor circles know very well that our upland birds of prey like the hen harrier, kestrel and our even rarer merlin population need urgent protection while in our lowlands the barn owl is hanging on by a thread and regarded as locally extinct in several areas of Northern Ireland.

Or could the real reason have been linked to a proposed introduction of red kites to County Down in July 2008? To state that hen harrier numbers were on the increase would seriously boost such a project. The public and RSPB members in Northern Ireland would see that we really do not have any Schedule 1 species of conservation concern and that the RSPB, as one of our statutory conservation bodies, was working very hard to conserve all our raptor species. We will really never know what their real motives were and what lay behind their thinking. Sadly, some people will believe what they are told while I and thankfully many others see the propaganda machine for what it is.

In March 2008, I was sad to read a joint paper in *Irish Birds* by RSPB Northern Ireland and Birdwatch Ireland, their counterparts in the Republic, concerning the status of the hen harrier. The paper, entitled 'The status of birds in Ireland: an analysis of conservation concern 2008–2013', specifically deals with the population status of birds in Ireland as a whole.

Species can be placed in three categories, red, amber or green, according to their population status and other factors. 'Red listed' means endangered or declining rapidly in number or range, 'amber listed' denotes that a species has declined moderately in recent years or has a very small but important population size, while 'green listed' applies to those species that require little direct conservation action but which need to be monitored closely in order to assess population trends.

Unbelievably, the hen harrier has now been removed from the red list and placed on the amber because of an 'increase' in their population . This was a direct result of the 2004 breeding survey in Northern Ireland and a subsequent survey in the Republic of Ireland in 2005 which drew their conclusions from unreliable counts. This happened despite a decrease in the overall population for the whole island from an estimated 250 to 300 pairs in the early 1970s to only 190 to 221 pairs.

I cannot and would not wish to speak for hen harriers in the Republic of Ireland nor for those charged with their overall protection and conservation but I can categorically say that there is not one person attached to RSPBNI at present who has an inkling about hen harriers in the Province. Even so, they are able to sit and make a crucial decision like this. Will they regret it in a few years' time? I would say that by 2013, there may not be too many of them left to study in our depleted uplands.

More remarkably, the outcome has been treated as a conservation success. It surely cannot count as one for Northern Ireland where the public and the birding fraternity as a whole have been totally misled by the 'cannot count properly' syndrome of 2004. The population may be increasing in the Republic of Ireland but I and my colleagues can testify that in County Antrim, never mind the rest of Northern Ireland, the population is definitely not on the up.

In all the years that Philip and I have been studying this species we have seen virtually no worthwhile conservation measures coming from RSPBNI. Neither has there been any work implemented in Northern Ireland by any government body to fully protect either the hen harrier, its moorland habitat, which particularly needs urgent attention, or any other vulnerable raptor species. It is therefore a travesty to call this a conservation success.

Apart from all this, the 2004 season as a whole was probably one of the more successful years for hen harriers in Antrim although 'could do better' might have been on its final report. The first of the three tree nests to be discovered was found in the original forest.on 5 June. One pair had definitely tree nested by 8 May but the remaining two males and a polyandrous female were not confirmed to be arboreal nesting until at least the next day. These three birds had reoccupied a ten metre high tree nest which had been used during the 1995 and 1996 breeding seasons. When no activity was observed by 26 May nor again by 5 June, I decided to visit the site to find out why it was now deserted.

On the forest floor were two freshly broken eggs – but more worrying was the nest site itself which contained little or no new nesting material. It appeared that the eggs had been laid or possibly dumped in haste by a female with no experience of tree nesting. The males too had no arboreal skills as their random efforts to occupy and secure the site had been abysmal. Little did I know that I would see this all again in just a few years' time.

Although there were only two nesting pairs in this forest despite the presence of a third male, the man employed to carry out the hen harrier survey stated that there were three breeding pairs. His inexperience of hen harriers in Antrim and of polyandry were obvious for all to see.

It seemed to be quite a year for polyandry as Fred Quinn informed me of another polyandrous female accompanied by two males at a ground nest in a north Antrim forest. This was the same forest in which he had first recorded this strange behaviour 27 years earlier in 1978. Once again the nest contained five chicks and by 18 July all five had fledged successfully.

With polyandry recorded at that location and only two nesting pairs in the original forest, our ace surveyor reported three pairs. Looking at just two cases, his estimate of six breeding pairs should only have been four and was therefore 33% inaccurate.

The second tree nest in the same forest, also 10 metres high, was found a week later on 12 June and did not seem to be very well constructed. On 29 June, after heavy overnight rain, two well grown and developed chicks were found sodden and huddled beneath the nest tree. Fortunately they were capable of flight and we fed them there with plucked meadow pipits that had fallen through the partially disintegrated nest before releasing them nearby. The remaining two chicks had fledged by 4 July with all four observed hiding in an adjacent firebreak prior to being fed by both adults.

The third tree nest in north Antrim was again around 10 metres high and firmly placed on the bole and side branches of a badly deformed trunk. Thankfully there were no problems to report with this nest throughout the season and when Philip and I returned to the site on 12 July, all three chicks had already fledged.

The season ended on a more frightening note for hen harriers when goshawks were observed holding territory and almost certainly breeding in at least four mature conifer forests in County Antrim, with displaying briefly observed at another plantation where the trees were still relatively young. On the good news front, no cases of persecution were reported.

As 2004 was an important survey year for hen harriers, I should mention another instance of miscounting. At a relatively young plantation in mid Antrim, only accessible through a private estate, the manager mentioned to me several times that nobody had asked for access in order to survey harriers in the nearby forest. The fact is that it would be easy, particularly for a stranger to the area, to drive past this forest and not even know it was there.

There were only two ground nesting pairs in this medium sized forest but the figures for the area later showed four. Both Philip and I had visited this forest for over ten years and had never in its history observed four pairs there. Looking at the three examples so far, for which the study gives ten pairs breeding or holding territory when there were in fact only six pairs, the survey figures are now inaccurate by a whopping 40%.

If this kind of miscounting based on inexperience was repeated across Antrim and Northern Ireland as a whole then this survey is obviously badly flawed and a totally inaccurate picture of the harrier population in 2004. The overall increase in numbers can also be partly attributed to the methodology used during the survey, which will always give inflated figures rather than a true reflection of the actual breeding population. Survey figures can always be manipulated to provide the figures you want.

Regrettably, this debacle was kept pretty quiet in Northern Ireland and no doubt elsewhere but the truth is simple: there never was a huge increase in hen harrier numbers in Antrim and neither was there a dramatic decrease. There was just a fluctuating and unstable population struggling to survive, having very few successful breeding seasons in recent years and suffering from an ecological imbalance, caused mainly by a combination of continuing conservation problems. Those, sadly, are being ignored by the people responsible for organising the hen harrier survey in the first place.

2005: polygyny and polyandry

It was now two decades since I had first laid eyes on a hen harrier in the uplands of County Antrim and as another season got underway, my enthusiasm for the species had not waned one iota. The weather for most of March was reasonable, to say the least, and April too was not that bad, but the sky dancing displays by resident males were again limited by, we assumed, a lack of females.

There were again around 14 pairs holding territory early in the season but, as in previous years, probably fewer than 50% were successful in their nesting attempts. Only two ground nests were found on open moorland, in mid and north Antrim, the remainder as usual being in young or mature conifer forests elsewhere. Of the five eggs laid at the site in mid Antrim, only three hatched, with the chicks fledging successfully in early July. All three, two males and a female, were ringed before they left the nest.

The second ground nest in north Antrim was discovered across the road from the ill-fated nest of 2003 and although it was not in an area where the heather was specifically burnt for red grouse, the birds had mysteriously deserted the area by 6 June. There had been four eggs in the nest when Philip and I visited it for the first time on 25 May, but when we visited it again on 12 June to find out why it was no longer active, we found it totally destroyed, with small pieces of eggshell strewn about. It seemed likely that depredation by a fox rather than persecution was responsible on this occasion.

Only two of the four tree nesting attempts were successful by the end of the season. One of those two, eight metres high, collapsed shortly before fledging, spilling all three chicks and most of the nesting material onto the ground. After only four days of rehabilitation at my home all three chicks could fly, so were taken back to their natal area for release on the moorland a short distance from the nest site. Once again, the positioning of the nest on very weak side branches rather than on the bole was probably responsible for its demise.

The second successful tree nest was in Slieveanorra Forest in north Antrim, around 15 miles from the previous location. This nest was at least ten metres high and appeared to be stoutly built on the bole of a deformed Sitka. It did at one stage give both Philip and me cause for concern as we found two broken eggs on the forest floor during a visit on 6 June. Thankfully, though, it held firm until all three chicks fledged around 18 July.

After the unexpected events of 2004, I expected 2005 to be a more normal year for hen harriers in the Antrim Plateau although they had practically never conformed to a normal breeding season since 1990. As the season progressed it became clear that polygyny and polyandry were, amazingly, occurring simultaneously in two south Antrim forests, no more than five kilometres apart as the crow flies.

Once again, as in 2004, five hen harriers, not four, were attempting to tree nest in the same forest. By 11 May, one pair appeared to be safely ensconced in a nine metre tree nest that had last been occupied in 2002 but by 5 June the nest had failed, apparently due to constant harassment by a pair of common buzzard. By 12 June, the polyandrous female and the two males at the second site had also abandoned their half-built eight metre nest due to the combination of wet and cold weather which prevailed for most of May and up to mid June. We later visited both nests, one of which was still completely intact while the other had collapsed, but no broken eggs or prey items were discovered below either.

A short distance away, at the younger of the two plantations, the more common polygyny was unexpectedly observed. In early May, a single pair had just begun ground nesting at the south end of the forest. On 15 May, I discovered that a second female was also ground nesting 300 metres further north but there was no sign of an additional male. Further observations in the area over the next ten days clearly showed that the resident male was provisioning both females.

By 21 June the polygynous male had lost his second partner but was still providing food for the original female who by now had three sprightly chicks. Once again the presence of two common buzzards may have contributed to the demise of the second ground nest which had contained two eggs on 25 May but the lone male never defended the site when the female was occasionally absent. The original nest was of course successful with all three chicks, two males and a female, already fledged by 11 July.

The discovery of polygyny and polyandry occurring so close to each other was probably unprecedented for this species in the Western Palaearctic and we were now seriously concerned about what exactly was happening within this unique harrier population. The polyandrous behaviour was more worrying than the more common polygyny, which had for decades been regularly recorded in UK harrier populations, with polyandry probably reflecting an imbalance of females to males in the population of the area.

There were most definitely warning signs that all was not well with the Antrim hen harrier population. Firstly, tree nesting and tree roosting had told us that the harriers were encountering serious habitat problems and consistently using forests and trees. Then came a lack of prolonged pre-breeding season displaying, or sky dancing, by males. Now there were these bouts of polygyny and, more commonly, polyandry. But no one out there seemed to be noticing.

The season ended on a high note when I discovered a pair of short-eared owls breeding in a north Antrim forest. It was the same forest and the same general area where a pair successfully bred in 2003. Birds had been present in a clear felled area from early May onwards and a nest containing three eggs was soon found amongst a pile of old brash. In early July the three chicks fledged successfully and remained in the vicinity of the nest site for over two weeks.

The expansion of goshawks in County Antrim continued unabated during 2005, probably to the detriment of the forest-dwelling hen harriers and other vulnerable species. At least six pairs were now known to have bred successfully, raising a minimum of seven young from only three of the nest sites. To my amazement, two of the six pairs were found breeding in one plantation but we did not know how many fledged at the remaining three sites.

These fearless predatory birds are known to wreak havoc on other avian species and mammals in coniferous and deciduous woodlands throughout the UK so I feared the same would happen, or may already have been happening, in some of Antrim's vast conifer plantations. The swift increase in the goshawk's breeding population in Northern Ireland since the late 1990s may eventually force the hen harrier, short-eared owl and possibly the merlin back out onto their traditional breeding grounds, heather moorland now so degraded that it could prove even more devastating for all three species.

2006: new beginnings

About five weeks into the 2006 breeding season, I was contacted by Dr. Robbie McDonald, then Centre Manager of Quercus, affiliated to Queen's University Belfast. In brief, Quercus is Northern Ireland's and the UK's first co-operative Research Centre for Biodiversity and Conservation Biology, established in 2003 as a partnership between the Environment and Heritage Service and Queen's University.

Quercus and Dr Tim Hipkiss were planning a two year project on breeding hen harriers. I met Tim at a field meeting in early May at Capanagh Forest in south Antrim with Robbie McDonald and Dr. Stuart Bearhop and decided that I would come on board to help with the project. Tim mentioned that he was struggling to find enough birds for a serious study and so my help and my years of field experience would be crucial to the overall success of the project. Within days we were in the field together, studying harriers and getting to know each other.

The study area and habitat were totally alien to Tim: his forte was more the study of breeding Tengmalm's owls in Sweden than harriers in the uplands of Northern Ireland. He was also working with the figures produced from the 2004 breeding survey so it didn't take long to work out why he felt he had been observing so few hen harriers in Antrim. I told him to put those figures completely from his mind.

I could see that Tim was puzzled by my dismissal of the figures but after only a few weeks of study in the Antrim Plateau, during which we visited every nook and cranny that I had got to know over the past two decades, it was clear that I was right about the numbers of harriers in the area. This was reflected at the end of the breeding season when all the year's data was collated, showing the true harrier population in Antrim rather than the false one from which he had been working over the previous weeks.

The 2006 breeding season was more intriguing than ever, despite the wet and cold weather that prevailed right through the vital incubation period, resulting in several complete failures, small broods, numerous addled eggs and, more importantly, poor fledging success. From early June and throughout most of July, we were greeted by excellent sunny and warm conditions but torrential rain during May had completely ruined the chances of a successful breeding season.

In total there were only 14 territorial pairs located in Antrim during 2006, all of which attempted breeding. There were only two known tree nest sites, one in south Antrim, which we found, the other in the north of the county which we looked for on several occasions but which we failed to find before the end of the season. Sadly, this was the lowest number of tree nests discovered since 2003, which regrettably summed up another unsuccessful season for harriers in the Antrim Plateau.

During April and May, two of the pairs were again present in the same south Antrim forest where polyandry had now become something of an annual event. By 11 May, one pair had already ground nested in a patch of degraded heather, not in the forest but at the south west corner of the plantation, around 50 metres from the forest edge. In contrast, at the north end of the forest, two grey males were relentlessly pursuing the resident female across the plantation and the adjacent moorland on both sides of the main road.

On 16 May, in the company of Tim Hipkiss, I observed the brace of males, one of which was a pale-plumaged old bird, the other a darker and much younger individual, circling over a block of tall Sitka close to the forest path. There was, though, no sign of the female. Could this be another polyandrous female or perhaps the same bird that had tried unsuccessfully to breed here in 2005?

Some 20 minutes elapsed. Suddenly, the female rose from the trees calling loudly in an agitated fashion. When she failed to return to what we presumed was a tree nest, Tim and I agreed that we should try to locate the site. Thirty minutes later, we discovered a freshly broken hen harrier egg lying on the ground approximately 100 metres in from the forest edge. As we peered up at the ten metre Sitka spruce, we could not locate a nest, only an array of side branches which clearly resembled one. It was directly below this strange arrangement of branches that the egg had been found.

When we returned to the same area on 22 May, all three birds were continually circling above the canopy on the opposite side of the forest path and probably no more than 200 metres from the first failed site. From a prominent vantage point further along the path, the female suddenly descended into the trees where she was possibly tree nesting again. The two males flew off in different directions but within a few minutes the female was in the air again and, just as on 16 May, she did not return to the new potential nest site.

After 15 minutes, with still no sign of the female returning, we took the bull by the horns and went looking for the nest site. After only 20 minutes of cold searching we discovered another two broken eggs lying below an 11 metre Sitka. Once again no nest was found but the formation of the side branches was similar to those we examined on the first tree six days earlier.

Tim had never before observed such strange behaviour and yet this was exactly what I had seen in 2004, in this same forest, at a totally different site but possibly by the same birds.

In early June the female was observed again but on this occasion only one male, the paler and more mature bird, was attending her. The dingy-plumaged younger bird had unexpectedly moved to a ground nest less than a kilometre away on the adjacent moorland but he was still in sight of what we now regarded as the resident pair. Like the pair at the south end of the plantation, his nest was approximately 50 metres from the forest edge.

The potential tree nesting pair had now moved again, this time to an adjacent block of conifers less than 100 metres from the second site and only 300 metres from the original location. After several sightings of both birds up to and on 18 June, including four spectacular food passes above the forest canopy, we decided after another airborne delivery on 23 June that the time was right to launch a search for the nest.

After a brief search, we eventually found it, only ten trees away from a drainage ditch and 38 rows in from the forest edge. The nest was 11 metres high and was precariously placed on the bole and side branches of a badly deformed Sitka spruce. In the past, poor tree selection and flimsily constructed nests have been problematic in Antrim and so this particular site did not appear too promising, considering this female's poor choices so far.

The nest began to fall apart due to heavy rain around the middle of July and on the 16th of that month, a downy chick, about ten days old, was found dead below the nest. By 27 July the nest had split in two and three days later a fully feathered chick, quite capable of flight, was found in a drain between two rows of conifers. On 5 August, when we visited the site again, the last of the three chicks was also found below the nest. This chick too was capable of sustained flight but was impeded by the low branches of the surrounding conifers.

Both these chicks were females, signified by their dark chocolate brown irides, and were extremely aggressive. They had been ably provisioned before we released them by dislodged meadow pipits which had fallen from the nest when it had collapsed. On 8 August, when I returned to the area with Linda, both were observed within metres of each other on the nearby moorland having been fed by both adults during a spectacular dual food pass. These were the 19th and 20th chicks that I had rescued from below those tree nests and released back to the wild and I was sure that they wouldn't be the last.

The two earlier attempts at tree nesting by the polyandrous female had failed dismally but they were similar in every way to what I had witnessed in 2004 and then briefly in 2005. Were the same trio of birds involved in those disasters as well? At present I can only speculate as to why polyandry and to a lesser extent polygyny are now consistently occurring in the Antrim hen harrier population. The observations that Philip, Tim and I had made over the previous three breeding seasons in particular (2004–2006) definitely pointed to a dearth of females in the Antrim Plateau or this behaviour would not have been a regular occurrence.

It is highly unlikely that earlier cases of polyandry or polygyny would have gone unnoticed; such strange and rarely recorded behaviour is likely to have been observed and mentioned by others observing harriers in this area. It does, though, take many years of field experience to identify such traits in harriers. I hope that further studies of this behaviour will reveal the real reasons why it happens and what implications it might have in the near future. Having said that, though, if we are to believe the inflated numbers created by the RSPB during the 2004 UK Hen Harrier Breeding Survey, then harriers in Antrim do not have problems such as this and are simply flying in 'unmentionable numbers'. If only that were true.

Perhaps a breakdown of the 14 breeding attempts in 2006 will persuade those sceptics who in the past have disbelieved my figures for this area. They also reveal the poor breeding success and productivity which has plagued this species every year from at least 2001.

Of the 14 recorded nesting attempts, seven (50%) were known to have completely failed with the outcome unknown. This was probably also the case at an eighth site. The probable failure of this eighth nest would increase the overall failure rate for Antrim to an abysmal 57% in 2006. One of the seven failed attempts was due to persecution, with the five eggs at a ground nest blatantly removed before hatching. This happened shortly after the perpetrator failed to poison both adults. A starling laced with poison was initially tied to a fence post close to the nest site where both birds occasionally perched.

The remaining four ground nests originally contained a total of 19 eggs, of which only 10 (52%) hatched. In total, the six active nests, including the two tree nests, produced a minimum of 25 eggs, which is equal to 4.1 eggs per nest but only 16 (64%) of these reached the hatching stage with 15 chicks (60%) managing to fledge successfully.

The two tree nests produced two and three fledged young respectively but only after two chicks were rescued from below the first nest and then released. Another chick was earlier found dead after falling from the same nest. If this tree nest had not been closely monitored these two chicks would also have perished, reducing the combined fledging rates for both sites from an initial 2.5 chicks per nest to a meagre 1.5 chicks per fledged nest.

Nothing goes to plan, especially in Northern Ireland where the weather can either make or break a hen harrier breeding season. At one stage in the season conditions appeared to be favourable and we hoped for large broods for the purposes of wing tagging, which would take place here for the first time. Unfortunately, due to the poor hatching rate in 2006, only three nestlings were wing tagged by Lorcan O'Toole of the Irish Raptor Study Group, one in south Antrim and two in the north of the county. The colour scheme used was left wing – dark blue, right wing – light blue.

The tagging was an attempt to monitor the autumn and winter movements of Northern Ireland's hen harriers and to identify important wintering sites. Although the three chicks did fledge successfully, they were sadly never observed during the winter of 2006, nor for that matter in 2007. Any future tagging therefore needs a minimum of at least ten or fifteen nestlings to be viable, but getting the required number of nestlings may not be easy, considering that the past few seasons have not been particularly fruitful.

In my 24 years of studying harriers in Northern Ireland, I have only ever observed three hen harriers sporting wing tags, the most recent in 2008 from the neighbouring Republic of Ireland, one in 2006 from England and one many years ago from Scotland. With very few from elsewhere ever recorded here, it would appear that recently fledged wing tagged hen harriers only migrate short distances from their natal area and probably within their country of origin, with of course the odd exception. It is no doubt exciting to trace the winter movements of certain birds like hen harriers and other large raptor species after they have fledged but very few survive the rigours of their first winter, which possibly explains why only the odd one is ever recorded here.

In early May 2006, I received a call from NIBA Records Secretary George Gordon regarding a pair of harriers that had been observed holding territory from before the end of April in a small coniferous wood in the Mourne Mountains, County Down. They had been seen by a Mrs Anne McComb who regularly frequented the Trassey Track area at the edge of the Mournes and believed that the harriers could be nesting in the nearby wood.

She was unable to meet me herself but after speaking with her several times in May and June, I spent 17 July in the area on my own and eventually managed to locate at least three and possibly four fledged young, along with both adults, about three kilometres south east of the wood. It was really hard work as the birds had already dispersed from their natal area and although I did not have time to find the nest on the day, I was delighted with the outcome. These were probably the first successful breeding hen harriers to be discovered in the Mournes since the late 1890s. The late C. D. Deane does mention a pair being seen there on 7 September 1952 but he was never given any proof of breeding. This was an amazing find, right up there with the very best of my many great hen harrier moments. It is not every day that one discovers a species breeding in an area where it has been missing for well over a century.

My sincere thanks for this fantastic record are due to two people: Anne McComb herself, whose intuitive judgement that hen harriers were nesting in her local patch led me to this historic pair of birds, and George Gordon, who when he realised the importance of Anne's information, took the time to pass it on to me.

I regret that I have not had the time to revisit the area since 2006 but rumours abound that other hen harriers may be breeding in and around the periphery of the Mournes. County Down has therefore been officially added to the four counties in Northern Ireland where this species breeds, with Armagh remaining the only exception.

Were these birds tree nesting, or were they just ground nesting on the periphery of the wood, where better all-round cover was probably available to them? Sadly, neither I nor Anne McComb could find the nest so both questions will have to remain unanswered for now.

Despite our best efforts, Philip, Tim and I did not manage to observe even one short-eared owl during the whole of 2006 but goshawks were still much in evidence in Antrim's mature conifer plantations, with six pairs once again discovered breeding. Only two sites were regularly monitored from a discreet distance and these appeared to show that at least four young fledged, two from each nest. Evidence in the form of a single pellet and several breast feathers discarded during a preening session were discovered within 20 metres of the hen harrier tree nest that we monitored in south Antrim, showing that one bird, probably the male, had remained there overnight.

2007: an early end to new beginnings

The weather during the spring of 2007 was in total contrast to that of the previous year, with virtually no heavy rain nor the usual bitterly cold spells that are a common feature in Northern Ireland during March. Instead we had basically dry and reasonably mild weather which continued well into April and May and was simply ideal for nesting harriers.

Then came the so-called summer months of June and July which unexpectedly brought some of the heaviest rain recorded here in recent history. Some parts of Belfast, along with other areas of the Province, suffered severe flooding over the five consecutive days from 12 to 16 June, with persistent heavy showers continuing after that. Many homes were flooded for days on end, with cars seen floating down several main thoroughfares close to the city centre. Many people here dismiss global warming as a joke but this summer's weather was anything but: it was a prime example of what we can expect again in the near future.

The Antrim uplands did not escape and many nests, both tree and ground, failed shortly after hatching took place, resulting in the deaths of many young chicks at the down stage of growth. Broods were also affected at nest sites in Fermanagh and south Tyrone, with several found dead in nests that were being regularly monitored. What had started so promisingly turned into just another dismal breeding season for hen harriers.

In total, 15 territories were occupied in Antrim during the 2007 breeding season, of which only 12 pairs definitely attempted breeding, a reduction of two nesting pairs from the previous year and an overall decrease for the area of 14%. In three of the territories, single males were observed displaying on several occasions but no females were ever recorded. This was most disappointing but not surprising, given the apparent dearth of females in recent years.

One such area, which unbelievably held only a single male, was Ballypatrick Forest in north Antrim. Two pairs were generally present every year, with the possibility of a third pair on the open moorland about three kilometres to the south east of the forest. For the first time in 22 years, no hen harriers bred in or beyond this forest. Dark forces were obviously again at work in this area which had suffered two known instances of blatant persecution in 2003.

Tim reported our findings about Ballypatrick Forest to RSPBNI, only to be told that we were not looking in the right places for the birds. It was a stupid thing to say, betraying a total lack of knowledge of hen harriers in the area. It was difficult for me, and probably for Tim, to take, considering my vast experience with the species over the years.

I think that blind panic had set in as we had told RSPBNI in 2005 and 2006 that the numbers quoted for Antrim in 2004 were totally incorrect. The breeding numbers that Tim and I had produced for 2006 and 2007 showed dramatic decreases of around 36% and 45% respectively, based on their survey figures for 2004. This was from a harrier population, to quote their own words, 'that is on the increase'. It might be on the Isle of Man and elsewhere in the UK, but it certainly is not in Antrim.

There were only two active tree nests, with a third possible, but both known sites ended in premature failure due to the prevailing weather conditions. The first site in south Antrim was the same nest that had been occupied in 2006 by the polyandrous female and her two male cohorts. On this occasion it was only briefly occupied, very possibly by the same trio of birds, with the site completely deserted by the end of May. Very little nesting material was ever added to bolster the nest in 2007 and as a result two broken eggs were found on the forest floor.

Prior to the demise of the first tree nest, Tim and I visited the site only once during May. As we made our way back to the main road we were met by another keen birder, Cameron Moore. While deep in conversation about this trio of birds, our attention was suddenly drawn to several raptors that appeared without warning over the adjacent moorland to our left. Right in our line of vision were a hunting peregrine falcon, a distant soaring goshawk, a male hen harrier and a male merlin, the harrier and merlin returning to their forest nest sites. It was an unexpected and unforgettable moment.

The second tree nest was found close to the main road at the largest conifer plantation in County Antrim. It was around 12 metres high, though possibly taller, as Tim, Philip and I did not physically visit the site although we were in the general area. This nest appeared to fail later in the annual breeding cycle, probably soon after hatching. There was possibly a third nest site to the east of the same forest but this was not substantiated during the season. The steady decline in tree nesting over the previous two or three years was most worrying but it probably went hand-in-hand with the overall situation in the Antrim Plateau.

What was also very worrying were the repeated visits in 2007 and probably also in 2006 by mainly unskilled field workers to some nest sites and to the areas where harriers were present. The second tree nest and the area it was in were visited a total of 29 times, not including the visits made by Philip, Tim and me to the general area. Multiple visits like this are totally irresponsible and unnecessary and could possibly have been to blame for the eventual failure of this nest. On 10 July 2005, Philip and I paid our first and only visit of the season to a ground nest in mid Antrim which we had been monitoring since early May. We needed to check the nest and record the number of chicks present prior to fledging. When we had done this, we hastily left the area to avoid further disturbance, not knowing that less than an hour later the same nest site would be visited again so that the three chicks could be ringed.

Things like this should not happen given proper co-ordination, and the persistent visiting of nest sites should cease immediately. If Philip and I had known that a visit was imminent, we would not have gone to the site that morning. Disturbance must be kept to the bare minimum to avoid depredation by the many foxes that inhabit these areas. Instead we inadvertently increase it.

The late Frances Hamerstrom who studied the Northern harrier in her beloved Wisconsin for over 30 years, and whom I had the pleasure of meeting in 1993, used to refer to those she employed to monitor harriers as 'gabboons'. I think of some of them here as 'moochers', totally inexperienced and clueless about how to study hen harriers correctly.

Both Philip and I have had the displeasure of watching several of them running around the Antrim Plateau like headless chickens, jumping out of their cars, map and pen in hand. We saw one in particular standing on the summit of a hill like a beacon, sitting down for a few moments before getting to his feet again, over and over again. He had no idea that an agitated male hen harrier was high above his head as a pair was nesting nearby. It said it all.

As the season progressed, I sensed that all was not well with Tim and his harrier studies. In early June, when we were once again in the Antrim Plateau, Tim dropped a bombshell and told us that he was giving up his job before the end of the present breeding season and returning to Sweden later that month with his wife Anna-Maria.

I sincerely wished Tim all the best for the future. I would miss his soft-spoken voice and cheery nature in the field but he had, above all, been a quick learner and good company during our all too brief time together in Antrim.

Tim's temporary replacement from Quercus, Conor Wilson, was not always available towards the latter stages of the season but I carried on regardless, more in the hope than the expectation of finding recently fledged harriers. To my horror, I managed to discover a total of only five fledglings from the few nests that were partially successful and three of those were from one ground nest. There were probably several more that went unnoticed but they were few and far between in 2007.

All in all, it was another disastrous season for hen harriers in Antrim and elsewhere in Northern Ireland and beyond. In south Ayrshire hen harrier breeding success was also badly affected by the extremely wet summer during 2007 as I observed several complete failures during an early June visit with my wife.

At this rate, it would take many years for the unique population in Northern Ireland to fully recover, if it ever were to do so. One thing was for certain: too few chicks had fledged in recent years to sustain a viable breeding population, due to a combination of poor weather, disturbance, depredation, persecution and the degraded moorland which explained the downward trend in successful breeding pairs, specifically in Antrim. It is fine to have 14 or so territorial pairs each season but why were they not all breeding successfully and producing the large broods which had been common a decade or so before? Was it really down to the problems we knew about or were there other underlying factors of which we were not yet aware? It would surely have been better for our conservation organisations to spend a little money examining the problems facing hen harriers than to persist with botched surveys and continual counts which achieved absolutely nothing.

For the second consecutive year, no short-eared owls were observed anywhere in the Antrim Plateau as the trend here shows that they usually return to breed in alternate years. Four visits to the hen harrier winter roost site in the Sperrins were also disappointing with only a single grey male present on two occasions, on one of which the bird flew on, presumably to roost elsewhere.

In the previous 21 years in the Antrim Plateau, one species of raptor had always managed to elude me: the fish eating osprey, a regular spring visitor. In this particular part of Antrim three reservoirs, well stocked with brown and rainbow trout, are to be found adjacent to the conifer forests that I frequent during my annual spring forays for hen harriers. On Sunday 15 April 2007 I happened to be in the right place at the right time when I observed a single osprey fishing at Altnahinch Reservoir, right in the heart of the Antrim Plateau. What a welcome sight it was, and well worth the twenty year wait.

2008: a poor year for hen harriers

The next two chapters, which deal with 2008 and 2009, take a more comprehensive look at my day-to-day hen harrier activities in the Antrim Plateau during the course of the breeding season. I detail the number of hours, days and months spent in the field, the locations that I visit at least eight times each season and the many miles clocked up every year. It is a long hard slog to complete the work to my satisfaction: it's a pleasure, but an unpaid one, and my findings are not always what people want to hear.

March 2008 roared in like the proverbial lion, with gale force winds, heavy rain, hail and intermittent but mainly light falls of snow in our uplands. This was a very poor month for the Province in terms of weather, with biting northerly winds blowing at up to 84 m.p.h and Antrim recorded as the wettest place in the UK on March 26.

Despite the conditions, my first visit of the season to several hen harrier locations in south Antrim went ahead on 4 March, but it came as no surprise that I did not observe a single harrier on the day. My next visit with Philip was more fruitful, as I recorded a pair of displaying goshawks on 16 March and my first grey male harrier of the year at Capanagh Forest a week later. The next day, Easter Monday, Linda and I visited our usual haunts in north Antrim and were met with a constant barrage of hail and snow flurries, but we did manage to catch a glimpse of a very pale-plumaged male near Slieveanorra, with two male merlins the highlight of the day.

In contrast with the early part of the month, the last few days of March and the first five days of April brought mild, sunny and reasonably warm weather to Northern Ireland with temperatures of 16 to 18 degrees recorded on most days. On 6 April, though, almost overnight, the wind changed to the north and in again came the snow and hail showers. Despite the change in the weather, Philip and I did manage that day to observe the same male at Capanagh Forest and, at two much larger plantations further north, a further two males, one being hastily escorted out of its former nesting area by a common buzzard. Once again no females were observed at any of the locations visited.

A few days later, the wind moved to the east where it remained for the next two weeks and although mainly dry and sunny weather prevailed during this period, it was bitterly cold. On 9 April, merlin aficionado Larry Toal told me about a displaying male at a different site in south Antrim and the next day I saw for myself two females and what was possibly the same male.

The 10th also brought the first sky dancing pair at nearby Capanagh Forest but the display was not prolonged and appeared to be nothing more than a token gesture, performed when both birds appeared to arrive simultaneously. At another forest in mid Antrim, a male and female were seen together at the north end of the plantation at around 12.20 p.m. but 35 minutes earlier, I had been very disturbed to see a low-flying male goshawk carrying a depredated male hen harrier. Three days later the partial remains and several feathers of this unfortunate male were found on the path at the south end of the forest.

The afternoon of 11 April was spent with a member of the NIRSG (Northern Ireland Raptor Study Group) at two well-known harrier locations in south and north Antrim. We first spent over two hours at Ballyboley Forest, making a fourth attempt to see harriers but failing. The rest of the day was spent in the Altnahinch area of Slieveanorra Forest. We had a pale-plumaged male at 5.15 p.m., followed at 6.20 p.m. by a much darker and younger male, but no female was seen on the day.

It would have been unheard of a few years ago to have to wait two hours to see a hen harrier but there simply are not the same numbers of birds around any more. There he saw that for himself but it's a pity that people in our conservation bodies who do not even study harriers refuse to take my word for it. You soon see the highs and lows in a harrier population when you have spent more than 20 years in an area, as Philip and I have done, and if we didn't, we wouldn't be doing our work properly. It is very frustrating and disheartening to report our findings to organisations which have their own agenda and are determined not to listen. Maybe they will believe my findings one day but it might by then be too late to save our local hen harriers.

The infrequency with which harriers are now being observed in Antrim has been raised by casual birdwatchers, during my lectures to local RSPB members' groups and by forestry staff so I am not the only one to complain about their scarcity in areas where once they were relatively common and easily observed. Cliff Dawson, who has studied breeding peregrine falcons in the Sperrins (Londonderry and Tyrone) for the last 30 years told me that he did not see a single hen harrier there in 2008 or 2009.

On 13 April, I spent another unproductive morning at Ballyboley Forest with a pair much in evidence at another nearby plantation. For the first time a male was present at Kane's Hill, but sadly no female. The same pair was probably again holding territory at the north end of the mid Antrim forest and on this occasion no goshawks were encountered. Further north there were again no birds at Elginny Hill but to the north east two new pairs were present in a further two forests. Returning home via Capanagh Forest, the pair seen there on 10 April were now firmly ensconced at the south end of the forest.

My next visit to the Antrim Plateau was with Philip on 20 April. We carefully checked all the usual harrier haunts in south and mid Antrim, the only additions being a second pair at the north end of a south Antrim forest, with a vigorously displaying male again at Kane's Hill, but once again there was no sign of a female.

In the north of the county a male and female were at Slieveanorra, as was a female goshawk, with a second pair displaying over conifers to the east of the Ballymoney Road. A female only was at Cushleake and what may have been a distant male was also briefly observed in the same area. Two pairs were seen displaying at nearby Ballypatrick Forest as were, typically, a male goshawk and an acrobatic pair of sparrowhawks.

At 11.40 a.m. on 27 April, Linda and I had an amazing start to the day with an unexpected wing tagged golden eagle passing low over our house in Dundonald. I found out that the bird was from the Irish release scheme in County Donegal. We went to Antrim in the afternoon and again saw no harriers at Ballyboley or Elginny Hill so it now looked highly unlikely that breeding would take place at either of these locations. The pairs at one mid Antrim and two south Antrim locations were thankfully still holding territory but there was still only a lone male at Kane's Hill.

The heavy showers that had practically been a daily feature much earlier in April had completely died out towards the end of the month and it was noticeably warmer and sunnier. Before April was out, we were blessed with beautiful and completely unseasonable weather which continued unbroken throughout the whole of May, with temperatures hitting the mid 70s most days. It was ideal weather for our nesting harriers. In contrast, the spring of 2007 had been extremely wet and cold and many clutches had been lost to the elements. We hoped that large clutches and broods would be the order of the day in 2008.

I had wanted for several years to visit the island of Mull, off the west coast of Scotland. Raptor Island, as it is sometimes known, hosts a wide variety of breeding raptor species such as golden and white-tailed eagle, short-eared owl and of course my favourite species, hen harriers. On 4 May, Linda and I set off for a week-long visit to the island, with the weather in our favour and the sun on our backs.

Before leaving home, I had contacted Paul Haworth, a freelance ecologist based on Mull who is deeply involved in a long-term ecological investigation of all the breeding raptor species on the island and his help and field experience during our visit was greatly appreciated. Harriers and of course the other raptor species thrive virtually unhindered on this unique island – they face no persecution and minimal depredation and there is little or no deliberate disturbance either to the birds or to their habitat. These four factors are responsible for many harrier nest failures in County Antrim.

The harrier's ground nesting habitat is badly degraded in many of the places that they regularly use, just as it is in Antrim, but it does not affect the breeding ecology of these birds. There were around 23 breeding pairs on the island in 2008, with approximately 70 chicks fledging. According to Paul, there is even a substantial hen harrier winter roost site on the island with up to 17 individuals recorded at one location in early November 2008 and several much smaller roosts scattered about the island. What a success story for this species on Mull, with obvious lessons for our local conservation organisations.

These figures speak volumes for Mull and many of the other offshore islands in Scotland such as Arran, Islay, the Uists and Orkney, where breeding hen harriers abound in comparison with their mainland counterparts. It is galling to think that all these islands are geographically smaller than the whole of Northern Ireland yet all support substantial and important breeding numbers of hen harriers.

If radical measures are not implemented soon in Northern Ireland by our so-called conservation bodies, most, if not all our breeding hen harriers could eventually be lost to these islands. That's a sobering thought for all of us to consider, seeing that Northern Ireland's hen harriers probably originated from several of these islands in the first place.

I was back in the real world and on the Antrim Plateau on 13 May. The weather was still fine and sunny, with birds apparently nesting except at Ballyboley, Elginny Hill and Kane's Hill, where surprisingly there was still only a lone male. Before I had gone on holiday there had been no more than 13 territorial pairs but numbers had now been reduced to 11, with the depredation of the male and the sudden disappearance of the female in the same forest, and the subsequent disappearance of the prospecting pair at Cushleake. As yet no tree nesting harriers had been located in the original forest or at other known forests in the Antrim Plateau.

A brief afternoon visit to south and mid Antrim on 18 May again found no harriers at Ballyboley or Elginny, with the single male at Kane's Hill still sky dancing and a second and completely new male displaying at a nearby forest. Regrettably, neither of these birds received a response from a wandering and, we hoped, unattached female. The two pairs at the original tree nesting forest were both now ground nesting with Michael Devlin monitoring one pair and Philip and I the other. This was sadly the first time since 1990 that a tree nest had not been discovered in this, the original tree nesting forest.

These two pairs were also discreetly monitored by two members of the Northern Ireland Raptor Study Group (NIRSG) due to the employment of a gamekeeper in the general area whose main interest was managing the adjoining moorland to accommodate red grouse. He had once told Tim Hipkiss and me that he had to keep it 'vermin free'. There is certainly a conflict of interests in this area and monitoring must continue indefinitely, both here and at two other adjacent breeding sites, as the success and fledging rates for harriers in this particular part of south Antrim in recent years has been abysmal.

Our next visit came on my birthday, 25 May, with Philip and I concentrating on the potential nesting site at Kane's Hill. Shortly after our arrival, the male was seen hunting over the nearby moorland and then carrying a small prey item back to the hillside where it was hastily despatched. There were no more bouts of persistent sky dancing so we wondered whether he had eventually found a mate who was now nesting. If so, this was almost certainly a late breeding attempt.

Although we had only ever observed a male in this area, it is also possible that we could have overlooked the presence of a female, completely fooled by her late egg laying and incubating duties and the male's ongoing acrobatic displays. After all, the Northern harrier has been described by Dunne, Sibley and Sutton in their book 'Hawks in Flight' as 'the great fooler'. Maybe this male and potential female had lived up to the nickname.

As we did not observe a female there that day, we got the impression that nesting had already been initiated. Why would the male still be present if there was no female and why would he have been regularly observed foraging in the area? We hoped our next visit would resolve our lingering doubts. Elsewhere a male was noted carrying prey to an unknown nest site at Slieveanorra with another two different males observed carrying prey to separate locations in another large forest further north, one of which later turned out to be an all-important tree nest.

I wanted to work out what was happening at Kane's Hill as soon as possible so I returned there with my wife on 27. May. Shortly after our arrival, we were greeted by the sight of what appeared to be an immature female hen harrier foraging over the adjacent moorland. The male was also present.

This female was almost certainly nesting on the hill as she landed at two different locations, at one of them with prey, and then simply disappeared into the deep heather. Was she already feeding chicks? It certainly seemed so. She was also vigorously defending the area, repeatedly mobbing a male kestrel and then seeing off a male peregrine falcon which was probably from nearby Slemish Mountain.

I could now finally confirm that there appeared to be 11 pairs attempting to breed in Antrim, rather than the ten we had thought. I would keep an open mind on those figures for now but they were probably accurate, given the amount of time and effort that Philip, Linda and I had spent searching for harriers in the Antrim Plateau that season.

Return visits to this area on 1, 7 and 15 June confirmed the presence of both harriers, with regular prey deliveries to the nest site in full swing, particularly on the 15th. There were almost certainly very young chicks in this nest, located on the north side of the hill, but how had we missed the female earlier in the season? Ground nesting females in most raptor species can become inconspicuous when necessary and harriers are no exception.

The weather had completely changed before my visit of 15 June. In came prolonged spells of cold, wet and blustery conditions, totally unsuitable for harriers with very young chicks. The spring had been absolutely fantastic and it was probably too much to expect a completely dry summer for once as well. The next few weeks were vitally important as they would dictate whether the harriers would have a great or another dismal breeding season in Antrim. There had been too many of the dismal variety in recent years and so a successful season was vital to bolster this vulnerable population.

I returned to Kane's Hill on the afternoon of 18 June in the company of two members of the NIRSG. As we approached the top of the hill, we were dismayed to find the south side of the hill completely burnt and still smouldering from an overnight fire. The north side of the hill, where the nest was located and which was one of the few places in Antrim where deep heather still existed, was also badly burnt. More importantly, there was no sign of the pair of hen harriers. Around 50% of the hill had been consumed by the fire and with it had gone the nest which must have contained an unknown number of downy chicks at that stage of the season.

The fire was probably malicious but it probably was not directed at the nesting harriers. These days, though, one can never tell who is keeping an eye on these birds so I kept an open mind at that stage of my enquiries. The incident was of course reported to the Police (PSNI), the Northern Ireland Environment Agency (NIEA) and RSPBNI. A similar fire had devastated part of the adjacent moorland in May 1999, when a pair of hen harriers and an even rarer pair of short-eared owls were nesting in the area. Those harriers too deserted the area post haste, while the owls succeeded in remaining as their nest was not in the immediate vicinity of the fire.

On 29 June I was amazed to observe the female again, if for the last time, while I saw what was possibly the same male on 3 July. It is unusual for a pair of harriers which have lost their nest so late in the season to remain nearby for any length of time: they usually desert the area within days of the failure and go their separate ways. It was going to be interesting to see if they returned to the same area to nest in 2009. I doubted it but had to remain positive and optimistic that they would.

After a well-earned family break and safari in Kenya, I returned to the Antrim Plateau around mid July for a final fortnight's work with Philip, rounding up what I hoped would be more outright successes than total failures.

Of the five nesting pairs in south and mid Antrim, only three nests produced young, giving a 60% success rate, but only five chicks were known to have fledged from these nests, one, two and three respectively, making 1.66 chicks per successful nest. The fledging success for hen harriers should average around 3.5 chicks per nest in order to sustain a viable and successful breeding population. These five pairs were teetering on the brink of extinction if these dismal rates continued in the future. With very small broods and an insignificant fledging success rate in recent years, the five chicks that did fledge in 2008 were barely replacing those birds lost from the previous season. Mortality rates are high with this species, with possibly only one or two of these five fledglings going to survive their first winter. As for the two failed pairs, the cause was unknown at the first site, with neither adult observed after 30 June. The outcome at the second nest was much clearer, as a malicious fire on the evening of 17 June completely destroyed the nest and an unknown number of chicks.

The six other nesting attempts in the north of the county were also a mixture of failures and reasonable successes. Of the two pairs we closely monitored in the Slieveanorra area, the more northerly pair at Altarichard was successful in rearing at least three chicks to the flying stage. The pair to the south appeared to have failed for some unknown reason as there was no sign of either adults or fledglings by 27 July.

At a further two plantations to the east of Slieveanorra there was again a mixed bag of results, which appeared to be becoming the norm in the Antrim Plateau in 2008, not for the first time in recent years. There were no telltale signs of life during several visits to the more northerly of the two forests where a pair had been present for the majority of the season. Once again the poor weather or possibly fox depredation may have been the cause of this and other recent nest failures, the weather being the more likely culprit at that late stage of the season.

There was a more positive outcome and most welcome news from the adjacent southerly plantation. After almost two hours of diligent observations on 20 July, we managed to locate the resident ground nesting pair with their four fledglings, with all six birds still present during our final visit of the season a week later.

At our final destination, the most northerly forest visited during our annual harrier studies, we found one pair present on 20 July. We do not know why the second pair suddenly vanished from the area: it could have been down to the weather, depredation or deliberate disturbance, as it had been a ground nest within the confines of the plantation. We could definitely not rule out persecution, as nests with eggs and chicks have been illegally and mysteriously removed from this forest in recent years, with one instance of chicks being blatantly killed and left in the nest for all to see during the 2003 breeding season.

All turned out well, as they were found to have unexpectedly moved to a moorland site approximately 2.5 kilometres south south-east of the forest. The nest was found by chance on 15 June by a schoolteacher Peter Laird when walking in the area. The nest contained four downy chicks, about one week old, all of which successfully fledged around mid July. It is a miracle that this nest survived at all as this whole area is manage-burned to accommodate red grouse with a female almost certainly shot there in 2003.

The good news was that the second pair was definitely tree nesting with both adults observed on two separate occasions carrying food to the site. This must have been a late nesting attempt, as food provisioning was again recorded on 27 July. As this was a late nest, we visited the area again on 3 August and this time observed three recently fledged chicks circling in unison above the canopy and landing on the nest on at least four occasions. We had no time to search for the nest, but it appeared to be another sky-scraper among trees that were at least 15 or 20 metres tall.

Of the six nesting pairs in north Antrim, a respectable four were successful, giving a 67% success rate, with a known total of 14 chicks fledging, three, four, three and four chicks respectively, an average of 3.5 chicks per successful nest. The heavy rain from mid June onwards appeared not to have had the same effect on the young chicks in these more northerly nests, resulting in satisfactory fledging rates. Breeding hen harriers in south Antrim appeared to have fared far worse than those in north Antrim so had the weather been better further north over the course of the season? I doubted it and wondered whether there were other reasons for the poor returns in the south of the county.

Overall, Philip and I were aware of 11 nesting pairs in the Antrim Plateau during 2008. That meant a 54.5 % success rate but from the 11 nesting attempts a minimum of only 20 chicks were known to have fledged, meaning a meagre 1.81 chicks per successful nest.

Disappointing annual figures like these are a recipe for disaster for the species but one of our leading conservation organisations leads me and others to believe that hen harriers are soaring in unmentionable numbers in Antrim and elsewhere in Northern Ireland. That organisation needs to stop living in cloud cuckoo land. The truth is that they have totally disregarded our findings in Northern Ireland in recent years, to their own detriment and sadly to that of the harriers.

Philip and I made only one visit to the winter roost site in the Sperrins, County Tyrone, in October 2008, and did not see any roosting hen harriers. Further visits were impossible, as the lock had been changed on the entrance we usually used, and regrettably we were not offered a new key to this site which we had been visiting for 17 years.

The poor weather conditions had not seemed to deter nesting goshawks or kestrels, as they, particularly the kestrels, had an exceptional year in Antrim. Kestrels have been a rare commodity in various parts of Northern Ireland in recent years and nowhere more so than in the Antrim Plateau.

To see one or two kestrels during the course of a day was once regarded as a good result: at least the species was still present in the area. But on 3 August, Philip and I observed in one day a record eight, mainly recently fledged juveniles. Then, on 7 September, we beat the record with 12, again mainly juveniles, with another three present two days later at a location we had not visited earlier in the week.

During my many visits to the Antrim Plateau in 2008, observed goshawk activity appeared to be much higher than in previous years. Philip had the same impression and he and my wife Linda had been privy to many spectacular sightings throughout the season. Even from my home in Dundonald, I could encounter on most days a soaring or hunting goshawk, as they are apparently living and breeding on the nearby Stormont Estate.

In the course of the season we managed to observe at least six breeding pairs in the eight conifer plantations we visited regularly, with numbers on a par with 2006 and 2007. A provisional total of seven recently fledged young were observed at four sites, with several others undoubtedly missed at the other two locations. Although my disturbance licence covers me to visit their nests as well as those of short-eared owl, I simply did not have the time to do so and for now had to be content with observing, admiring and recording them.

On 23 July, towards the end of the season, I received a most welcome email from my raptor colleague Larry Toal who had observed a single short-eared owl at the Star Bog in south Antrim, only two kilometres from Capanagh Forest. Both Philip and I had watched this area many times on our way to the forest but had never observed any 'shorties' in the area. During the breeding season this species too can be very discreet about its nesting habits, so if there had been a pair present, both of us had missed them.

I visited the area to look for them early on the morning of 26 July and to my amazement found not one but four short-eared owls. Two appeared to be recently fledged juveniles, as their plumage was slightly darker overall than that of the adults, and to my surprise all four obligingly remained static for a full 15 minutes, perched on a line of fence posts about 75 metres from my roadside vantage point.

I stayed there for more than two hours and had just that one view of them. I was lucky, for when Philip and I returned to the area the following day, there was not an owl in sight. This was the first breeding record that I am aware of in Antrim since 2005 and was a superb consolation prize for what had been another poor hen harrier breeding season.

2009: more hen harrier woe

After a long and bitterly cold winter, I was really looking forward to the spring of 2009 and the prospect of much milder weather. Perhaps I was beginning to feel my age: since turning 60, I had found the winters very hard. There is nothing like having the sun shining on your back as you head up into the Antrim Plateau at the start of another harrier year. It boosts your flagging morale and gets your adrenaline flowing for the work to come in the months ahead. I never give up hoping for warm and sunny weather in March or even April even though I know the chances are slim.

Long before the start of the 2009 hen harrier breeding season, I had decided that after 24 years this would be the last I would spend scientifically studying the species in the Antrim Plateau. In future years, Philip, Linda and I will continue to monitor these beautiful raptors, but as nothing more than a hobby. I regret that after all these years I cannot categorically say that I am leaving the future of this species in safe hands: far from it. I have little or no confidence that any of our statutory conservation bodies or any other affiliated organisation will fully protect this species and help preserve its declining numbers and habitat.

The year started on a sour note. On February 27 2009 I watched a BBC news bulletin which maligned the goshawk – described accurately enough by Chris Packham on Springwatch as an 'avian terminator' – as one of the main predators of red grouse on English grouse moors. First, it was the hen harrier, then the peregrine falcon, now the shooting lobby had added the goshawk to the ever-growing list of unwanted predators. I wondered which species will be condemned and persecuted next? The late Derek Ratcliffe, famous for his studies of the peregrine falcon in the UK, put it neatly: 'If they do not want to stop killing birds of prey, then they can stop shooting red grouse'. I quite agree. All this, and the breeding season had not even started.

On Sunday, 1 March, I made my first visit of the new season to locations in south and mid Antrim in search of early hen harrier activity. I decided on an earlier than normal spring visit because of a spell of mild weather with which we had been blessed over the previous two weeks. I wanted to take full advantage of it as poor weather was forecast for later in the week.

When I arrived at the north end of Capanagh Forest, I met up with my old friend and local merlin expert Larry Toal. I did not observe any harriers here but was intrigued to see a pair of merlins perching on a line of fence posts on the nearby moorland and then copulating before my very eyes. Although breeding would not take place until late April or early May, as in hen harriers, these birds were obviously establishing a pair bond early in the season and, more importantly, holding territory.

Visits to a further two forests also drew a blank on the harrier front as did complete recces of the Star Bog and Kane's Hill area. I hoped for more success on a visit to my final forest of the day in mid Antrim. As I drove along the narrow private road to get to my elevated destination, a bird suddenly flew low from right to left, no more than five metres in front of my car.

I could not believe my eyes. It was a male great spotted woodpecker, complete with the telltale red spot on the back of its head and red undertail coverts. Interestingly, seconds earlier I'd seen a bird of similar size, colour and jizz flying swiftly into the adjacent woodland which contained a mixture of mature coniferous and deciduous trees. It could quite possibly have been the female as both sightings took me completely by surprise. A 30 minute search of the area did not lead to any more sightings, nor did I hear the customary drumming associated with woodpeckers. Later, having reported it to George Gordon, the Records Secretary for the Northern Ireland Birdwatchers Association, my sighting turned out to have been the first recent record for this species in County Antrim, with previous ones in Counties Armagh and, mainly, Down. In 2007, this species appeared to breed in Down, apparently the first confirmed breeding since prehistoric times (Irish Birds 8, Num. 3. 2008).

My visit to the nearby forest over the course of the next two hours proved fruitful as, surprisingly, I saw a pair of hen harriers together, the first of the year for me, over the plantation.

On the way home I was given a sharp reminder that spring might not have arrived after all. Torrential hail and rain, so heavy that I was forced at one stage to stop my car, meant that winter was for the moment still with us.

On 8 March, Philip and I made our way into the southern uplands. Overnight it had turned bitterly cold and windy and light snow had begun to fall. We intended to make our first visit to the northern reaches of the Antrim Plateau but heavy snow and treacherous road conditions forced us to turn back at Newtown Crommelin. For the second week in a row, we had to be content with visiting known harrier haunts in south and mid Antrim.

The only hen harrier we observed during the course of the day was a female quartering the moorland in search of prey at Carnalbanagh, where a male had been seen by Larry Toal a fortnight earlier. This was the second female seen in a week in mid Antrim, which was most notable as adult males are more likely to be encountered than females on early season visits The five other locations we visited drew a blank in terms of harriers but we did manage to observe five buzzards, probably the same male merlin that we'd seen the week before at Capanagh and a totally different pair of merlins at another forestry plantation.

We had a reasonably successful day in the field, considering the weather conditions, but after a long and severe winter we were hoping for a sunny and slightly warmer day next time out.

When the overnight fog eventually cleared, 15 March was a good day to be out searching for hen harriers, especially for my first visit of the season to north Antrim. Single males were eventually observed at Slieveanorra, Ballypatrick Forest, and Glenariff and on the way home a female was seen perching on a willow bush below Elginny Hill, apparently concentrating on a particular patch of heather for a potential prey item,. The favourable conditions meant sightings of buzzard, kestrel, merlin and sparrowhawk but surprisingly no goshawks.

The first signs of spring were definitely seen that day, with singing skylarks a joy to watch as they hung on fluttering wings, two coveys of red grouse seen and heard calling at two locations in south Antrim and newly-born lambs at every turn. A great day out was spoiled by the return of fly-tipping and vandalism around the scenic Slieveanorra area. Household rubbish, dead sheep and, more disturbingly, a boom complete with black oil had been dumped in a nearby stream where in February 2008 I had observed an otter. Large piles of cow manure had even been dumped in adjacent lay-bys, with fires lit in several places to try and dispose of the household litter. Even road signs had been torn down and dumped in a nearby river. It was an absolute disgrace and local inhabitants and farmers were almost certainly to blame.

With no harriers observed in north and parts of mid and south Antrim on 20 March, due mainly to lingering hill fog followed by hazy conditions, I was hoping for better luck on 29 March. After the early morning frost had cleared, I was treated to a glorious day's weather in south and mid Antrim before I set off on a family holiday to the Gambia on 1 April.

I managed to observe all our seven diurnal species of raptor during the course of the day, plus the pair of great spotted woodpeckers that I had first observed on 1 March. Visiting six locations, three in south and three in mid Antrim, I saw only two male hen harriers, one in each area, and no territorial females, which over the course of the day was most disappointing.

In the late afternoon, while watching Capanagh Forest from a prominent roadside vantage point, I met up with my old friend Gary Wilkinson. He and several birding colleagues were returning from a field trip in north Antrim and had observed three grey males and one female hen harrier at two well known locations to the north east of Slieveanorra. This was fantastic news, as sightings in that huge area of moorland and forest had been sporadic in recent weeks, to say the least. Hopefully, most pairs of hen harriers would be in place by the time I returned from holiday, making my task much easier over the weeks to come.

Thanks to the vigilance of Larry Toal I was able to fill in two of my three harrier blanks in south Antrim for 29 March. Firstly, a hunting female had drifted over the moorland to the north of Shillanavogey Wood shortly after I had left the area. Then, 30 minutes later, Larry observed another female circling just west of Killylane reservoir near Ballyboley Forest. It was of course possible that these two females were just passing through as they were only briefly observed by Larry.

On 31 March I paid an impromptu visit to four harrier locations, three in south and one in mid Antrim, before setting off on holiday the following day. The weather was superb, sunny and warm with the temperature touching 17 degrees, so I was hoping for a successful afternoon. However, I saw no harriers at two of the south and the mid Antrim locations despite eight buzzards being much in evidence there.

Then our luck changed. At our last forest location, viewed from a prominent roadside vantage point, Linda and I had a female flying low over the eastern edge of the plantation at 2.45 p.m. followed at 2.54 p.m. by a male. This, unbelievably, was only my second pair of the new season after a very slow start. I hoped it would not be my last.

The weather was again in our favour on 19 April, as Philip and I set off for another full day's raptor watching at five different harrier haunts in south and mid Antrim. We spent over nine and a half hours at these well-known locations, visiting four of them twice, both morning and afternoon, with the most distant site eating up over two hours of our precious time.

Over the day we managed to observe 23 raptors of six species, of which only one was a hen harrier, a female. 16 buzzards dominated 69.5% of the total, the majority of them seen displaying over nearby conifer plantations which did not bode well for hen harriers wishing to nest there. Among the remaining six birds there were no goshawks but two kestrels, two sparrowhawks, a single merlin and a peregrine falcon.

When I arrived home I received an unexpected telephone call from Dot Blakely, the leader of WWT Castle Espie Birdwatching Club, who had taken a small party of birders on a field trip to Capanagh Forest specifically to look for hen harriers and merlins. Like Philip and me, they had observed no hen harriers despite spending well over two hours searching for them and wondered where they had all gone. We both hoped that the worrying lack of harriers in south and mid Antrim was not a sign of things to come in 2009.

Productivity in the Ballyboley-Capanagh-Shillanavogey triangle is dangerously low. Before the arrival of a gamekeeper in the area, employed to manage the moorland solely for red grouse, there were generally between four and six breeding pairs annually, yet in 2008 there were only two pairs which reared a meagre three chicks between them. I am paranoid about gamekeepers and would not trust them with the welfare of birds of prey on their land, as in 1995 I observed their handiwork towards mammals and raptors on an estate in the Highlands of Scotland which resulted in a successful prosecution by the RSPB. One thing is for sure: hen harriers are genuinely decreasing in this particular part of Antrim and that is very worrying indeed.

On 26 April, after the overnight rain and hill fog had eventually cleared, Philip and I spent most of our day looking for territorial hen harriers in north Antrim. We were not to be disappointed. At the vast area of moorland and conifers that encompasses the summit of Slieveanorra, we had a hunting male in one area at 9 a.m. followed an hour later by our first sky dancing male of the year, complete with a very pale-plumaged female, probably older than normal. In the same general area, we watched in horror as a pair of agitated merlins tried to defend their nest against four hooded crows, sadly losing both the battle and their nest.

At another well known location we had a third male hen harrier, perching and preening halfway up a tall Sitka, but no female was seen. In the same area we also had a small covey of at least four or five red grouse, calling and surprisingly showing well. We had already observed three of Northern Ireland's rarest birds in this one area so the day was going from strength to strength.

At another partially felled plantation further north, a very pale silvery-grey adult male harrier was seen in the company of a female for well over 20 minutes, which was most pleasing, as breeding harriers have been extremely scarce in this particular area in recent years. Before leaving we also had the resident pair of merlins and, not surprisingly, a soaring male goshawk.

Several hours later, when we were checking two separately named but adjoining forests to the south east of that plantation, we immediately discovered a territorial pair of hen harriers at one and a single male at the other. When travelling south later in the afternoon, we again checked the Elginny area for harriers and, as in the early morning, found none there. There were also no harriers at Kane's Hill, with the 2008 fire there probably having put off any returning birds for this year.

Finally, we reached Capanagh Forest where we watched the area for one and a half hours from our roadside vantage point but to no avail. A couple who had been birdwatching in the same area for two hours before we arrived told us that they too had failed to observe any hen harriers. This was the second week in a row that no birds had been seen there despite over six hours of joint observations. Despite these disappointments in mid and south Antrim, this had been without doubt our best day of the 2009 season so far.

Sunday, 3 May was a mainly sunny and blustery day with the odd heavy shower and a noticeable slight drop in temperature from the previous day. Nevertheless, Linda and I, along with the dog, Willow the Weimaraner, set off early for a full day's birding. We thoroughly searched three harrier locations in south Antrim and two in mid Antrim over an eight and a half hour period.

The results were again disappointing. Only one pair were located in the area I have christened the Ballyboley Triangle in south Antrim. Working on instinct and from previous experience, I firmly believed that there was at least one more pair, although possibly no more than one in this area which was simply proving elusive. In mid Antrim, as expected, a polygynous male and two receptive females first observed on 12 April were still active above the forest canopy during our two hour visit there.

In its heyday, south and mid Antrim could hold a maximum of eight or nine pairs of breeding hen harriers, while in 2009 we would be lucky to encounter three or four pairs at the most in these areas, making at least a whopping 50% decrease. Yet this species has been removed from the Red List of endangered species and placed on the much lower Amber List of birds of only medium conservation concern. What a farcical decision and, more importantly, what an insult to the species and to the two people here who study it with such care. I have nothing against, say, black-headed and herring gull which remain on the Red List and which are probably genuinely in decline. How, though, they can take precedence over the hen harrier which is even less numerous, especially in Northern Ireland, is a complete and utter mystery to me.

As well as rare raptor species, we also, of course, have several species of rare mammals in Northern Ireland and four of those were much in evidence on 3 May. To our amazement we saw three red deer, several Irish hares, a single otter and an ever rarer red squirrel on that single day: a very welcome sight to make up for the scarcity of harriers.

Two days later I was reliably informed by a fully-qualified BTO ringer that he had tried to enter Ballypatrick Forest Park on 3 May and had been politely turned away because a car rally was underway. I had also recently noticed that tree felling was taking place at Parkmore Forest, which continued later into the month despite the presence of a pair of territorial hen harriers. I had thought both these issues resolved a long time ago but some things, it seemed, never change.

Following a visit on 10 May to all known harrier localities in north Antrim, two of the three sites in mid Antrim and all of the known sites in south Antrim, Philip and I were extremely disappointed with the final outcome of more than ten hours in the field. Although harriers were seen holding territory, particularly in the north of the county, serious gaps were appearing, as we had noted in previous weeks, in mid and south Antrim.

If our calculations were correct – and we hoped they would be proved wrong at a later date – then there were possibly only two pairs and a polygynous threesome holding territory in the whole of mid and south Antrim. Weeks earlier, two pairs had been regularly observed holding territory at two different sites in south Antrim but both pairs had been very elusive of late and could already have been nesting. In truth, we felt we were probably being a little pessimistic, making excuses for not having seen them of late, and believed them still to be present in both areas.

On 12 May Linda and I spent over six hours in south and mid Antrim frantically searching for territorial or nesting hen harriers with only minimal success. Once again, the polygynous male with his two attentive females was observed in mid Antrim with only a single hunting male noted in the south of the county. That evening, though, I was reliably informed by Walter Veale that he and a friend had observed at least one of the two southerly pairs still holding territory, which was very welcome news indeed.

Our provisional figures for the whole of the Antrim Plateau were still liable to make grim reading at the end of the 2009 season with only eight probable and one possible pairs observed so far. If we concluded that there were only nine pairs compared with eleven pairs in 2008, then that would be an 18% decrease from the previous year and a massive 27% decline if there were only eight pairs present. Overall, if one were truly to believe the numbers that were created during the RSPB Breeding Survey in 2004 – and regrettably some people still did – then this would amount to a staggering 64% decline in the Antrim population over the five years from 2004 to 2009. Could that really be possible?

On Wednesday 13 May, I received a very interesting phone call from Stephen Murphy of Natural England who studies hen harriers in the Forest of Bowland in Lancashire. He wanted to know how our numbers were doing, as his were well down from 2008 and he was starting to wonder if he was imagining things. Numbers had also declined in several other known haunts in England and he had just heard that they were possibly down in parts of northern Scotland as well. This anecdotal evidence was not what I really wanted to hear but it did confirm our worst fears: that the species was not only in trouble in County Antrim and possibly the whole of Northern Ireland, but probably right across parts of the UK mainland as well. It was proof that Linda, Philip and I and others are not crying wolf about the way numbers had dwindled in the Antrim Plateau in the past decade. When the **** eventually hits the fan here, and it undoubtedly will, I wonder what lame excuses our so-called conservation organisations will come up with for the imminent collapse of the species. They have failed miserably.

A brief visit to the three locations in south Antrim on 17 May did confirm the presence of two males hunting in the same plantation where my reliable informant Walter Veale had observed a breeding pair five days earlier. Unfortunately the persistent heavy rain and a strong southeasterly wind which had prevailed for the past week cut my visit badly short. My observations appeared to show that nesting had probably started at one of the sites and not at the other, as my good friend Keith Glasgow confirmed the presence of a hunting female in the same general area on 20 May, showing that nesting was already a week late for this second pair.

Over the Bank Holiday weekend, I spent 24 May in south and mid Antrim and

25 May in the northern parts. On the 24th, the weather, though dry and dull, did appear to reveal that the second pair in south Antrim were not yet nesting as both male and female were seen together over rough pasture for more than 20 minutes that morning. I had my first cuckoo of the year but sadly did not hear it calling and had to wait until 31 May for that long-anticipated moment. I only observed two cuckoos in the whole of the Antrim Plateau during 2009 which ties in with the overall decline of the species throughout the whole of the UK.

May 25 was again dull and overcast and heavy rain had moved into all areas by early afternoon. We did manage to see a hunting male near the Byvore Bridge at Slieveanorra and the same female as before, physically attacking a buzzard at the second site in south Antrim. Nesting was probably already occurring and she would simply have been defending the site in a territorial dispute with the much larger bird. The male, to our surprise, was nowhere to be seen.

When we reached Capanagh Forest at 2 p.m. rain was definitely in the air and by 2.15 p.m. it was bouncing off the main road adjacent to the forest. Suddenly, to our surprise, a large bird of prey rose briefly from the trees and flew low through the upper branches of the canopy to another location further to our right. It was a red kite but its all-too-brief appearance and the murky conditions meant that we could not see if it was sporting wing tags. Although we remained in the area for a further hour the kite did not take to the air again, quite sensibly, given the torrential rain.

One of the all too few ground nests discovered in 2009 was another unique event for the Antrim hen harrier population. On 12 April 2009 and during subsequent visits throughout the month to a semi-mature conifer plantation in mid Antrim, two female hen harriers and a single male had been regularly observed displaying and closely associating. As this behaviour is not uncommon during April, I dismissed their close association as nothing more than a pre-breeding display in the absence of a second male.

When I briefly returned to the area on 2 May and again the day after, I was amazed to find all three birds still together but now moved from what had been a central position within the forest to an out-of-the-way location further north. Regular bouts of sky dancing between all three birds were again observed with still no sign of a second male. From their behaviour, it appeared to me that this was a polygynous threesome but as nesting had not yet started I would have to wait a further week or so to be sure.

On 10 May, after a brief interval, the male was seen carrying prey to what was almost certainly a ground nest. I identified the area where he landed as no female took to the air for a customary food pass. Twenty minutes later the male appeared again with prey and landed in exactly the same spot as before, with, once again, no female rising to relieve him of his quarry. If this was a polygynous male, I would have expected him to land at a second ground nest but that did not occur that day. A further two prey deliveries were noted in the afternoon, both delivered to the same site with again no sign of a female.

It was possible that there was only a normal breeding pair here now and that the female was busy egg laying or incubating, which would explain her non-appearance. Or had the second female moved on elsewhere? It was not appropriate at this stage of the season to investigate so I hoped to get the information I needed on my next visit. In recent years, the normally rarer polyandry had occurred more often than polygyny in the Antrim hen harrier population so to find the more common form of this behaviour occurring might suggest a dearth of males in this area. I found that hard to believe.

Due to the curious and as yet unexplained nature of this behaviour, Philip and I visited the area again on 13 May. Shortly after our arrival, we noticed two females in the air with the male nearby carrying prey. On his arrival, both females suddenly landed in what seemed to be the spot that I had been watching a few days earlier, followed immediately by the male. This was undoubtedly a polygynous male but were both his females sharing the same nest? Or was there a second nest nearby which I could not see? When the male reappeared with more prey and landed in exactly the same area, my theory seemed to be confirmed – there was only one nest.

After two more individual prey items were delivered on 30 May, one of the females briefly leaving the nest to accept the first prey item in a spectacular mid-air food pass, I decided to look for the nest. When I got to within five metres of where I suspected it was, I discovered two freshly broken harrier eggs lying on the ground as if they had been purposely ejected from the nest. As I discreetly approached to within three or four metres of the nest, both females took to the air simultaneously and began to bombard me from above, deliberately ushering me away from the area before I had managed to photograph the nest.

A brief glance before I left, though, told me there were six eggs in the nest in addition to the two found earlier, none of which had hatched. Both females continued with their low-level bombardment, the male uttering yikkering calls, probably in response to my unwanted presence. In my 24 years of studying hen harriers, I really can count on the fingers of one hand the number of times I have been dive-bombed by aggressive birds, male or female, but these two females in particular were very territorial. This was an exceptional threesome.

A visit on 10 June was mainly to find out if all three harriers were still present and to see if their highly unusual nesting attempt was progressing satisfactorily. As it was a very warm and sunny day, it came as no surprise to see both females soaring in tandem about 200 metres east of the nest site. There was no sign of the male.

When I briefly visited the nest, I discovered that only three of the remaining six eggs had hatched. Three downy chicks, two of which were much smaller than the first born, were lying beside the three unhatched eggs and I duly photographed the nest for record purposes. The three unhatched eggs were probably addled or infertile and unlikely to hatch at this late stage of the season so I left them in the nest where they could be used by either female, if required.

The nest was surprisingly clean, given that three adults and now three sprightly chicks were in regular attendance. Apart from the surrounding heather being encrusted with crystallised white excreta, there were no pellets, prey remains, moulted feathers or hatched eggshells in or around the vicinity of the nest site. The two broken eggs discovered on 30 May had also vanished, presumably eaten by the adults as an extra source of calcium or by marauding hooded crows. The nest itself was larger than normal, probably because of the shared incubation duties by the two females and because three birds were flying in and out.

I arrived at the nest site at 10 a.m. on 13 June and again watched from a discreet distance, with both females arriving with prey within ten minutes of each other. Before landing, both briefly circled low over the nest and as the second female prepared to descend, the first female immediately took to the air and flew off in a westerly direction. Prey was again delivered by both females at noon and at 12.20 p.m. respectively, with again no sign of the resident male. Had he deserted and left the two females to feed and rear the three chicks? Desertion by males is not uncommon at this stage of the breeding season and I had witnessed this many times at both ground and tree nests in Antrim over the years.

Due to a week-long family break I did not visit the site again until 21 June. Both females were still present and very active, with on-the-hour prey deliveries to the nest. During these frequent visits, I noticed that one of the females would spend more time than the other at the nest, with this interesting behaviour also recorded on 13 June. Was there a significant age difference or a seniority status between these females, with presumably the elder taking overall charge at the nest? Without the aid of a hide, this question and a host of others would remain unanswered. As on my previous two visits, the male was not observed.

I returned briefly on 1 and 3 July with less frequent activity recorded, although both females were still in attendance. A distant male, who made no attempt to visit the nest, was also observed. A visit on 10 July saw a flurry of activity by both females, with food provisioning occurring at an incredible rate. In just 57 minutes, six prey items were brought to the nest, all of which appeared to be small birds. From past experience, it appeared that fledging was imminent.

I was unable to visit the area again until 16 July when, after an hour of no observations, I decided to visit the nest site as I thought fledging might have occurred in my absence. On arrival, I found that the nest had been vacated and the three unhatched eggs had disappeared, presumably eaten by the females or fed to the pre-fledging chicks.

Around 20 metres to my left and completely unaware of my presence were the three fledglings, feeding furiously on the shared carcass of a freshly killed rabbit. As neither female was present, I discreetly retreated for fear of flushing the contented fledglings and bringing the unwanted wrath of both females down upon myself for a second time. All five birds were seen again on 19 and 25 July but, surprisingly, not again after that.

Polygyny in hen harriers has been well documented over the years, mainly in Orkney but rarely in Northern Ireland or the island of Ireland as a whole, but this case was unique to the Antrim population. Searching through the vast amounts of hen harrier literature available to me, I eventually came across a single paper by Nic Picozzi who witnessed a similar occurrence on the east mainland of Orkney on 12 June 1981. There he was shown a nest with eight eggs, which had originally been ten, and two females paired with an adult male. His first impressions were that one of the brown harriers was a first-year male (ringtail), but both proved to be adult females, one positively identified by a leg ring, the other by eye colour as eight and four years old respectively. I must add that Nic Picozzi's later observations were made with the help of a hide which I unfortunately did not have at my disposal during my study.

His observations began shortly after the first chick had hatched but, as it was very light in weight, he fostered a two day old chick and a hatching egg to the nest on 20 June to be certain that the adults had viable chicks to rear. This was an important factor in the partial success of this nest as only four of the remaining eight eggs hatched; the chicks seen alive weighed only 14.5 g and 16 g and all sadly died within no more than three days of hatching. Such light chicks apparently never survive but both foster chicks fledged successfully.

Nic Picozzi correctly believed that had he not intervened and fostered chicks to the nest, no young would have been produced at this site, as has often been the case in other species when nests have been recorded with two females in attendance. He added that his observations in Orkney were particularly interesting for two reasons. Firstly, female harriers are very aggressive towards each other in spring so the sight of two hens sitting side by side with no aggression was a complete surprise. Secondly, the cooperation between the hens, which even involved food being caught by one and taken by the other to feed the young, appeared to be unprecedented in raptors.

Unfortunately, I was not privy to all the goings-on at the 2009 nest in which incubation duties, the feeding of the young, nest sanitation, hunting and the obligatory food provisioning were almost certainly shared by the two females, particularly when the resident male disappeared prior to hatching. It is of course possible that his desertion may have been due to the total dominance of both females and not of his own accord. I did notice that both females appeared to take full control of his duties when hatching was imminent, which possibly kept him from visiting the nest and providing his fair share of food. In addition he showed no aggression towards human intrusion, unlike his two mates He was a relatively young and possibly inexperienced male, to judge by his conspicuous dark mantle and upperwing coverts, and that may also have had an overall bearing on his premature departure.

Over the past 24 years, I have witnessed many unusual forms of hen harrier behaviour, including this case of polygyny, polyandry, tree nesting and of course tree roosting. Remarkably, this was the first time I had ever observed this particular facet of their complicated lifestyle in Northern Ireland and so it ranks high on my ever-growing list of exceptional feats associated with this species' ecology in County Antrim. It is unbelievable that this nest succeeded without human intervention while the Orkney nest would undoubtedly have failed without it. I talked about this strange form of behaviour to my good friend Colin Shawyer who has studied breeding barn owls across the UK mainland for over 30 years. He has occasionally recorded two female barn owls sharing one nest and the same male and in a sense I was relieved to know that other raptor species indulge in this behaviour too.

As for harriers elsewhere in the Antrim Plateau, the weather was absolutely superb throughout most of June and July and apart from the odd thundery shower it was scorching hot for weeks on end, with temperatures touching 26 degrees. The month of June tends to be one of the quieter times for the birds and for their observer. It can best be described as time-consuming: going back over old ground until I work out which pairs have nested and which pairs have failed, waiting for anything up to two hours until the male arrives with prey to provision his mate, proving that the pair has been successful and allowing me to move on to where the next pair are nesting.

By the end of June 2009, and only with great difficulty, Philip and I had been able to find around 50% of the eight or nine pairs that had held territory earlier in the season. It was very disappointing but followed the trend that had developed over recent years among hen harriers in Antrim. Early season figures of, say, eight or nine pairs look well on paper and occasionally flatter even me but it is the number of successful pairs at the end of each season which counts. That number is generally lower than the number at the start. Because the weather had been so fine, the decline in breeding pairs and nest failures could not be blamed solely on a wet spring or summer, as in previous years. It is now a regular occurrence, showing that all is not well with the breeding ecology of this species in the Antrim Plateau.

What disappointed us most during our observations was the apparent absence of tree nesting pairs in any of Antrim's mature forests. Most striking of all, and for the second consecutive year, was a lack of tree nests in the original plantation which had been partially felled earlier in the year, particularly the third of the forest towards the south end. This meant that for the first time since 1990 there were likely to be no tree nests anywhere in the Antrim Plateau. I am an optimist, though, and hoped that some other eagle-eyed birder would find one somewhere.

This was probably, though, the end of tree nesting as we knew it. There had not been enough successful tree nests or, for that matter, ground nests over at least the previous seven or eight years to sustain the phenomenon or the population. Tree nesting had not ceased because of a lack of suitable trees, as there were plenty in those vast plantations. Neither had it stopped because the birds had returned to nest on prime tracts of open moorland, as there were very few of those. It had come to an end simply because the population had been highly unsuccessful in recent years and was now sadly in freefall. Gone were the days when hen harriers reared big broods of five or six chicks to the fledging stage. Recent years had seen broods of one or two or even no chicks at all at some nests, with little likelihood of the young surviving beyond their first winter. I am bitterly disappointed with how things turned out in 2009 and devastated that I may never again in my lifetime see hen harriers tree nesting in County Antrim.

My visits to the Antrim Plateau during June and part of July were not as regular as normal, because of the unexpected discovery of a pair of breeding marsh harriers in County Down. It is not every day that one is able to study breeding marsh harriers in Northern Ireland so I am afraid that they briefly overshadowed my beloved hen harriers.

On 17 July David Nixon and my colleague Philip McHaffie spent over eight hours hopelessly searching for any recently fledged hen harriers in parts of south, mid and north Antrim, at Slieveanorra. To their dismay they did not observe a single harrier, never mind a fledgling. During a visit two days later, Philip and I spent a similar length of time at all but one known locations in mid Antrim. Once again no fledglings were observed anywhere and apart from one brief sighting of an adult male in north east Antrim, our day was very disappointing.

On 22 July I was contacted by Cliff Dawson regarding the presence of hen harriers at the forest roost site in the Sperrins, County Tyrone. When I told him that I had stopped visiting the area in October 2008, not only because of access problems but because no harriers were roosting there, he confirmed my worst fears. He too had not observed a single hen harrier in that area during his regular visits to monitor breeding peregrine falcons in 2008 and 2009. It was satisfying to know that other competent raptor observers were now confirming what I had said over and over again: that this species was declining almost everywhere it occurred in Northern Ireland.

Goshawks breeding secretively deep in Antrim's claustrophobic plantations showed a mixed bag of results in 2009. Although singletons had been observed at four conifer plantations in Antrim since late March, our first vigorously displaying pair of goshawks were not observed until 10 May at a forest in the north of the county. What a performance they both gave, especially the much smaller male, as he tumbled out of control and wing clapped close to his mate high above the canopy. Then, in an instant, they disappeared, only to return ten minutes later to repeat the whole mystifying sequence.

During June and July we had more success, with at least four or five pairs definitely present in the Plateau's forests. From our observations, particularly towards the end of July and early August, it appeared that all five pairs were successful, with at least one fledgling seen at each site. Over the past few years the population in Antrim had remained relatively stable with around four to six breeding pairs known to us annually. To be frank, it is the ones we do not know about and which are rarely seen that are giving us the most concern. The four to six pairs quoted may only be the tip of the iceberg in the Antrim Plateau.

On a scorching 31 May, Linda and I had our first short-eared owl of the new season in mid Antrim. The bird was seen flying low to our left over a large expanse of heather before hastily landing in a small circular patch of long grass at the lower edge of the sloping moorland, where it remained partially visible only with the aid of a good pair of binoculars. Although we continued to watch the area for some 45 minutes, we did not see a second owl but another may well have been present nearby. The bird we saw appeared to be nesting as it maintained a firm presence while we were there. We hoped that further observations would reveal a nesting pair as this species last nested in this area back in 1999. A late afternoon visit on 8 June revealed for the first time two birds together, almost certainly a breeding pair. The birds then became very inconspicuous and we doubted that they were still present in the area. Then, on 28 July, after a gap of several weeks without a definite sighting of either bird, the two adults, along with three fledglings were seen about 50 metres north of the nest site. I must admit to breathing a sigh of relief, as I had thought the nest had failed.

A brief sighting on 14 June of a single 'shortie' in a former breeding haunt, a recently planted area of a north Antrim forest, led to a brief search for a nest or a second bird but neither was found. Several follow-up visits to the area towards the end of June and in mid July unfortunately turned out negative.

As for hen harriers – leaving aside the three chicks that fledged successfully on 16 July from the polygynous nesting attempt in mid Antrim – Linda and I did eventually come across several other recently fledged birds in south Antrim on 31 July and with Philip in north Antrim on 2 August. In total, we had six along with the three in the polygynous nest which were still present on 31 July. We hoped that there were others that we had missed but did not expect many more, as this had been another woeful season for hen harriers in the Antrim Plateau.

2009: a grand harrier finale

It was the crowning glory: 24 years of scientific study of the hen harrier on the Antrim Plateau were coming to an end yet led unexpectedly to the discovery of another *Circus* species, a pair of breeding Western marsh harriers in County Down, the first to breed in the Province for well over 150 years.

At 11.15 a.m. on Wednesday, 3 June, my wife Linda and I were taking a leisurely drive southward in the North Down area, making the most of the exceptional weather we had been having. My wife and I rarely birdwatch in County Down so this random visit was based on nothing more than balmy weather, wanting a change in scenery from my hen harrier study area in County Antrim and a little bit of Irish luck.

Our attention was drawn to two large dark birds of prey in the air to the west of the busy main road that leads from Comber to the historic town of Downpatrick. We at first took them to be a pair of common buzzard, which are relatively numerous in this area, but once we had quickly parked our car and given the birds a second look, we discovered to our amazement that they were a pair of marsh harriers.

We watched in total shock. It seemed that we had just missed an aerial food pass as the female, carrying an unidentified but large prey item, instantly dropped down into a large marshy area or reedbed. The male continued to circle high above the site for a full ten minutes before flying off in an easterly direction towards nearby Strangford Lough.

The site these birds had chosen is known locally as the Flow Dam and is only six miles from our home in Dundonald. This large reedbed lies approximately six or seven metres below the level of the main road and is almost surrounded by tall trees and bushes, apart from a small open area at the north eastern end from where the site can easily be viewed. The marsh was blooming with common reedmace or bulrush and dotted in many places with many small willow bushes. The surrounding area is hilly and consists of mainly green fields with sheep and cattle freely grazing and a few houses and several farms also in view.

More importantly, it appeared that this pair were almost certainly breeding and had already initiated a nest, hence the food pass and the sudden return by the female to the reedbed. I wondered how long the birds had been here and why nobody had observed them before now, as the site was close to a very busy main road and a nearby side road which leads right past the northern end of the marsh. I could only think that the site was well masked from view by tall trees and that the reedbed lies well below the level of the main road.

So, from 3 June until fledging, I decided to watch the site on an almost daily basis, either in the morning, afternoon or evening, with the help of Linda and Philip. This would give me the chance to try to age both birds by studying their plumage in greater detail, my initial findings having been unsatisfactory due to the brief and distant views I had on my first observation. In fact, both birds tended to be as inconspicuous as possible, which is apparently normal behaviour for nesting marsh harriers, with long waits of up to two hours considered the norm for a sighting of either bird. This elusive behaviour was probably the reason why neither bird had been observed before 3 June.

After several good views of both birds' plumages in subsequent weeks, I concluded that the male was probably a second-summer bird or possibly older, due to his dingy off-white underwings which still showed slight traces of a dark trailing edge on the secondaries and a faint hint of a dark band on the tail. All these are normally clean cut and pure white on an adult male.

The female also appeared to be a sub-adult bird but my first and brief observations of her seemed to show slight traces of rufous streaking on the head, crown and throat. Later views of her revealed a more creamy texture to those parts and a slightly dark chocolate brown body. There was only a hint of a pale breast band but not all individuals have one. The customary creamy patches on the front edge of the upperwings were not as clean cut as on an adult bird but these probably vary from individual to individual. As for age, it is harder to age a female marsh harrier than a male. In males, full adult plumage is attained in the third or fourth calendar year and the age of younger birds can be gauged more clearly by their varying plumages.

I had seriously thought of visiting the nest for historic and record purposes but as some members of the extended marsh harrier family are vulnerable to disturbance and possible desertion, I cancelled my request to the NIEA for a disturbance licence. This decision was unanimously agreed between with my wife and Philip, setting aside personal gain in the name of conservation and allowing these historic birds to breed here in relative peace and safety. I also considered the reedbed to be treacherous underfoot with hidden dangers for the unwary and any nest visit would undoubtedly have drawn unwanted attention to the area.

During the incubation period, it came as no surprise to observe the male regularly arriving with prey from the direction of Strangford Lough, as there appeared to be no other wetland areas nearby. History tells us that during the 19th century, the islands Mahee and Reagh were notable breeding places on the Lough. I myself observed a female or immature bird near Castle Espie on 7 September 2003. Even then the marsh harrier enjoyed the bird-rich and varied food supply provided by this superb area and continued to do so in 2009.

From 23 June, there was a dramatic increase in the daily food provisioning by both male and female of an unknown number of chicks. On two separate occasions brown rats were brought to the nest as well as what was almost certainly a coot, to judge by its dumpy shape and what seemed to be black colouring. On the whole it was really hard to determine the exact nature of the prey items as the nest was situated towards the south end of the marsh, close to several small willow bushes which occasionally masked our view of the incoming adults.

After a flurry of activity on the evening of 29 June, Linda and I decided to visit the site at around 7.30 the following morning, as very hot conditions were forecast for later in the day. On arrival, we were immediately treated to the sight of a recently fledged juvenile which had not been present when Philip and I had left the area at 9.45 the previous evening. This bird perched precariously on top of one of the small willow bushes close to the nest, a common trait in recently fledged marsh harriers. A further visit that evening revealed the same rufous-crowned individual with no more fledglings observed.

The male was not present during visits to the area on 1 and 2 July but a second chick had fledged by the morning of the 2nd. It is not unusual for males of this species to disappear shortly after one chick has fledged or before they all have, with similar behaviour recorded at hen harrier tree and ground nests in County Antrim. We also noticed that morning that the female did not make any further visits to the nest as she appeared to concentrate fully on her brood of two, as both were fed on at least two occasions several metres from the nest. Had all her chicks now fledged? All three birds were present on 3 July but again the male was absent.

As Linda and I were away on a brief family holiday to marsh and hen harrier country in Leighton Moss and South Ayrshire from 4 to 8 July, I did not visit the site until the evening of July 9. To my surprise there was no sign of the female or the two fledglings and by now the male appeared to be long gone from the area. Two visits on the morning and evening of July 10 also drew a complete blank, as did an afternoon visit on 11 July followed by two further morning visits on 12 and 13 July. A random evening visit by Linda and me on 20 July did, however, result in a brief sighting of the male. The wanderer had returned.

On the evening of 23 July, George Gordon informed me, as did Joe Doolan from Irishbirding.com, of a female marsh harrier that had been seen one mile east of the Quoile Pondage, only about eight miles as the crow flies from the nest site. That bird may have been the female associated with this nest site as we very rarely get a passage of migrating marsh harriers so early in the season. We hoped for further sightings, particularly of the two fledglings and the male, over the weeks to come.

We were now really worried about why all three birds seemed to have left their natal grounds so soon after fledging, as it is common for recently fledged young harriers of all *Circus* species and at least one of the adults to remain in the area for up to two weeks prior to their dispersal. We could only hope that all three birds were safe and well and had just moved a short distance from the nest site to an area where food would be more easily obtained, probably along the shore of nearby Strangford Lough. The thought that both chicks could have been depredated by a passing red fox did also cross my mind.

Given that it takes a pair of marsh harriers between seven and ten days to fully construct a nest followed by the crucial incubation period of around 33 to 35 days and at least a further 35 days until fledging, we calculated that this breeding pair had probably been present at this site from at least the first or second week of April and yet had gone unrecorded. This was amazing, given that the majority of Northern Ireland's birders are based in County Down and nearby Belfast. The annual spring migration route of the marsh harrier is generally along the east coast of Ireland, so the easterly counties of Antrim, Armagh and of course Down hold the majority of our annual records, with the more westerly counties of Fermanagh, Londonderry and Tyrone minimally represented to date. The eventual arrival of a breeding pair in County Down was probably to have been expected, and sooner rather than later. It's sad to think that, when at last it did occur, the birds could have come and gone unnoticed but for a chance sighting.

Surprisingly, only a handful of the 100 or so records that have graced our shores since 1954 have been positively identified as males. The majority, therefore, have tended to be either females or immature birds but as immature birds sport similar plumage details to females, some of them could of course have been misidentified.

In recent years, there have been rumours and counter-rumours of marsh harriers breeding in the Republic of Ireland in the likes of Tacumshin and Lady's Island Lake in County Wexford and at other suitable locations. Whether these unconfirmed reports are true or not, it can only be a matter of time before this species recolonises our island once again, having been driven to extinction in Northern Ireland by the end of the 19th century and in the Republic by the end of the first two decades of the 20th century.

I hope this ground-breaking pair will return to the same or another suitable reedbed in 2010 and again breed successfully, as the marsh harrier has been missing from Northern Ireland and the Irish Breeding List for far too long. I will certainly be more vigilant in future and will definitely be on the lookout for them over the coming years, whether in County Down or in any other part of Northern Ireland.

Final thoughts

As Frank Sinatra so eloquently put it: 'Regrets, I've had a few ...' and over the years, so have I.

I made up my mind towards the end of 2008 that the following breeding season would be the last I spent in scientific study of the hen harrier or any other species in Northern Ireland. I had seriously considered bowing out in 2010 after completing 25 years of study but in my own best interests decided to go while I still had my sanity.

I did not come to this decision lightly. After many weeks of soul searching and lengthy discussions with my wife Linda, my raptor colleague of 21 years, Philip McHaffie and other respected friends, I decided for personal reasons to leave the raptor scene with my head held high, knowing that I had tried to do my best for hen harriers under extremely difficult circumstances and over years of growing frustration.

I will continue to follow the mixed fortunes of this beautiful bird of prey in the Antrim Plateau, hopefully in a more relaxed and enjoyable manner with the ever-loyal Linda and Philip still by my side in the field. I remember Linda once asking me why, when it should be a lovely and relaxing way of life, the study of birds in Northern Ireland involved so much back stabbing and sour grapes. That perceptive comment cut right to the heart of why I have decided to bow out.

It is obvious to me that harrier work has become more about money and personal gain than about doing anything constructive and long lasting to conserve our highly vulnerable hen harrier population. Talks, more talks, never ending counts and report after report: Nero fiddles while Rome burns. For well over two decades, nobody else in Northern Ireland wanted to study hen harriers, until, that is, money became available for a report on the species. Then the main protagonists, Philip McHaffie and I, were not even consulted prior to its publication.

That most recent report, published in early 2009, which I believe to be the second on hen harriers to be commissioned by the NIEA in three years, is riddled with inconsistencies and, if accepted and implemented in its present form, could have a detrimental effect on the long-term future of the hen harrier, not only in County Antrim but the whole of Northern Ireland.

To my bitter disappointment, I was not asked to peer review or contribute to this report, despite having 23 years' experience and being the only person apart from Philip McHaffie to have studied this species in Northern Ireland. I could have passed many useful and positive comments on to the four authors, two of whom in particular had no experience of studying hen harriers locally while the third had only limited knowledge of their ecology here.

Three or four of the report's flaws stand out. Firstly, it states 'that the hen harrier's ecological requirements are less well known in Northern Ireland than in the UK'. This is totally incorrect. Secondly, it states that 'surprisingly little research has been conducted on hen harriers in Northern Ireland', despite the ongoing research work by Philip McHaffie and myself. We have worked diligently and painstakingly for well over two decades, publishing numerous papers and articles on this species' ecology in the Antrim Plateau and elsewhere in Northern Ireland. Then, to our astonishment, several of our papers were in fact referred to throughout the report, making a complete nonsense of the earlier quote.

Thirdly, it was assumed that the only trees suitable for the purposes of tree nesting were those Sitkas aged 30 years or more, when in fact the majority of my tree nesting records are from trees aged between 15 and 25 years and around 20 years on average, although occasionally slightly younger.

Fourthly, the availability of deformed trees with multiple leaders, upon which the harriers build their nests, was briefly mentioned in the report as 'unknown'. If the local experts had studied harriers here as they say they have, and closely examined the trees for this anomaly as I have done, they would soon have discovered that there are many such Sitkas in Antrim's conifer plantations.

The authors also suggested that small clutch sizes, low rates of polygyny and probable low rates of breeding initiation may be due to limited food supply. Having studied the diet and availability of prey for the past 19 years (1991–2009) and published a unique paper on the subject, I can categorically state that a lack of food is not the problem: it is down to the combination of factors clearly outlined in this book. In fact, during the 2009 breeding season, Philip and I encountered no shortage of meadow pipits and starlings, both adults and fledglings, throughout the Antrim Plateau.

Probably the most ludicrous of all their ideas was the proposed creation of a network of fully trained and eventually skilled and paid volunteer raptor fieldworkers who would systematically study hen harriers in Northern Ireland and report their annual findings. It is and always has been virtually impossible to get anyone interested in committing to do such work and it is very rare for Philip and me to encounter anyone out studying this species, as we do, in great detail. As far as I am concerned, this idea is pie in the sky and by the time these measures are implemented there may well be no harriers left for people to study.

I would say to the three local authors that before writing up a report of this magnitude and importance, one has to have studied the hen harrier locally, in great detail, over a long period of time, especially when addressing subjects like its ecology in Northern Ireland. Hen harriers in Northern Ireland live a totally different lifestyle from those in the rest of the UK while those in Antrim live differently from those in other parts of the Province, so their ecology must be kept totally separate when writing or referring to them. You could say that the less one knows about hen harriers, the more expert one becomes.

If a conservation organisation asked me to write an important report or comment on the future of the barn owl or the peregrine falcon in Northern Ireland, I would refuse point blank. I know virtually nothing about either species' ecology or lifestyle here and it would not be appropriate of me to intrude into another person's study species without first consulting the species experts.

This poorly thought out and contradictory report was the final straw for both Philip and me as we cannot endorse something that is likely to affect the future of this species in our uplands. I would therefore ask those involved, and the authors of any future reports on hen harriers in Northern Ireland, to refrain from referencing our work without our permission as we totally distance ourselves from this report and will almost certainly do so from others in the near future. The report states that the local authors had 'personal communication' with me, which is untrue, as I was not aware that a report was pending. It was kept totally confidential.

To be truthful, I would not have minded if the three local authors in particular had seriously studied the hen harrier here and decided to publish a report. I would have fully supported them. To do such a thing behind a supposed raptor colleague's back is, though, totally unforgivable as far as Philip and I are concerned. I would advise them to go out and spend valuable time studying hen harriers for themselves, as we have done over the past 24 and 21 years respectively, and save themselves from making haphazard assumptions and embarrassing, contradictory remarks about other people's hard-earned findings.

Once again people are playing at conservation to the detriment of a species. If this report is regarded by the NIEA as the definitive way forward for the hen harrier in Northern Ireland then they need to look again. By the time this book is published, the fate of the species in Northern Ireland may well have been decided.

Lastly, I would remind those who hope to publish any future reports on the hen harrier that we may only get one chance to get our house in order regarding its future and, more importantly, its long-term survival in our uplands. This has to be put right at the first time of asking, as we may not get a second opportunity. I will no doubt be criticised for criticising, but that is my last word on this highly emotive subject.

This is not the way I would have chosen to end my scientific study of the hen harrier but sometimes we don't have a choice in these things. Comments like 'Things have moved on here scientifically' make Philip and me think that we are getting far too old for this. Now is the right time to leave things to the so-called experts that we seem to have here all of a sudden, many of whom we have never observed in the field.

I would like to point out that in all my years of studying and reporting on the hen harrier in Northern Ireland, I was never offered or received any remuneration locally to support our harrier studies. We were grateful for donations from the Hawk and Owl Trust and used money from our own pockets to keep these studies alive. I would add that mileage expenses for the work that Philip and I carried out here were apparently available for the first time in 2008, but we refused to claim them for personal reasons.

I and many other people in Northern Ireland think that our main conservation organisations would be better employed in trying to secure the long-term future of the hen harrier, the merlin, barn owl and dwindling numbers of kestrels than to have embarked on the so-called reintroduction of the red kite in July 2008. I say 'so-called' as it remains highly doubtful whether the red kite was ever a breeding resident in Northern Ireland. I have scrupulously researched the species' history myself: there is no archaeological evidence of it having been here and no ornithological records were kept here before the 19th century. The failure to meet those criteria was almost certainly the reason why the introduction scheme did not take place in 2007 in tandem with the reintroduction of the species in County Wicklow.

I worked on the erection of the holding cages prior to the kites' arrival in South Down in early 2008 and have to admit that their presence in Northern Ireland is a most welcome sight. The more raptors, the better as far as I am concerned, but definitely not if they come at the expense of our native species. Only when we have got our conservation house in order can we start introducing or reintroducing flagship species like red kites and ospreys.

In England there are at present proposals to reintroduce white-tailed eagles in Norfolk and a project is underway in north-east Scotland. Numerous red kites have already been reintroduced nationwide, not forgetting the ospreys at Rutland Water. Great bustards have been released and have now bred on Salisbury Plain, with corncrakes on the Nene Washes and common crane reintroductions in the pipeline for the Norfolk Broads. Yet the hen harrier is now classed as a very rare and declining native species, particularly in England where field-workers' comments are being totally disregarded by the statutory conservation organisations. In fact hen harrier field workers across the UK, including Philip McHaffie and myself, feel that they never have been listened to.

Where, I ask, do our priorities lie? Do they lie with continuing reintroductions at the expense of our indigenous species? Surely the future of the hen harrier must be secured before we proceed with further reintroductions? Common sense should prevail but I wonder whether it will ever be allowed to.

So this will be my final book on harriers, dedicated solely to the mixed fortunes of the hen harrier in Northern Ireland. The hen harrier is an absolutely delightful bird to behold and to have studied for so many years in the wilds of the now sadly degenerated Antrim Plateau. I hope its long-term future in the area can be fully secured.

You may be wondering what the future holds for me in terms of harrier studies. Well, I have been invited back for a fourth time by my good friend Henk Castelijns to Saeftinghe in south west Holland to monitor wintering hen and Western marsh harriers with the Zeeland Raptor Working Group. Again by personal invitation, I am hoping to visit the Tay reedbeds in east central Scotland to study breeding marsh harriers under the guidance of Steve Moyes and Harry Bell. I have also had open invitations to revisit Madagascar to study the endangered Madagascar marsh harrier and similarly to Australia, where I would like to spend further time studying the original tree nesting spotted harrier.

Locally, I still intend to carry on with my very popular and worthwhile raptor education work using my captive-bred owls in schools across the religious divide in Northern Ireland. I will also continue my work at other important venues such as WWT Castle Espie where I spent nine happy years until my visits were temporarily interrupted by illness and by the full-scale redevelopment of the area in 2008. Most recently, I have been voluntarily visiting the local branches of the charity Speechmatters with my owls, working with people of all ages who have suffered strokes: challenging, worthwhile and highly rewarding work.

While I will always remain deeply passionate about all birds of prey and owls, my real love is the hen harrier and the other 15 members and one subspecies of the genus *Circus* which have given me so much pleasure and excitement for well over two decades. These are the birds that make the hair stand up on the back of my neck every time I see one, whether it be a hen harrier in the Antrim Plateau or a spotted harrier in far-off Australia. It is an amazing thrill to see any wild creature in its natural environment and one that should never be taken for granted.

It has been a labour of love for me to write In the Shadow of Slemish, a modern day history of the hen harrier in County Antrim. It has also been a real privilege for me to study this species in great detail and as an ardent raptor lover; I could not have chosen a better subject on which to spend the past 24 years. What started out as a passing interest soon became a hobby and then a passion. I hope that anyone reading this book will enjoy it and sense that passion for hen harriers shining through on every page.

Over the years I have been asked, again and again, how I have managed it: finding all those hen harrier tree nests and even harriers breeding in the Mournes and discovering other breeding raptor species like goshawk, short-eared owl, red kite and marsh harrier?

The answer is simple: you have to be out in the field on a regular basis. Since my early retirement from full-time employment in 2003, I have been out in the Antrim Plateau on at least four days every week, averaging between eight and ten hours every day. Before my retirement, my visits were limited to weekends and at least one evening per week. You also need help from a network of friends – several of mine have been regular informants for years – and I have also had the long-lasting friendship and support of my colleague Philip McHaffie and my long-suffering wife Linda. It has not all been down just to me and others have played a big part in the successes I have enjoyed.

It is important to remember that the Antrim Plateau will die if we constantly neglect its natural inhabitants like the graceful hen harrier and fail to manage their habitat. This will happen sooner rather than later at the present rate of decline for both species and habitat alike. It's a sobering thought and is probably in line with Dr. Rob Simmons' intuitive remarks 'that in 25 years or less, harriers and other species may only survive in protected reserves'.

The protection of our environment and its wildlife is an obligation, not a choice, so a habitat unfit for birds of prey is also one unfit for man. I wait in hope for a visionary – or indeed anyone with some common sense and practical skills – to see what we are doing to our birds and our landscape.

Nothing beats the excitement of seeing hen harriers in the wild and it's a spectacle laid on for us entirely free of charge. We simply cannot afford to lose these magnificent raptors, probably the most beautiful of them all, from our uplands. Finally, if we do lose the Hen Harrier, it will probably be due to habitat loss, so there will be no re-introducing a species where there is no habitat.

Scientific Names

Birds

African Marsh Harrier *Circus ranivorus*
Barn Owl *Tyto alba*
Blackbird *Turdus merula*
Black Harrier *Circus maurus*
Black-headed Gull *Larus ridibundus*
Black Kite *Milvus migrans*
Chaffinch *Fringilla coelebs*
Cinereous Harrier *Circus cinereus*
Common Buzzard *Buteo buteo*
Common Crane *Grus grus*
Common Kestrel *Falco tinnunculus*
Corncrake *Crex crex*
Cuckoo *Cuculus carnorus*
Curlew *Numenius arquata*
Dunlin *Calidris alpina*
Eastern Marsh Harrier *Circus spilonotus*
European Eagle Owl *Bubo bubo*
Fieldfare *Turdus pilaris*
Golden Eagle *Aquila chrysaetos*
Golden Plover *Pluvialis apricaria*
Goshawk *Accipiter gentilis*
Great Bustard *Otis tarda*
Great Spotted Woodpecker *Dendrocopos major*
Harrier Hawk *Polyboroides typus*
Hen Harrier *Circus cyaneus*

Herring Gull *Larus argentatus*
Honey Buzzard *Pernis apivorus*
Hooded Crow *Corvus corone*
House Sparrow *Passer domesticus*
Lapwing *Vanellus vanellus*
Long-eared Owl *Asio otus*
Long-winged Harrier *Circus buffoni*
Madagascar Marsh Harrier *Circus macrosceles*
Magpie *Pica pica*
Meadow Pipit *Anthus pratensis*
Merlin *Falco columbarius*
Mistle Thrush *Turdus viscivorus*
Montagu's Harrier *Circus pygargus*
North-African race of Western Marsh Harrier *Circus aeruginosus harterti*
Northern Harrier *Circus hudsonius*
Osprey *Pandion haliaetus*
Pallid Harrier *Circus macrourus*
Papuan Harrier *Circus spilothorax*
Peregrine Falcon *Falco peregrinus*
Pied Harrier *Circus melanoleucos*
Raven *Corvus corax*
Red Grouse *Lagopus lagopus*
Red Kite *Milvus milvus*
Reunion Harrier *Circus maillardi*
Robin *Erithacus rubecula*
Short-eared Owl *Asio flammeus*
Skylark *Alauda arvensis*
Snipe *Gallinago gallinago*
Sparrowhawk *Accipiter nisus*
Spotted Harrier *Circus assimilis*
Starling *Sturnus vulgaris*
Stonechat *Saxicola torquata*
Swainson's Hawk *Buteo swainsoni*
Swamp Harrier *Circus approximans*
Tengmalm's Owl *Aegolius funereus*
Western Marsh Harrier *Circus aeruginosus*
White-tailed Eagle *Haliaeetus albicilla*
Woodpigeon *Columba palumbus*

Wren *Troglodytes troglodytes*

Mammals

Badger *Meles meles*
Brown Rat *Rattus norvegicus*
Domestic Cattle *Bos taurus*
Domestic Chicken *Gallus gallus domesticus*
Domestic Homing (Racing) Pigeon *Columba livia domestica*
Domestic Sheep *Ovis aries*
Irish Hare *Lepus timidus hibernicus*
Irish Stoat *Mustela erminea hibernica*
Mink *Mustela vison*
Otter *Lutra lutra*
Pygmy Shrew *Sorex minutus*
Rabbit *Oryctolagus cuniculus*
Red Deer *Cervus elaphus*
Red Fox *Vulpes vulpes*
Red Squirrel *Sciurus vulgaris*
Ring-tailed Possum *Pseudocheirus peregrinus*
Short-tailed Vole *Microtus agrestis*
Wood Mouse *Apodemus sylvaticus*

Reptiles

Viviparous Lizard *Lacerta vivipara*

Insects

Ground Beetle *Carabus violaceus*

Fish

Brown Trout *Salmo trutta*
Rainbow Trout *Oncorhynchus mykiss*

Plants

Bell Heather *Erica cinerea*
Bracken *Pteridium aquilinum*
Casuarina *Casuarina spp.*
Common Cottongrass *Eriophorum angustifolium*
Common Elder *Sambucus nigra*

Common Gorse *Ulex europaeus*
Common Hawthorn *Crataegus monogyna*
Common Reed *Phragmites australis*
Eucalyptus *Eucalyptus spp.*
European Larch *Larix decidua*
Ling Heather *Calluna vulgaris*
Mahoe Tree *Melicytus ramiflorus*
Oak *Quercus spp.*
Pine Tree *Pinus spp.*
Purple Moor Grass *Molinia caerulea*
Sedge *Cladium spp.*
Sitka Spruce *Picea sitchensis*
Snowberry Bush *Symphoricarpos rivularis*
Soft Rush *Juncus effusus*
Sugar Cane *Saccharum officinarum*
Tawa Tree *Beilschmiedia tawa*
Tea-tree *Leptospermum scoparium*
Wheat *Triticum spp.*
Willow *Salix spp.*

Tables

Table 1 Bird and mammal diet by number of individuals identified to species (1991- 1995), from a total of 160 pellets (148 from ground and tree nests in County Antrim and 12 from the winter roost in County Tyrone), which contained 260 prey items. Pellets analysed by the late Dr. Roger Clarke.

Species	Number	%
Meadow Pipit	83	31.9
Skylark	42	16.2
Starling	67	25.8
Red Grouse	2	0.8
Snipe	3	1.2
Unidentified passerines	7	2.7
Lagomorph (rabbit/hare)	33	12.7
Small mammals (Pygmy Shrew and Wood Mouse)	11	4.2
Unidentified beetle remains	12	4.5
Totals	260	100

Table 2 Bird and mammal diet by number of individuals identified to species (1996 – 2005), from a total of 310 pellets (300 from ground and tree nests in County Antrim and 10 from the winter roost in County Tyrone), which contained 453 prey items. Pellets analysed by Don Scott.

Species	Number	%
Meadow Pipit	147	32.5
Starling	130	28.7
Skylark	63	14.0
Red Grouse	5	1.1
Snipe	12	2.6
Curlew	8	1.8
Chaffinch	4	0.9
House Sparrow	3	0.6
Lagomorph (rabbit/hare)	43	9.5
Badger	1	0.2
Pygmy Shrew	10	2.2
Wood Mouse	9	2.0
Viviparous Lizard	4	0.9
Beetle remains	14	3.0
Totals	453	100

Table 3 Bird and mammal diet by number of individuals identified to species (2006 – 2009), from a total of 130 pellets, all from ground and tree nests in County Antrim, which contained 240 prey items. Pellets analysed by Don Scott.

Species	Number	%
Meadow Pipit	76	31.7
Starling	65	27.1
Skylark	35	14.6
Red Grouse	2	0.8
Snipe	5	2.1
Curlew	3	1.2
Chaffinch	2	0.8
Stonechat	1	0.4

Table 3 *Continued*

Species	Number	%
Blackbird	1	0.4
Lagomorph (rabbit/hare)	25	10.5
Pygmy Shrew	7	3.0
Wood Mouse	6	2.5
Brown Rat	2	0.8
Viviparous Lizard	2	0.8
Beetle remains	8	3.3
Totals	240	100

Bibliography

Books related to Harriers

Clarke, R. 1990. *Harriers of the British Isles.* Shire, Princes Risborough.

Clarke, R. 1995. *The Marsh Harrier.* Hamlyn, London.

Clarke, R. 1996. *Montagu's Harrier.* Arlequin Press, Chelmsford.

Hamerstrom, F. 1986. *Harrier, Hawk of the Marshes.* Smithsonian Press, Washington.

Scott, D. 2008. *Harriers, Journeys around the World.* Tiercel Publishing, Wheathampstead.

Simmons, R. E. 2000. *Harriers of the World.* Oxford University Press, Oxford.

Verma, A. 2007. *Harriers in India: A Field Guide.* Wildlife Institute of India, Dehradu.

Watson, D. 1977. *The Hen Harrier.* Poyser, Berkhamsted.

Weis, H. 1923. *Life of the Harrier in Denmark.* Wheldon and Wesley, London.

General Bibliography

Andris, K. Saumer, F. and Trillmich, F. 1970. *Beobachtungen an Schlafplatzen der Kornweihe (Hen Harrier) in der Oberrheinebene.* (Sleeping places of the Hen Harrier in the Upper Rhine valley). Vogelwelt 91: 184–191.

Armstrong, E. A. 1940. *Birds of the Grey Wind.* Oxford University Press, London.

Baker-Gabb, D. J. 1984. *The Evolution of Tree-nesting and the origin of the Spotted Harrier.* Corella 8: 67–69.

Baker-Gabb, D. J. 1985. *Autumn breeding by the Spotted Harrier.* Australian Bird Watcher 11: 48.

Bourne, W. R. P. 1992. *What happens when Hen Harriers nest above ground?* Irish Birds 4: 564–565.

Brown, L. and Amadon, D. 1968. *Eagles, Hawks and Falcons of the World.* Country Life Books, Hamlyn London.

Cramp, S. and Simmons, K. E. L. 1980. *The Birds of the Western Palaearctic.* Vol 2. Oxford.

Cupper, J. and L. 1981. *Hawks in Focus.* Jaclin Enterprises, Mildura. Australia.

D'Arcy, G. 1988. *The Animals of Ireland.* Appletree Press, Belfast.

Deane, C. D. 1954. *Handbook of the Birds of Northern Ireland.* Belfast Museum Publication.

DeCandido, R. and Allen, D. 2006. *Nocturnal hunting by Peregrine Falcons at the Empire State Building, New York City.* The Wilson Journal of Ornithology 118(1): 53–58.

Dunne, P. Sibley, D. and Sutton, C. 1988. *Hawks in Flight.* Houghton Mifflin Company, Boston.

Gleichner, W. and Naumann, C. 1985. *Extreme Rohrweihen horststandorte.* Der Falke 32: 263.

Gray, R. and Anderson, T. 1869. *Birds of Ayrshire and Wigtownshire.*

Hedley, L. A. 1985. *Another example of tree nesting Harriers.* Notornis 32: 22.

Hesketh, B. and Murphy, B. 2004. *Female harrier the belle of the moor.* Bird Watching Magazine: June Issue, 2004.

Hesketh, B. 2009. *They hunt by night (Hen Harrier).* Birdwatch Magazine: March Issue 2009.

Hollands, D. 2003. *Eagles Hawks and Falcons of Australia.* Bloomings Books, Melbourne.

Hutchinson, C. D. 1989. *Birds in Ireland.* Poyser, Calton.

Jardine, Sir W. 1834–1838. *Natural History of the Birds of Great Britain and Ireland.*

Kennedy, P. G. Ruttledge, R. F. and Scroope, C. F. 1954. *The Birds of Ireland.* Oliver and Boyd, Edinburgh.

Klau, W. L. 1985. *Spotted Harriers nesting on the Nullarbor Plain.* Australian Bird Watcher 11: 46–48.

Kropp, von R. and Munch, C. 1979. *Beobachtungen an Schlafplatzen uberwinternder Kornweihen (Hen Harrier) in der Renchniederung (Mittelbaden).* Okologie der Vogel (Ecology of Birds) 1: 165–179.

Kunstmuller, I. and Hlavac, V. 1988. *Unusually nesting of the Marsh Harrier on the pine-tree top.* Buteo 3: 43–46.

Lynas, P. Newton, S. F. and Robinson, J. A. 2007. *The status of birds in Ireland: an analysis of conservation concern 2008–2013.* Irish Birds 8: 149–166.

Mackenzie, W. 1841. *History of Galloway.* Kirkcudbright. 2 Vols.

Messenger, B. 1990. *Tree nesting Harriers.* Notornis 37: 172.

Mellon, C. Allen, D. and Scott, D. 2005. *Proposed Special Protection Areas for Hen Harriers in Northern Ireland.* Report for EHS by Allen and Mellon Environmental Ltd: 1–41.

Miles, J. 2002. *The Return of the Jacobite.* Miles and Miles of Countryside. Castle Carrock.

Naoroji, R. 2006. *Birds of Prey of the Indian Subcontinent.* Christopher Helm. London.

Newton, S. Donaghy, A. Allen, D. and Gibbons, D. 1999. *Birds of Conservation Concern in Ireland.* Irish Birds 6: 333–344.

O'Flynn, W.J. 1983. *Population changes of the Hen Harrier in Ireland.* Irish Birds 2: 337–343.

Olsen, P. 1995. *Australian Birds of Prey.* The John Hopkins University Press, Baltimore, Maryland.

Perry, K. W. 1986. *The Irish Dipper.* Published Privately.

Picozzi, N. 1980. *Food, growth, survival and sex ratio of nestling Hen Harriers in Orkney.* Ornis Scandinavica 11: 1–11.

Picozzi, N. 1983. *Two hens, but a single nest: an unusual case of polygyny by Hen Harriers in Orkney.* British Birds 76: 123–128.

Picozzi, N. 1984. *Breeding biology of polygynous Hen Harriers in Orkney.* Ornis Scandinavica 15: 1–10.

Ritchie, J. 1920. *The Influence of Man on Animal Life in Scotland.*

Russell, R. W. 1991. *Nocturnal flight by migrant 'diurnal' raptors.* Journal of Field Ornithology 62: 505–508.

Rutz, C. 2003. *Post-fledging dispersal of Northern Goshawks in an urban environment.* Vogelwelt 124: 93–101.

Scharf, W. C. and Balfour, E. 1971. *Growth and Development of Nestling Hen Harriers.* Ibis 113.

Schipper, W. J. A. 1973. *A Comparison of prey selection in Sympatric Harriers, in Western Europe.* Le Gerfaut 63: 17–120.

Schropfer, L. 1988. *First nesting of the Marsh Harrier on a shrub in West Bohemia.* Buteo 3: 39–42.

Scott, D. Clarke, R. and Shawyer, C. R. 1991. *Hen Harriers breeding in a tree nest.* Irish Birds 4: 413–417.

Scott, D. 1991/92. *Winter Roosts of Hen Harriers in Northern Ireland.* Northern Ireland Bird Report: 78–79. N.I.B.A.

Scott, D. Clarke, R. and McHaffie, P. 1992. *Hen Harriers successfully breeding in a tree nest of their own construction.* Irish Birds 4: 566–570.

Scott, D. 1993. *Hen Harriers tree nest again in 1993.* Northern Ireland Bird Report: 69–71. N.I.B.A.

Scott, D. and Clarke, R. 1993. *Taking to the Trees.* Bird Watching Magazine: February Issue, 1993.

Scott, D. Clarke, R. and Shawyer, C. R. 1993/94. *Tree-nesting Hen Harriers – Evolution in the making?* The Raptor 21: 53–56.

Scott, D. and Clarke, R. 1994. *First records of tree roosting by Hen Harriers in Northern Ireland.* Northern Ireland Bird Report: 84–89. N.I.B.A.

Scott, D. 1996. *Records of Albinism in Ireland's Hen Harrier Population.* Northern Ireland Bird Report: 101–106. N.I.B.A.

Scott, D. 1997. *Short-eared Owl Breeding in Northern Ireland in 1997.* Northern Ireland Bird Report: 108–110. N.I.B.A.

Scott, D. 1997. *Hen Harrier records from Copeland Bird Observatory.* Northern Ireland Bird Report: 111–115. N.I.B.A.

Scott, D. 1998. *The Ecology of a Hen Harrier Winter Roost.* Northern Ireland Bird Report: 105–116. N.I.B.A.

Scott, D. 1999. *Goshawk – Breeding in Northern Ireland.* Northern Ireland Bird Report: 114–119. N.I.B.A.

Scott, D. 1999. *Influx of Short-eared Owls and Hen Harriers into Northern Ireland during 1999.* Northern Ireland Bird Report: 120–127. N.I.B.A.

Scott, D. 2000. *The Uplands of Antrim – A moorland habitat under threat from humans, and the implications for ground nesting Raptors and other species.* Northern Ireland Bird Report: 98–101. N.I.B.A.

Scott, D. 2000. *Marking a decade of tree nesting by Hen Harriers in Northern Ireland, 1991–2000.* Irish Birds 6: 586–589.

Scott, D. and McHaffie, P. 2001. *The demise of a Hen Harrier roost site.* Northern Ireland Bird Report: 107–110. N.I.B.A.

Scott, D. 2002. *How many species of Harrier are there? – and my quest to find them all.* Northern Ireland Bird Report: 126–129. N.I.B.A.

Scott, D. and McHaffie, P. 2002. *Attempted nesting of the Red Kite in Northern Ireland during 2002.* Irish Birds 7: 131–132.

Scott, D. and McHaffie, P. 2003. *What impact do Buzzard and Goshawk have on other raptors in coniferous forest? – preliminary findings.* Irish Birds 7: 267–269.

Scott, D. 2003/04. *Polygamy – a new phase in Hen Harrier Ecology.* Northern Ireland Bird Report: 149–151. N.I.B.A.

Scott, D. 2004. *Four in a row for tree nesting Hen Harriers, in 2002.* Irish Birds 7: 440.

Scott, D. 2005. *The diet of Hen Harriers in Northern Ireland 1991–2005.* Irish Birds 7: 597–599.

Scott, D. and Hipkiss, T. 2006. *Tree-nesting behaviour by a polyandrous female Hen Harrier.* Irish Birds 8: 139–141.

Scott, D. and Clarke, R. 2007. *Comparing the success of Hen Harrier tree nests and ground nests in the Antrim Hills, 1990–2006.* Irish Birds 8: 315–318.

Scott, D. and McHaffie, P. 2008. *Hen Harrier killed at wind farm site in County Antrim.* Irish Birds 8: 436–437.

Scott, D. and McHaffie, P. 2009. *Do Buzzard and Goshawk harass, depredate and displace Hen Harriers, in coniferous forest during the winter months? – A preliminary study.* Irish Birds 8: In Press.

Scott, D. Scott, L. and McHaffie, P. 2009. *Unexpected Breeding of the Marsh Harrier in County Down, during 2009.* Northern Ireland Bird Report and Irish Birds: In Press.

Scott, D. 2009. *Two females and one male, but only a single ground nest: an unusual case of polygyny by Hen Harriers in County Antrim, in 2009*: Unpublished as yet.

Selby, P. J. 1825–1833. *Illustrations of British Ornithology.*

Simecek, K. 1992. *Neobvykle hnizdeni, motaka pochopa, na jizni Morave. (Unusual breeding of Marsh Harrier in South Moravia).* Ziva 4: 183.

Sim, I. M. W. Dillon, I. A. Eaton, M. A. Etheridge, B. Lindley, P. Riley, H. Saunders, R. Sharpe, C. and Tickner, M. 2007. *Status of the Hen Harrier in the UK and Isle of Man in 2004, and a comparison with the 1988/89 and 1998 surveys.* Bird Study 54: 256–267.

Skinner, J. F. 1979. *Puzzling behaviour of Harriers.* Notornis 26: 119.

Swieton, Z. and Marek, J. 1979. *Neobvykle zahnizdeni, motaka pilicha (An unusual nesting of Hen Harrier).* Zpravodaj Klubu sokolniku 11: 23.

Thompson, Wm. 1849–56. *The Natural History of Ireland.* Reeve, Benham and Reeve, London.

Turner, Dr. W. 1544. *Avium Praecipuarum.* Trans. A. H. Evans, 1903.

Ussher, R. J. and Warren, R. 1900. *The Birds of Ireland.* Gurney and Jackson, London.

Viktora, L. 1992. *Neobvykle hnizdeni, motaka pochopa, (Unusual breeding of Marsh Harrier).* Ziva 4: 182.

Watson, D. 1991. *Hen Harriers breeding in a tree nest: further comments.* Irish Birds 4: 418–420.

Watters, J. J. 1853. *The Natural History of The Birds Of Ireland.* McGlashan. Dublin.

Whilde, A. 1993. *Threatened Mammals, Birds, Amphibians and Fish in Ireland.* Irish Red Data Book 2: Vertebrates. Belfast HMSO.

Witherby, H. F. 1938–41. *The Handbook of British Birds.*